Hudibras by Samuel Butler

Samuel Butler was born on 4th December 1835 at the village rectory in Langar, Nottinghamshire.

His relationship with his parents, especially his father, was largely antagonistic. His education began at home and included frequent beatings, as was all too common at the time.

Under his parents' influence, he was set to follow his father into the priesthood. He was schooled at Shrewsbury and then St John's College, Cambridge, where he obtained a first in Classics in 1858.

After Cambridge he went to live in a low-income parish in London 1858–59 as preparation for his ordination into the Anglican clergy; there he discovered that baptism made no apparent difference to the morals and behaviour of his new peers. He began to question his faith. Correspondence with his father about the issue failed to set his mind at peace, inciting instead his father's wrath.

As a result, the young Butler emigrated in September 1859 to New Zealand. He was determined to change his life.

He wrote of his arrival and life as a sheep farmer on Mesopotamia Station in 'A First Year in Canterbury Settlement' (1863). After a few years he sold his farm and made a handsome profit. But the chief achievement of these years were the drafts and source material for much of his masterpiece 'Erewhon'.

Butler returned to England in 1864, settling in rooms in Clifford's Inn, near Fleet Street, where he would live for the rest of his life.

In 1872, he published his Utopian novel 'Erewhon' which made him a well-known figure.

He wrote a number of other books, including a moderately successful sequel, 'Erewhon Revisited' before his masterpiece and semi-autobiographical novel 'The Way of All Flesh' appeared after his death. Butler thought its tone of satirical attack on Victorian morality too contentious to publish during his life time and thereby shied away from further potential problems.

Samuel Butler died aged 66 on 18th June 1902 at a nursing home in St John's Wood Road, London. He was cremated at Woking Crematorium, and accounts say his ashes were either dispersed or buried in an unmarked grave.

Index of Contents

PART I

CANTO I

THE ARGUMENT

Sir Hudibras his passing worth,
The manner how he sallied forth;
His arms and equipage are shown;
His horse's virtues, and his own.
Th' adventure of the bear and fiddle
Is sung, but breaks off in the middle.

When civil dudgeon first grew high,
And men fell out they knew not why?
When hard words, jealousies, and fears,
Set folks together by the ears,
And made them fight, like mad or drunk,
For Dame Religion, as for punk;
Whose honesty they all durst swear for,
Though not a man of them knew wherefore:
When Gospel-Trumpeter, surrounded
With long-ear'd rout, to battle sounded,
And pulpit, drum ecclesiastick,
Was beat with fist, instead of a stick;
Then did Sir Knight abandon dwelling,
And out he rode a colonelling.
A wight he was, whose very sight wou'd
Entitle him Mirror of Knighthood;
That never bent his stubborn knee
To any thing but Chivalry;
Nor put up blow, but that which laid
Right worshipful on shoulder-blade;
Chief of domestic knights and errant,
Either for cartel or for warrant;

Great on the bench, great in the saddle,
That could as well bind o'er, as swaddle;
Mighty he was at both of these,
And styl'd of war, as well as peace.
(So some rats, of amphibious nature,
Are either for the land or water).
But here our authors make a doubt
Whether he were more wise, or stout:
Some hold the one, and some the other;
But howsoe'er they make a pother,
The diff'rence was so small, his brain
Outweigh'd his rage but half a grain;
Which made some take him for a tool
That knaves do work with, call'd a fool,
And offer to lay wagers that
As MONTAIGNE, playing with his cat,
Complains she thought him but an ass,
Much more she wou'd Sir HUDIBRAS;
(For that's the name our valiant knight
To all his challenges did write).
But they're mistaken very much,
'Tis plain enough he was no such;
We grant, although he had much wit,
H' was very shy of using it;
As being loth to wear it out,
And therefore bore it not about,
Unless on holy-days, or so,
As men their best apparel do.
Beside, 'tis known he could speak GREEK
As naturally as pigs squeek;
That LATIN was no more difficile,
Than to a blackbird 'tis to whistle:
Being rich in both, he never scanted
His bounty unto such as wanted;
But much of either would afford
To many, that had not one word.
For Hebrew roots, although they're found
To flourish most in barren ground,
He had such plenty, as suffic'd
To make some think him circumcis'd;
And truly so, he was, perhaps,
Not as a proselyte, but for claps.

He was in LOGIC a great critic,
Profoundly skill'd in analytic;
He could distinguish, and divide
A hair 'twixt south, and south-west side:
On either which he would dispute,

Confute, change hands, and still confute,
He'd undertake to prove, by force
Of argument, a man's no horse;
He'd prove a buzzard is no fowl,
And that a lord may be an owl,
A calf an alderman, a goose a justice,
And rooks Committee-men and Trustees.
He'd run in debt by disputation,
And pay with ratiocination.
All this by syllogism, true
In mood and figure, he would do.
For RHETORIC, he could not ope
His mouth, but out there flew a trope;
And when he happen'd to break off
I' th' middle of his speech, or cough,
H' had hard words,ready to show why,
And tell what rules he did it by;
Else, when with greatest art he spoke,
You'd think he talk'd like other folk,
For all a rhetorician's rules
Teach nothing but to name his tools.
His ordinary rate of speech
In loftiness of sound was rich;
A Babylonish dialect,
Which learned pedants much affect.
It was a parti-colour'd dress
Of patch'd and pie-bald languages;
'Twas English cut on Greek and Latin,
Like fustian heretofore on satin;
It had an odd promiscuous tone,
As if h' had talk'd three parts in one;
Which made some think, when he did gabble,
Th' had heard three labourers of Babel;
Or CERBERUS himself pronounce
A leash of languages at once.
This he as volubly would vent
As if his stock would ne'er be spent:
And truly, to support that charge,
He had supplies as vast and large;
For he cou'd coin, or counterfeit
New words, with little or no wit:
Words so debas'd and hard, no stone
Was hard enough to touch them on;
And when with hasty noise he spoke 'em,
The ignorant for current took 'em;
That had the orator, who once
Did fill his mouth with pebble stones
When he harangu'd, but known his phrase

He would have us'd no other ways.
In MATHEMATICKS he was greater
Than TYCHO BRAHE, or ERRA PATER:
For he, by geometric scale,
Could take the size of pots of ale;
Resolve, by sines and tangents straight,
If bread or butter wanted weight,
And wisely tell what hour o' th' day
The clock does strike by algebra.
Beside, he was a shrewd PHILOSOPHER,
And had read ev'ry text and gloss over;
Whate'er the crabbed'st author hath,
He understood b' implicit faith:
Whatever sceptic could inquire for,
For ev'ry why he had a wherefore;
Knew more than forty of them do,
As far as words and terms cou'd go.
All which he understood by rote,
And, as occasion serv'd, would quote;
No matter whether right or wrong,
They might be either said or sung.
His notions fitted things so well,
That which was which he could not tell;
But oftentimes mistook th' one
For th' other, as great clerks have done.
He could reduce all things to acts,
And knew their natures by abstracts;
Where entity and quiddity,
The ghosts of defunct bodies fly;
Where truth in person does appear,
Like words congeal'd in northern air.
He knew what's what, and that's as high
As metaphysic wit can fly;
In school-divinity as able
As he that hight, Irrefragable;
A second THOMAS, or, at once,
To name them all, another DUNCE:
Profound in all the Nominal
And Real ways, beyond them all:
For he a rope of sand cou'd twist
As tough as learned SORBONIST;
And weave fine cobwebs, fit for skull
That's empty when the moon is full;
Such as take lodgings in a head
That's to be let unfurnished.
He could raise scruples dark and nice,
And after solve 'em in a trice;
As if Divinity had catch'd

The itch, on purpose to be scratch'd;
Or, like a mountebank, did wound
And stab herself with doubts profound,
Only to show with how small pain
The sores of Faith are cur'd again;
Although by woeful proof we find,
They always leave a scar behind.
He knew the seat of Paradise,
Could tell in what degree it lies;
And, as he was dispos'd, could prove it,
Below the moon, or else above it.
What Adam dreamt of, when his bride
Came from her closet in his side:
Whether the devil tempted her
By a High Dutch interpreter;
If either of them had a navel:
Who first made music malleable:
Whether the serpent, at the fall,
Had cloven feet, or none at all.
All this, without a gloss, or comment,
He could unriddle in a moment,
In proper terms, such as men smatter
When they throw out, and miss the matter.

For his Religion, it was fit
To match his learning and his wit;
'Twas Presbyterian true blue;
For he was of that stubborn crew
Of errant saints, whom all men grant
To be the true Church Militant;
Such as do build their faith upon
The holy text of pike and gun;
Decide all controversies by
Infallible artillery;
And prove their doctrine orthodox
By apostolic blows and knocks;
Call fire and sword and desolation,
A godly thorough reformation,
Which always must be carried on,
And still be doing, never done;
As if religion were intended
For nothing else but to be mended.
A sect, whose chief devotion lies
In odd perverse antipathies;
In falling out with that or this,
And finding somewhat still amiss;
More peevish, cross, and splenetick,
Than dog distract, or monkey sick.

That with more care keep holy-day
The wrong, than others the right way;
Compound for sins they are inclin'd to,
By damning those they have no mind to:
Still so perverse and opposite,
As if they worshipp'd God for spite.
The self-same thing they will abhor
One way, and long another for.
Free-will they one way disavow,
Another, nothing else allow:
All piety consists therein
In them, in other men all sin:
Rather than fail, they will defy
That which they love most tenderly;
Quarrel with minc'd-pies, and disparage
Their best and dearest friend, plum-porridge;
Fat pig and goose itself oppose,
And blaspheme custard through the nose.
Th' apostles of this fierce religion,
Like MAHOMET'S, were ass and pidgeon,
To whom our knight, by fast instinct
Of wit and temper, was so linkt,
As if hypocrisy and nonsense
Had got th' advowson of his conscience.

Thus was he gifted and accouter'd;
We mean on th' inside, not the outward;
That next of all we shall discuss:
Then listen, Sirs, it follows thus
His tawny beard was th' equal grace
Both of his wisdom and his face;
In cut and dye so like a tile,
A sudden view it would beguile:
The upper part thereof was whey;
The nether, orange mix'd with grey.
This hairy meteor did denounce
The fall of scepters and of crowns;
With grisly type did represent
Declining age of government;
And tell with hieroglyphick spade,
Its own grave and the state's were made.
Like SAMPSON'S heart-breakers, it grew
In time to make a nation rue;
Tho' it contributed its own fall,
To wait upon the publick downfal,
It was monastick, and did grow
In holy orders by strict vow;
Of rule as sullen and severe

As that of rigid Cordeliere.
'Twas bound to suffer persecution
And martyrdom with resolution;
T' oppose itself against the hate
And vengeance of th' incensed state;
In whose defiance it was worn,
Still ready to be pull'd and torn;
With red-hot irons to be tortur'd;
Revil'd, and spit upon, and martyr'd.
Maugre all which, 'twas to stand fast
As long as monarchy shou'd last;
But when the state should hap to reel,
'Twas to submit to fatal steel,
And fall, as it was consecrate,
A sacrifice to fall of state;
Whose thread of life the fatal sisters
Did twist together with its whiskers,
And twine so close, that time should never,
In life or death, their fortunes sever;
But with his rusty sickle mow
Both down together at a blow.
So learned TALIACOTIUS from
The brawny part of porter's bum
Cut supplemental noses, which
Wou'd last as long as parent breech;
But when the date of NOCK was out,
Off drop'd the sympathetic snout.

His back, or rather burthen, show'd,
As if it stoop'd with its own load:
For as AENEAS bore his sire
Upon his shoulders thro' the fire,
Our Knight did bear no less a pack
Of his own buttocks on his back;
Which now had almost got the upper-
Hand of his head, for want of crupper.
To poise this equally, he bore
A paunch of the same bulk before;
Which still he had a special care
To keep well-cramm'd with thrifty fare;
As white-pot, butter-milk, and curds,
Such as a country-house affords;
With other vittle, which anon
We farther shall dilate upon,
When of his hose we come to treat,
The cupboard where he kept his meat.

His doublet was of sturdy buff,

And tho' not sword, yet cudgel-proof;
Whereby 'twas fitter for his use,
Who fear'd no blows, but such as bruise.

His breeches were of rugged woollen,
And had been at the siege of Bullen;
To old King HARRY so well known,
Some writers held they were his own.
Thro' they were lin'd with many a piece
Of ammunition bread and cheese,
And fat black-puddings, proper food
For warriors that delight in blood.
For, as we said, he always chose
To carry vittle in his hose,
That often tempted rats and mice
The ammunition to surprise:
And when he put a hand but in
The one or t' other magazine,
They stoutly in defence on't stood,
And from the wounded foe drew blood;
And 'till th' were storm'd and beaten out,
Ne'er left the fortify'd redoubt.
And tho' Knights Errant, as some think,
Of old did neither eat nor drink,
Because, when thorough desarts vast,
And regions desolate, they past,
Where belly-timber above ground,
Or under, was not to be found,
Unless they graz'd, there's not one word
Of their provision on record;
Which made some confidently write,
They had no stomachs, but to fight.
'Tis false: for ARTHUR wore in hall
Round table like a farthingal,
On which with shirt pull'd out behind,
And eke before, his good Knights din'd.
Though 'twas no table, some suppose,
But a huge pair of round trunk hose;
In which he carry'd as much meat
As he and all the Knights cou'd eat,
When, laying by their swords and truncheons,
They took their breakfasts, or their nuncheons.
But let that pass at present, lest
We should forget where we digrest,
As learned authors use, to whom
We leave it, and to th' purpose come,

His puissant sword unto his side,

Near his undaunted heart, was ty'd;
With basket-hilt, that wou'd hold broth,
And serve for fight and dinner both.
In it he melted lead for bullets,
To shoot at foes, and sometimes pullets,
To whom he bore so fell a grutch,
He ne'er gave quarter t' any such.
The trenchant blade, Toledo trusty,
For want of fighting, was grown rusty,
And ate unto itself, for lack
Of somebody to hew and hack.
The peaceful scabbard where it dwelt
The rancour of its edge had felt;
For of the lower end two handful
It had devour'd, 'twas so manful;
And so much scorn'd to lurk in case,
As if it durst not shew its face.
In many desperate attempts,
Of warrants, exigents, contempts,
It had appear'd with courage bolder
Than Serjeant BUM invading shoulder.
Oft had it ta'en possession,
And pris'ners too, or made them run.

This sword a dagger had t' his page,
That was but little for his age;
And therefore waited on him so,
As dwarfs upon Knights Errant do.
It was a serviceable dudgeon,
Either for fighting or for drudging.
When it had stabb'd, or broke a head,
It would scrape trenchers, or chip bread;
Toast cheese or bacon; tho' it were
To bait a mouse-trap, 'twould not care.
'Twould make clean shoes; and in the earth
Set leeks and onions, and so forth.
It had been 'prentice to a brewer,
Where this and more it did endure;
But left the trade, as many more
Have lately done on the same score.

In th' holsters, at his saddle-bow,
Two aged pistols he did stow,
Among the surplus of such meat
As in his hose he cou'd not get.
These wou'd inveigle rats with th' scent,
To forage when the cocks were bent;
And sometimes catch 'em with a snap

As cleverly as th' ablest trap.
They were upon hard duty still,
And ev'ry night stood centinel,
To guard the magazine i' th' hose
From two-legg'd and from four-legg'd foes.

Thus clad and fortify'd, Sir Knight
From peaceful home set forth to fight.
But first with nimble, active force
He got on th' outside of his horse;
For having but one stirrup ty'd
T' his saddle, on the further side,
It was so short, h' had much ado
To reach it with his desp'rate toe:
But, after many strains and heaves,
He got up to the saddle-eaves,
From whence he vaulted into th' seat,
With so much vigour, strength and heat,
That he had almost tumbled over
With his own weight, but did recover,
By laying hold on tail and main,
Which oft he us'd instead of rein.

But now we talk of mounting steed,
Before we further do proceed,
It doth behoves us to say something
Of that which bore our valiant bumkin.
The beast was sturdy, large, and tall,
With mouth of meal, and eyes of wall.
I wou'd say eye; for h' had but one,
As most agree; tho' some say none.
He was well stay'd; and in his gait
Preserv'd a grave, majestick state.
At spur or switch no more he skipt,
Or mended pace, than Spaniard whipt;
And yet so fiery, he wou'd bound
As if he griev'd to touch the ground:
That CAESAR's horse, who, as fame goes
Had corns upon his feet and toes,
Was not by half so tender hooft,
Nor trod upon the ground so soft.
And as that beast would kneel and stoop
(Some write) to take his rider up,
So HUDIBRAS his ('tis well known)
Wou'd often do to set him down.
We shall not need to say what lack
Of leather was upon his back;
For that was hidden under pad,

And breech of Knight, gall'd full as bad.
His strutting ribs on both sides show'd
Like furrows he himself had plow'd;
For underneath the skirt of pannel,
'Twixt ev'ry two there was a channel
His draggling tail hung in the dirt,
Which on his rider he wou'd flurt,
Still as his tender side he prick'd,
With arm'd heel, or with unarm'd kick'd:
For HUDIBRAS wore but one spur;
As wisely knowing, cou'd he stir
To active trot one side of's horse,
The other wou'd not hang an arse.

A squire he had, whose name was RALPH,
That in th' adventure went his half:
Though writers, for more stately tone,
Do call him RALPHO; 'tis all one;
And when we can with metre safe,
We'll call him so; if not, plain RALPH:
(For rhyme the rudder is of verses,
With which like ships they steer their courses.)
An equal stock of wit and valour
He had laid in; by birth a taylor.
The mighty Tyrian Queen, that gain'd
With subtle shreds a tract of land,
Did leave it with a castle fair
To his great ancestor, her heir.
From him descended cross-legg'd Knights,
Fam'd for their faith, and warlike fights
Against the bloody cannibal,
Whom they destroy'd both great and small.
This sturdy Squire, he had, as well
As the bold Trojan Knight, seen Hell;
Not with a counterfeited pass
Of golden bough, but true gold-lace.
His knowledge was not far behind
The Knight's, but of another kind,
And he another way came by 't:
Some call it GIFTS, and some NEW-LIGHT;
A liberal art, that costs no pains
Of study, industry, or brains.
His wit was sent him for a token,
But in the carriage crack'd and broken.
Like commendation nine-pence crook'd,
With — To and from my love — it look'd.
He ne'er consider'd it, as loth
To look a gift-horse in the mouth;

And very wisely wou'd lay forth
No more upon it than 'twas worth.
But as he got it freely, so
He spent it frank and freely too.
For Saints themselves will sometimes be
Of gifts, that cost them nothing, free.
By means of this, with hem and cough,
Prolongers to enlighten'd stuff,
He cou'd deep mysteries unriddle
As easily as thread a needle.
For as of vagabonds we say,
That they are ne'er beside their way;
Whate'er men speak by this New Light,
Still they are sure to be i' th' right.
'Tis a dark-lanthorn of the Spirit,
Which none see by but those that bear it:
A light that falls down from on high,
For spiritual trades to cozen by
An Ignis Fatuus, that bewitches
And leads men into pools and ditches,
To make them dip themselves, and sound
For Christendom in dirty pond
To dive like wild-fowl for salvation,
And fish to catch regeneration.
This light inspires and plays upon
The nose of Saint like bag-pipe drone,
And speaks through hollow empty soul,
As through a trunk, or whisp'ring hole,
Such language as no mortal ear
But spirit'al eaves-droppers can hear:
So PHOEBUS, or some friendly muse,
Into small poets song infuse,
Which they at second-hand rehearse,
Thro' reed or bag-pipe, verse for verse.

Thus RALPH became infallible
As three or four-legg'd oracle,
The ancient cup, or modern chair;
Spoke truth point-blank, tho' unaware.

For MYSTICK LEARNING, wond'rous able
In magick Talisman and Cabal,
Whose primitive tradition reaches
As far as ADAM'S first green breeches:
Deep-sighted in intelligences,
Ideas, atoms, influences;
And much of Terra Incognita,
Th' intelligible world, cou'd say:

A deep OCCULT PHILOSOPHER,
As learn'd as the wild Irish are,
Or Sir AGRIPPA; for profound
And solid lying much renown'd.
He ANTHROPOSOPHUS, and FLOUD,
And JACOB BEHMEN understood:
Knew many an amulet and charm,
That wou'd do neither good nor harm:
In ROSY-CRUCIAN lore as learned,
As he that Vere adeptus earned.
He understood the speech of birds
As well as they themselves do words;
Cou'd tell what subtlest parrots mean,
That speak, and think contrary clean:
What Member 'tis of whom they talk,
When they cry, Rope, and walk, knave, walk.
He'd extract numbers out of matter,
And keep them in a glass, like water;
Of sov'reign pow'r to make men wise;
For drop'd in blear thick-sighted eyes,
They'd make them see in darkest night
Like owls, tho' purblind in the light.
By help of these (as he profess'd)
He had First Matter seen undress'd:
He took her naked all alone,
Before one rag of form was on.
The Chaos too he had descry'd,
And seen quite thro', or else he ly'd:
Not that of paste-board which men shew
For groats, at fair of Barthol'mew;
But its great grandsire, first o' the name,
Whence that and REFORMATION came;
Both cousin-germans, and right able
T' inveigle and draw in the rabble.
But Reformation was, some say,
O' th' younger house to Puppet-play.
He cou'd foretel whats'ever was
By consequence to come to pass;
As death of great men, alterations,
Diseases, battles, inundations.
All this, without th' eclipse o' th' sun,
Or dreadful comet, he hath done,
By inward light; away as good,
And easy to be understood;
But with more lucky hit than those
That use to make the stars depose,
Like Knights o' th' post, and falsely charge
Upon themselves what others forge:

As if they were consenting to
All mischiefs in the world men do:
Or, like the Devil, did tempt and sway 'em
To rogueries, and then betray 'em.
They'll search a planet's house, to know
Who broke and robb'd a house below:
Examine VENUS, and the MOON,
Who stole a thimble or a spoon;
And tho' they nothing will confess,
Yet by their very looks can guess,
And tell what guilty aspect bodes,
Who stole, and who receiv'd the goods.
They'll question MARS, and, by his look,
Detect who 'twas that nimm'd a cloke:
Make MERCURY confess, and 'peach
Those thieves which he himself did teach.
They'll find, i' th' physiognomies
O' th' planets, all men's destinies.;
Like him that took the doctor's bill,
And swallow'd it instead o' th' pill
Cast the nativity o' th' question,
And from positions to be guess'd on,
As sure as it' they knew the moment
Of natives birth, tell what will come on't.
They'll feel the pulses of the stars,
To find out agues, coughs, catarrhs;
And tell what crisis does divine
The rot in sheep, or mange in swine
In men, what gives or cures the itch;
What makes them cuckolds, poor or rich;
What gains or loses, hangs or saves;
What makes men great, what fools or knaves,
But not what wise; for only of those
The stars (they say) cannot dispose,
No more than can the Astrologians.
There they say right, and like true Trojans.
This RALPHO knew, and therefore took
The other course, of which we spoke.

Thus was the accomplish'd Squire endu'd
With gifts and knowledge, per'lous shrew'd.
Never did trusty Squire with Knight,
Or Knight with Squire, e'er jump more right.
Their arms and equipage did fit,
As well as virtues, parts, and wit.
Their valours too were of a rate;
And out they sally'd at the gate.
Few miles on horseback had they jogged,

But Fortune unto them turn'd dogged;
For they a sad adventure met,
Of which anon we mean to treat;
But ere we venture to unfold
Atchievements so resolv'd and bold,
We shou'd as learned poets use,
Invoke th' assistance of some muse:
However, criticks count it sillier
Than jugglers talking to familiar.
We think 'tis no great matter which
They're all alike; yet we shall pitch
On one that fits our purpose most
Whom therefore thus do we accost:

Thou that with ale, or viler liquors,
Did'st inspire WITHERS, PRYN, and VICKARS,
And force them, tho' it was in spite
Of nature and their stars, to write;
Who, as we find in sullen writs,
And cross-grain'd works of modern wits,
With vanity, opinion, want,
The wonder of the ignorant,
The praises of the author, penn'd
B' himself, or wit-insuring friend;
The itch of picture in the front,
With bays and wicked rhyme upon't;
All that is left o' th' forked hill,
To make men scribble without skill;
Canst make a poet spite of fate,
And teach all people to translate,
Tho' out of languages in which
They understand no part of speech;
Assist me but this once, I 'mplore,
And I shall trouble thee no more.

In western clime there is a town,
To those that dwell therein well known;
Therefore there needs no more be said here,
We unto them refer our reader;
For brevity is very good,
When w' are, or are not, understood.
To this town people did repair,
On days of market, or of fair,
And, to crack'd fiddle, and hoarse tabor,
In merriment did drudge and labor.
But now a sport more formidable
Had rak'd together village rabble:
'Twas an old way of recreating,

Which learned butchers call bear-baiting:
A bold advent'rous exercise,
With ancient heroes in high prize:
For authors do affirm it came
From Isthmian or Nemean game:
Others derive it from the bear
That's fix'd in northern hemisphere,
And round about the pole does make
A circle like a bear at stake,
That at the chain's end wheels about,
And overturns the rabble-rout.
For after solemn proclamation,
In the bear's name, (as is the fashion,
According to the law of arms,
To keep men from inglorious harms,)
That none presume to come so near
As forty foot of stake of bear,
If any yet be so fool-hardy,
T' expose themselves to vain jeopardy,
If they come wounded off, and lame,
No honour's got by such a maim;
Altho' the bear gain much, b'ing bound
In honour to make good his ground,
When he's engag'd, and takes no notice,
If any press upon him, who 'tis;
But let's them know, at their own cost,
That he intends to keep his post.
This to prevent, and other harms,
Which always wait on feats of arms,
(For in the hurry of a fray
'Tis hard to keep out of harm's way,)
Thither the Knight his course did steer,
To keep the peace 'twixt dog and bear;
As he believ'd he was bound to do
In conscience, and commission too;
And therefore thus bespoke the Squire.

We that are wisely mounted higher
Than constables in curule wit,
When on tribunal bench we sit,
Like speculators shou'd foresee,
From Pharos of authority,
Portended mischiefs farther then
Low Proletarian tything-men:
And therefore being inform'd by bruit,
That dog and bear are to dispute;
For so of late men fighting name,
Because they often prove the same;

(For where the first does hap to be,
The last does coincidere;)
Quantum in nobis, have thought good,
To save th' expence of Christian blood,
And try if we, by mediation
Of treaty and accommodation,
Can end the quarrel and compose
The bloody duel without blows.
Are not our liberties, our lives,
The laws, religion and our wives,
Enough at once to lie at stake
For Cov'nant and the Cause's sake?
But in that quarrel dogs and bears,
As well as we must venture theirs
This feud, by Jesuits invented,
By evil counsel is fomented:
There is a MACHIAVILIAN plot,
(Tho' ev'ry Nare olfact is not,)
A deep design in't, to divide
The well-affected that confide,
By setting brother against brother,
To claw and curry one another.
Have we not enemies plus satis,
That Cane & Angue pejus hate us?
And shall we turn our fangs and claws
Upon our own selves, without cause?
That some occult design doth lie
In bloody cynarctomachy,
Is plain enough to him that knows
How Saints lead brothers by the nose.
I wish myself a pseudo-prophet,
But sure some mischief will come of it;
Unless by providential wit,
Or force, we averruncate it.
For what design, what interest,
Can beast have to encounter beast?
They fight for no espoused cause,
Frail privilege, fundamental laws,
Not for a thorough reformation,
Nor covenant, nor protestation,
Nor liberty of consciences,
Nor Lords and Commons ordinances;
Nor for the church, nor for church-lands,
To get them in their own no hands;
Nor evil counsellors to bring
To justice that seduce the King;
Nor for the worship of us men,
Though we have done as much for them.

Th' AEgyptians worshipp'd dogs, and for
Their faith made internecine war.
Others ador'd a rat, and some
For that church suffer'd martyrdom.
The Indians fought for the truth
Of th' elephant and monkey's tooth,
And many, to defend that faith,
Fought it out mordicus to death.
But no beast ever was so slight,
For man, as for his God, to fight.
They have more wit, alas! and know
Themselves and us better than so.
But we, who only do infuse
The rage in them like Boute-feus;
'Tis our example that instils
In them th' infection of our ills.
For, as some late philosophers.
Have well observ'd, beasts, that converse
With man, take after him, as hogs
Get pigs all the year, and bitches dogs.
Just so, by our example, cattle
Learn to give one another battle.
We read, in NERO's time, the heathen,
When they destroy'd the Christian brethren,
Did sew them in the skins of bears,
And then set dogs about their ears:
From thence, no doubt, th' invention came
Of this lewd antichristian game.

To this, quoth RALPHO, Verily
The point seems very plain to me.
It is an antichristian game,
Unlawful both in thing and name.
First, for the name: the word, bear-baiting
Is carnal, and of man's creating:
For certainly there's no such word
In all the scripture on record;
Therefore unlawful, and a sin;
And so is (secondly) the thing.
A vile assembly 'tis, that can
No more be prov'd by scripture than
Provincial, classic, national;
Mere human-creature cobwebs all.
Thirdly, it is idolatrous;
For when men run a whoring thus
With their inventions, whatsoe'er
The thing be, whether dog or bear,
It is idolatrous and pagan,

No less than worshipping of DAGON.

Quoth HUDIBRAS, I smell a rat;
RALPHO, thou dost prevaricate:
For though the thesis which thou lay'st
Be true ad amussim, as thou say'st;
(For that bear-baiting should appear
Jure divino lawfuller
Than synods are, thou dost deny,
Totidem verbis; so do I;)
Yet there's a fallacy in this;
For if by sly HOMAEOSIS,
Tussis pro crepitu, an art
Under a cough to slur a f—t
Thou wou'dst sophistically imply,
Both are unlawful, I deny.

And I (quoth RALPHO) do not doubt
But bear-baiting may be made out,
In gospel-times, as lawful as is
Provincial or parochial classis;
And that both are so near of kin,
And like in all, as well as sin,
That put them in a bag, and shake 'em,
Yourself o' th' sudden would mistake 'em,
And not know which is which, unless
You measure by their wickedness:
For 'tis not hard t'imagine whether
O' th' two is worst; tho' I name neither.

Quoth HUDIBRAS, Thou offer'st much,
But art not able to keep touch.
Mira de lente, as 'tis i' th' adage,
Id est, to make a leek a cabbage;
Thou'lt be at best but such a bull,
Or shear-swine, all cry, and no wool;
For what can synods have at all
With bear that's analogical?
Or what relation has debating
Of church-affairs with bear-baiting?
A just comparison still is
Of things ejusdem generis;
And then what genus rightly doth
Include and comprehend them both?
If animal both of us may
As justly pass for bears as they;
For we are animals no less,
Altho' of different specieses.

But, RALPHO, this is not fit place
Nor time to argue out the case:
For now the field is not far off,
Where we must give the world a proof
Of deeds, not words, and such as suit
Another manner of dispute;
A controversy that affords
Actions for arguments, not words;
Which we must manage at a rate
Of prowess and conduct adequate
To what our place and fame doth promise,
And all the godly expect from us,
Nor shall they be deceiv'd, unless
We're slurr'd and outed by success;
Success, the mark no mortal wit,
Or surest hand can always hit:
For whatsoe'er we perpetrate,
We do but row, we're steer'd by Fate,
Which in success oft disinherits,
For spurious causes, noblest merits.
Great actions are not always true sons
Of great and mighty resolutions;
Nor do th' boldest attempts bring forth
Events still equal to their worth;
But sometimes fail, and, in their stead,
Fortune and cowardice succeed.
Yet we have no great cause to doubt;
Our actions still have borne us out;
Which tho' they're known to be so ample,
We need not copy from example.
We're not the only persons durst
Attempt this province, nor the first.
In northern clime a val'rous Knight
Did whilom kill his bear in fght,
And wound a fiddler; we have both
Of these the objects of our wroth,
And equal fame and glory from
Th' attempt of victory to come.
'Tis sung, there is a valiant Mamaluke
In foreign land, yclep'd —
To whom we have been oft compar'd
For person, parts; address, and beard;
Both equally reputed stout,
And in the same cause both have fought:
He oft in such attempts as these
Came off with glory and success;
Nor will we fail in th' execution,
For want of equal resolution.

Honour is like a widow, won
With brisk attempt and putting on;
With ent'ring manfully, and urging;
Not slow approaches, like a virgin.

'Tis said, as yerst the Phrygian Knight,
So ours with rusty steel did smite
His Trojan horse, and just as much
He mended pace upon the touch;
But from his empty stomach groan'd
Just as that hollow beast did sound,
And angry answer'd from behind,
With brandish'd tail and blast of wind.
So have I seen, with armed heel,
A wight bestride a Common-weal;
While still the more he kick'd and spurr'd,
The less the sullen jade has stirr'd.

PART I

CANTO II

THE ARGUMENT

The catalogue and character
Of th' enemies best men of war;
Whom, in bold harangue, the Knight
Defies, and challenges to fight.
H' encounters Talgol, routs the Bear,
And takes the Fiddler prisoner,
Conveys him to enchanted castle;
There shuts him fast in wooden bastile.

There was an ancient sage philosopher,
That had read ALEXANDER Ross over,
And swore the world, as he cou'd prove,
Was made of fighting and of love:
Just so romances are; for what else
Is in them all, but love and battels?
O' th' first of these we've no great matter
To treat of, but a world o' th' latter;
In which to do the injur'd right
We mean, in what concerns just fight.
Certes our authors are to blame,
For to make some well-sounding name

A pattern fit for modern Knights
To copy out in frays and fights;
Like those that a whole street do raze
To build a palace in the place.
They never care how many others
They kill, without regard of mothers,
Or wives, or children, so they can
Make up some fierce, dead-doing man,
Compos'd of many ingredient valors,
Just like the manhood of nine taylors.
So a Wild Tartar, when he spies
A man that's handsome, valiant, wise,
If he can kill him, thinks t' inherit
His wit, his beauty, and his spirit
As if just so much he enjoy'd
As in another is destroy'd
For when a giant's slain in fight,
And mow'd o'erthwart, or cleft down right,
It is a heavy case, no doubt;
A man should have his brains beat out
Because he's tall, and has large bones;
As men kill beavers for their stones.
But as for our part, we shall tell
The naked truth of what befel;
And as an equal friend to both
The Knight and Bear, but more to troth,
With neither faction shall take part,
But give to each his due desert;
And never coin a formal lie on't,
To make the Knight o'ercome the giant.
This b'ing profest, we've hopes enough,
And now go on where we left off.

They rode; but authors having not
Determin'd whether pace or trot,
(That is to say, whether tollutation,
As they do term't, or succussation,)
We leave it, and go on, as now
Suppose they did, no matter how;
Yet some from subtle hints have got
Mysterious light, it was a trot:
But let that pass: they now begun
To spur their living-engines on.
For as whipp'd tops, and bandy'd balls,
The learned hold, are animals;
So horses they affirm to be
Mere engines made by geometry;
And were invented first from engines,

As Indian Britons were from Penguins.
So let them be; and, as I was saying,
They their live engines ply'd, not staying
Until they reach'd the fatal champain,
Which th' enemy did then encamp on;
The dire Pharsalian plain, where battle
Was to be wag'd 'twixt puissant cattle
And fierce auxiliary men,
That came to aid their brethren,
Who now began to take the field,
As Knight from ridge of steed beheld.
For as our modern wits behold,
Mounted a pick-back on the old,
Much further oft; much further he,
Rais'd on his aged beast cou'd see;
Yet not sufficient to descry
All postures of the enemy;
Wherefore he bids the Squire ride further,
T' observe their numbers, and their order;
That when their motions he had known
He might know how to fit his own.
Meanwhile he stopp'd his willing steed,
To fit himself for martial deed.
Both kinds of metal he prepar'd,
Either to give blows, or to ward:
Courage and steel, both of great force,
Prepar'd for better, or for worse.
His death-charg'd pistols he did fit well,
Drawn out from life-preserving vittle.
These being prim'd, with force he labour'd
To free's sword from retentive scabbard
And, after many a painful pluck,
From rusty durance he bail'd tuck.
Then shook himself, to see that prowess
In scabbard of his arms sat loose;
And, rais'd upon his desp'rate foot,
On stirrup-side he gaz'd about,
Portending blood, like blazing star,
The beacon of approaching war.
RALPHO rode on with no less speed
Than Hugo in the forest did;
But far more in returning made;
For now the foe he had survey'd,
Rang'd as to him they did appear,
With van, main battle, wings, and rear.
I' the head of all this warlike rabble,
CROWDERO march'd, expert and able.
Instead of trumpet and of drum,

That makes the warrior's stomach come,
Whose noise whets valour sharp, like beer
By thunder turn'd to vinegar,
(For if a trumpet sound, or drum beat,
Who has not a month's mind to combat?)
A squeaking engine he apply'd
Unto his neck, on north-east side,
Just where the hangman does dispose,
To special friends, the knot of noose:
For 'tis great grace, when statesmen straight
Dispatch a friend, let others wait.
His warped ear hung o'er the strings,
Which was but souse to chitterlings:
For guts, some write, e'er they are sodden,
Are fit for music, or for pudden;
From whence men borrow ev'ry kind
Of minstrelsy by string or wind.
His grisly beard was long and thick,
With which he strung his fiddle-stick;
For he to horse-tail scorn'd to owe,
For what on his own chin did grow.
Chiron, the four-legg'd bard, had both
A beard and tail of his own growth;
And yet by authors 'tis averr'd,
He made use only of his beard.
In Staffordshire, where virtuous worth
Does raise the minstrelsy, not birth;
Where bulls do chuse the boldest king,
And ruler, o'er the men of string;
(As once in Persia, 'tis said,
Kings were proclaim'd by a horse that neigh'd;)
He bravely venturing at a crown,
By chance of war was beaten down,
And wounded sore. His leg then broke,
Had got a deputy of oak:
For when a shin in fight is cropp'd,
The knee with one of timber's propp'd,
Esteem'd more honourable than the other,
And takes place, though the younger brother.

Next march'd brave ORSIN, famous for
Wise conduct, and success in war:
A skilful leader, stout, severe,
Now marshal to the champion bear.
With truncheon, tipp'd with iron head,
The warrior to the lists he led;
With solemn march and stately pace,
But far more grave and solemn face;

Grave as the Emperor of Pegu
Or Spanish potentate Don Diego.
This leader was of knowledge great,
Either for charge or for retreat.
He knew when to fall on pell-mell;
To fall back and retreat as well.
So lawyers, lest the bear defendant,
And plaintiff dog, should make an end on't,
Do stave and tail with writs of error,
Reverse of judgment, and demurrer,
To let them breathe a while, and then
Cry whoop, and set them on agen.
As ROMULUS a wolf did rear,
So he was dry-nurs'd by a bear,
That fed him with the purchas'd prey
Of many a fierce and bloody fray;
Bred up, where discipline most rare is,
In military Garden Paris.
For soldiers heretofore did grow
In gardens, just as weeds do now,
Until some splay-foot politicians
T'APOLLO offer'd up petitions
For licensing a new invention
They'd found out of an antique engine,
To root out all the weeds that grow
In public gardens at a blow,
And leave th' herbs standing. Quoth Sir Sun,
My friends, that is not to be done.
Not done! quoth Statesmen; yes, an't please ye,
When it's once known, you'll say 'tis easy.
Why then let's know it, quoth Apollo.
We'll beat a drum, and they'll all follow.
A drum! (quoth PHOEBUS;) troth, that's true;
A pretty invention, quaint and new.
But though of voice and instrument
We are the undoubted president,
We such loud music don't profess:
The Devil's master of that office,
Where it must pass, if't be a drum;
He'll sign it with Cler. Parl. Dom. Com.
To him apply yourselves, and he
Will soon dispatch you for his fee.
They did so; but it prov'd so ill,
Th' had better let 'em grow there still.
But to resume what we discoursing
Were on before, that is, stout ORSIN:
That which so oft, by sundry writers,
Has been applied t' almost all fighters,

More justly may b' ascrib'd to this
Than any other warrior, (viz.)
None ever acted both parts bolder,
Both of a chieftain and a soldier.
He was of great descent and high
For splendour and antiquity;
And from celestial origine
Deriv'd himself in a right line.
Not as the ancient heroes did,
Who, that their base-births might be hid,
(Knowing they were of doubtful gender,
And that they came in at a windore)
Made Jupiter himself and others
O' th' gods, gallants to their own mothers,
To get on them a race of champions,
(Of which old Homer first made Lampoons.)
ARCTOPHYLAX, in northern spheres
Was his undoubted ancestor:
From him his great forefathers came,
And in all ages bore his name.
Learned he was in med'c'nal lore;
For by his side a pouch he wore,
Replete with strange Hermetic powder,
That wounds nine miles point-blank wou'd solder;
By skilful chemist, with great cost,
Extracted from a rotten post;
But of a heav'nlier influence
Than that which mountebanks dispense;
Tho' by Promethean fire made,
As they do quack that drive that trade.
For as when slovens do amiss
At others doors, by stool or piss,
The learned write, a red-hot spit
B'ing prudently apply'd to it,
Will convey mischief from the dung
Unto the part that did the wrong,
So this did healing; and as sure
As that did mischief this would cure.

Thus virtuous ORSIN was endu'd
With learning, conduct, fortitude,
Incomparable: and as the prince
Of poets, HOMER sung long since
A skilful leech is better far
Than half an hundred men of war,
So he appear'd; and by his skill,
No less than dint of sword, cou'd kill

The gallant BRUIN march'd next him,
With visage formidably grim,
And rugged as a Saracen,
Or Turk of Mahomet's own kin;
Clad in a mantle della guerre
Of rough impenetrable fur;
And in his nose, like Indian King,
He wore, for ornament, a ring;
About his neck a threefold gorget.
As rough as trebled leathern target;
Armed, as heralds cant, and langued;
Or, as the vulgar say, sharp-fanged.
For as the teeth in beasts of prey
Are swords, with which they fight in fray;
So swords, in men of war, are teeth,
Which they do eat their vittle with.
He was by birth, some authors write,
A Russian; some, a Muscovite;
And 'mong the Cossacks had been bred;
Of whom we in diurnals read,
That serve to fill up pages here,
As with their bodies ditches there.
SCRIMANSKY was his cousin-german,
With whom he serv'd, and fed on vermin;
And when these fail'd, he'd suck his claws,
And quarter himself upon his paws.
And tho' his countrymen, the Huns,
Did stew their meat between their bums
And th' horses backs o'er which they straddle,
And ev'ry man eat up his saddle;
He was not half so nice as they,
But eat it raw when 't came in's way.
He had trac'd countries far and near,
More than LE BLANC, the traveller;
Who writes, he spous'd in India,
Of noble house, a lady gay,
And got on her a race of worthies,
As stout as any upon earth is.
Full many a fight for him between
TALGOL and ORSIN oft had been
Each striving to deserve the crown
Of a sav'd citizen; the one
To guard his bear; the other fought
To aid his dog; both made more stout
By sev'ral spurs of neighbourhood,
Church-fellow-membership, and blood
But TALGOL, mortal foe to cows,
Never got aught of him but blows;

Blows, hard and heavy, such as he
Had lent, repaid with usury.

Yet TALGOL was of courage stout,
And vanquish'd oft'ner than he fought:
Inur'd to labour, sweat and toil,
And like a champion shone with oil.
Right many a widow his keen blade,.
And many fatherless had made.
He many a boar and huge dun-cow
Did, like another Guy, o'erthrow;
But Guy with him in fight compar'd,
Had like the boar or dun-cow far'd
With greater troops of sheep h' had fought
Than AJAX or bold DON QUIXOTE:
And many a serpent of fell kind,
With wings before and stings behind,
Subdu'd: as poets say, long agone
Bold Sir GEORGE, St. GEORGE did the dragon.
Nor engine, nor device polemic,
Disease, nor doctor epidemic,
Tho' stor'd with deletory med'cines,
(Which whosoever took is dead since,)
E'er sent so vast a colony
To both the underworlds as he:
For he was of that noble trade
That demi-gods and heroes made,
Slaughter and knocking on the head;.
The trade to which they all were bred;
And is, like others, glorious when
'Tis great and large, but base if mean.
The former rides in triumph for it;
The latter in a two-wheel'd chariot
For daring to profane a thing
So sacred with vile bungling.

Next these the brave MAGNANO came;
MAGNANO, great in martial fame.
Yet when with ORSIN he wag'd fight,
'Tis sung, he got but little by't.
Yet he was fierce as forest boar,
Whose spoils upon his back he wore,
As thick as AJAX' seven-fold shield,
Which o'er his brazen arms he held:
But brass was feeble to resist
The fury of his armed fist:
Nor cou'd the hardest ir'n hold out
Against his blows, but they wou'd through't.

In MAGIC he was deeply read
As he that made the brazen head;
Profoundly skill'd in the black art;
As ENGLISH MERLIN for his heart;
But far more skilful in the spheres
Than he was at the sieve and shears.
He cou'd transform himself in colour
As like the devil as a collier;
As like as hypocrites in show
Are to true saints, or crow to crow.

Of WARLIKE ENGINES he was author,
Devis'd for quick dispatch of slaughter:
The cannon, blunderbuss, and saker,
He was th' inventor of, and maker:
The trumpet, and the kettle-drum,
Did both from his invention come.
He was the first that e'er did teach
To make, and how to stop, a breach.
A lance he bore with iron pike;
Th' one half wou'd thrust, the other strike;
And when their forces he had join'd,
He scorn'd to turn his parts behind.

He TRULLA lov'd; TRULLA, more bright
Than burnish'd armour of her Knight:
A bold virago, stout and tall,
As JOAN of FRANCE, or English MALL.
Thro' perils both of wind and limb,
Thro' thick and thin, she follow'd him,
In ev'ry adventure h' undertook,
And never him or it forsook.
At breach of wall, or hedge surprize,
She shar'd i' th' hazard and the prize:
At beating quarters up, or forage,
Behav'd herself with matchless courage;
And laid about in fight more busily
Than the Amazonian dame Penthesile.

And though some criticks here cry shame,
And say our authors are to blame,
That (spite of all philosophers,
Who hold no females stout, but bears;
And heretofore did so abhor
That women should pretend to war,
'They wou'd not suffer the stoutest dame
To swear by HERCULES'S name)

Make feeble ladies, in their works,
To fight like termagants and Turks;
To lay their native arms aside,
 Their modesty, and ride astride;
 To run a-tilt at men, and wield
 Their naked tools in open field;
 As stout ARMIDA, bold TRALESTRIS,
 And she that wou'd have been the mistress
 Of GUNDIBERT; but he had grace,
And rather took a country lass;
They say, 'tis false, without all sense,
But of pernicious consequence
To government, which they suppose
Can never be upheld in prose;
Strip nature naked to the skin,
You'll find about her no such thing.
It may be so; yet what we tell
Of TRULLA that's improbable,
Shall be depos'd by those who've seen't,
Or, what's as good, produc'd in print:
And if they will not take our word,
We'll prove it true upon record.

The upright CERDON next advanc't,
Of all his race the valiant'st:
CERDON the Great, renown'd in song,
Like HERC'LES, for repair of wrong:
He rais'd the low, and fortify'd
The weak against the strongest side:
Ill has he read, that never hit
On him in Muses' deathless writ.
He had a weapon keen and fierce,
That through a bull-hide shield wou'd pierce,
And cut it in a thousand pieces,
Tho' tougher than the Knight of Greece his,
With whom his black-thumb'd ancestor
Was comrade in the ten years war:
For when the restless Greeks sat down
So many years before Troy town,
And were renown'd, as HOMER writes,
For well-soal'd boots no less than fights,
They ow'd that glory only to
His ancestor, that made them so.
Fast friend he was to REFORMATION,
Until 'twas worn quite out of fashion.
Next rectifier of wry LAW,
And wou'd make three to cure one flaw.
Learned he was, and could take note,

Transcribe, collect, translate, and quote.
But PREACHING was his chiefest talent,
Or argument, in which b'ing valiant,
He us'd to lay about and stickle,
Like ram or bull, at conventicle:
For disputants, like rams and bulls,
Do fight with arms that spring from skulls.

Last COLON came, bold man of war,
Destin'd to blows by fatal star;
Right expert in command of horse;
But cruel, and without remorse.
That which of CENTAUR long ago
Was said, and has been wrested to
Some other knights, was true of this;
He and his horse were of a piece.
One spirit did inform them both;
The self-same vigour, fury, wroth:
Yet he was much the rougher part,
And always had a harder heart;
Although his horse had been of those
That fed on man's flesh, as fame goes.
Strange food for horse! and yet, alas!
It may be true, for flesh is grass.
Sturdy he was, and no less able
Than HERCULES to clean a stable;
As great a drover, and as great
A critic too, in hog or neat.
He ripp'd the womb up of his mother,
Dame Tellus, 'cause she wanted fother
And provender wherewith to feed
Himself, and his less cruel steed.
It was a question, whether he
Or's horse were of a family
More worshipful: 'till antiquaries
(After th' had almost por'd out their eyes)
Did very learnedly decide
The business on the horse's side;
And prov'd not only horse, but cows,
Nay, pigs, were of the elder house:
For beasts, when man was but a piece
Of earth himself, did th' earth possess.

These worthies were the chief that led
The combatants, each in the head
Of his command, with arms and rage,
Ready and longing to engage.
The numerous rabble was drawn out

Of sev'ral counties round about,
From villages remote, and shires,
Of east and western hemispheres
From foreign parishes and regions,
Of different manners, speech, religions,
Came men and mastiffs; some to fight
For fame and honour, some for sight.
And now the field of death, the lists,
Were enter'd by antagonists,
And blood was ready to be broach'd,
When HUDIBRAS in haste approach'd,
With Squire and weapons, to attack 'em:
But first thus from his horse bespake 'em:
What rage, O citizens! what fury
Doth you to these dire actions hurry?
What oestrum, what phrenetic mood,
Makes you thus lavish of your blood,
While the proud Vies your trophies boast
And unreveng'd walks — ghost?
What towns, what garrisons might you
With hazard of this blood subdue,
Which now y'are bent to throw away
In vain, untriumphable fray!
Shall SAINTS in civil bloodshed wallow
Of Saints, and let the CAUSE lie fallow?
The Cause for which we fought and swore
So boldly, shall we now give o'er?
Then, because quarrels still are seen
With oaths and swearings to begin,
The SOLEMN LEAGUE and COVENANT
Will seem a mere God-dam-me rant;
And we, that took it, and have fought,
As lewd as drunkards that fall out.
For as we make war for the King
Against himself the self-same thing,
Some will not stick to swear we do
For God and for Religion too:
For if bear-baiting we allow,
What good can Reformation do?
The blood and treasure that's laid out,
Is thrown away, and goes for nought.
Are these the fruits o' th' PROTESTATION,
The Prototype of Reformation,
Which all the Saints, and some, since Martyrs,
Wore in their hats like wedding garters,
When 'twas resolv'd by either house
Six Members quarrel to espouse?
Did they for this draw down the rabble,

With zeal and noises formidable,
And make all cries about the town
Join throats to cry the Bishops down?
Who having round begirt the palace,
(As once a month they do the gallows,)
As members gave the sign about,
Set up their throats with hideous shout.
When tinkers bawl'd aloud to settle
Church discipline, for patching kettle:
No sow-gelder did blow his horn
To geld a cat, but cry'd, Reform.
The oyster-women lock'd their fish up,
And trudg'd away, to cry, No Bishop.
The mouse-trap men laid save-alls by,
And 'gainst Ev'l Counsellors did cry.
Botchers left old cloaths in the lurch,
And fell to turn and patch the Church.
Some cry'd the Covenant instead
Of pudding-pies and ginger-bread;
And some for brooms, old boots and shoes,
Bawl'd out to Purge the Commons House.
Instead of kitchen-stuff, some cry,
A Gospel-preaching Ministry;
And some, for old suits, coats, or cloak,
No Surplices nor Service-Book.
A strange harmonious inclination
Of all degrees to Reformation.
And is this all? Is this the end
To which these carr'ings on did tend?
Hath public faith, like a young heir,
For this ta'en up all sorts of ware,
And run int' every tradesman's book,
'Till both turn'd bankrupts, and are broke?
Did Saints for this bring in their plate,
And crowd as if they came too late?
For when they thought the Cause had need on't,
Happy was he that could be rid on't.
Did they coin piss-pots, bowls, and flaggons,
Int' officers of horse and dragoons;
And into pikes and musquetteers
Stamp beakers, cups, and porringers!
A thimble, bodkin, and a spoon,
Did start up living men as soon
As in the furnace they were thrown,
Just like the dragon's teeth b'ing sown.
Then was the Cause of gold and plate,
The Brethren's off'rings, consecrate,
Like th' Hebrew calf, and down before it

The Saints fell prostrate, to adore it
So say the wicked — and will you
Make that sarcasmus scandal true,
By running after dogs and bears?
Beasts more unclean than calves or steers.
Have pow'rful Preachers ply'd their tongues,
And laid themselves out and their lungs;
Us'd all means, both direct and sinister,
I' th' pow'r of Gospel-preaching Minister?
Have they invented tones to win
The women, and make them draw in
The men, as Indians with a female
Tame elephant inveigle the male?
Have they told Prov'dence what it must do,
Whom to avoid, and whom to trust to?
Discover'd th' enemy's design,
And which way best to countermine?
Prescrib'd what ways it hath to work,
Or it will ne'er advance the Kirk?
Told it the news o' th' last express,
And after good or bad success,
Made prayers, not so like petitions,
As overtures and propositions,
(Such as the army did present
To their creator, th' Parliament,)
In which they freely will confess
They will not, cannot acquiesce,
Unless the work be carry'd on
In the same way they have begun,
By setting Church and Common-weal
All on a flame, bright as their zeal,
On which the Saints were all a-gog,
And all this for a bear and dog?
The parliament drew up petitions
To itself, and sent them, like commissions,
To well-affected persons down,
In ev'ry city and great town,
With pow'r to levy horse and men,
Only to bring them back agen:
For this did many, many a mile,
Ride manfully in rank and file,
With papers in their hats, that show'd
As if they to the pillory rode.
Have all these courses, these efforts,
Been try'd by people of all sorts,
Velis & remis, omnibus nervis
And all t'advance the Cause's service?
And shall all now be thrown, away

In petulant intestine fray?
Shall we that in the Cov'nant swore,
Each man of us to run before
Another, still in Reformation,
Give dogs and bears a dispensation?
How will Dissenting Brethren relish it?
What will malignants say? videlicet,
That each man Swore to do his best,
To damn and perjure all the rest!
And bid the Devil take the hin'most,
Which at this race is like to win most.
They'll say our bus'ness, to reform
The Church and State, is but a worm;
For to subscribe, unsight, unseen,
To an unknown Church-discipline,
What is it else, but before-hand
T'engage, and after understand?
For when we swore to carry on
The present Reformation,
According to the purest mode
Of Churches best reformed abroad,
What did we else, but make a vow
To do we know not what, nor how?
For no three of us will agree,
Where or what Churches these should be;
And is indeed the self-same case
With theirs that swore et caeteras;
Or the French League, in which men vow'd
To fight to the last drop of blood.
These slanders will be thrown upon
The Cause and Work we carry on,
If we permit men to run headlong
T' exorbitances fit for Bedlam
Rather than Gospel-walking times,
When slightest sins are greatest crimes.
But we the matter so shall handle,
As to remove that odious scandal.
In name of King and parliament,
I charge ye all; no more foment
This feud, but keep the peace between
Your brethren and your countrymen;
And to those places straight repair
Where your respective dwellings are.
But to that purpose first surrender
The FIDDLER, as the prime offender,
Th' incendiary vile, that is chief
Author and engineer of mischief;
That makes division between friends,

For profane and malignant ends.
He, and that engine of vile noise,
On which illegally he plays,
Shall (dictum factum) both be brought
To condign punishment, as they ought.
This must be done; and I would fain see
Mortal so sturdy as to gain-say:
For then I'll take another course,
And soon reduce you all by force.
This said, he clapp'd his hand on sword,
To shew he meant to keep his word.

But TALGOL, who had long supprest
Inflamed wrath in glowing, breast,
Which now began to rage and burn as
Implacably as flame in furnace,
Thus answer'd him: — Thou vermin wretched
As e'er in measled pork was hatched;
Thou tail of worship, that dost grow
On rump of justice as of cow;
How dar'st thou, with that sullen luggage
O' th' self, old ir'n, and other baggage,
With which thy steed of bones and leather
Has broke his wind in halting hither;
How durst th', I say, adventure thus
T' oppose thy lumber against us?
Could thine impertinence find out
To work t' employ itself about,
Where thou, secure from wooden blow,
Thy busy vanity might'st show?
Was no dispute a-foot between
The caterwauling Brethren?
No subtle question rais'd among
Those out-o-their wits, and those i' th' wrong;
No prize between those combatants
O' th' times, the Land and Water Saints;
Where thou might'st stickle without hazard
Of outrage to thy hide and mazzard;
And not for want of bus'ness come
To us to be so troublesome,
To interrupt our better sort
Of disputants, and spoil our sport?
Was there no felony, no bawd,
Cut-purse, no burglary abroad;
No stolen pig, nor plunder'd goose,
To tie thee up from breaking loose?
No ale unlicens'd, broken hedge,
For which thou statute might'st alledge,

To keep thee busy from foul evil,
And shame due to thee from the Devil?
Did no committee sit, where he
Might cut out journey-work for thee?
And set th' a task, with subornation,
To stitch up sale and sequestration;
To cheat, with holiness and zeal,
All parties, and the common-weal?
Much better had it been for thee,
H' had kept thee where th' art us'd to be;
Or sent th' on bus'ness any whither,
So he had never brought thee hither.
But if th' hast brain enough in skull
To keep itself in lodging whole,
And not provoke the rage of stones
And cudgels to thy hide and bones
Tremble, and vanish, while thou may'st,
Which I'll not promise if thou stay'st.
At this the Knight grew high in wroth,
And lifting hands and eyes up both,
Three times he smote on stomach stout,
From whence at length these words broke out:

Was I for this entitled SIR,
And girt with trusty sword and spur,
For fame and honor to wage battle,
Thus to be brav'd by foe to cattle?
Not all that pride that makes thee swell
As big as thou dost blown-up veal;
Nor all thy tricks and sleights to cheat,
And sell thy carrion for good meat;
Not all thy magic to repair
Decay'd old age in tough lean ware;
Make nat'ral appear thy work,
And stop the gangrene in stale pork;
Not all that force that makes thee proud,
Because by bullock ne'er withstood;
Though arm'd with all thy cleavers, knives,
And axes made to hew down lives,
Shall save or help thee to evade
The hand of Justice, or this blade,
Which I, her sword-bearer, do carry,
For civil deed and military.
Nor shall those words of venom base,
Which thou hast from their native place,
Thy stomach, pump'd to fling on me,
Go unreveng'd, though I am free:
Thou down the same throat shalt devour 'em,

Like tainted beef, and pay dear for 'em.
Nor shall it e'er be said, that wight
With gantlet blue, and bases white,
And round blunt truncheon by his side,
So great a man at arms defy'd
With words far bitterer than wormwood,
That would in Job or Grizel stir mood.
Dogs with their tongues their wounds do heal;
But men with hands, as thou shalt feel.

This said, with hasty rage he snatch'd
His gun-shot, that in holsters watch'd;
And bending cock, he levell'd full
Against th' outside of TALGOL'S skull;
Vowing that he shou'd ne'er stir further,
Nor henceforth cow nor bullock murther.
But PALLAS came in shape of rust,
And 'twixt the spring and hammerthrust
Her Gorgon shield, which made the cock
Stand stiff, as t'were transform'd to stock.
Mean while fierce TALGOL, gath'ring might,
With rugged truncheon charg'd the Knight;
But he with petronel upheav'd,
Instead of shield, the blow receiv'd.
The gun recoil'd, as well it might,
Not us'd to such a kind of fight,
And shrunk from its great master's gripe,
Knock'd down and stunn'd by mortal stripe.
Then HUDIBRAS, with furious haste,
Drew out his sword; yet not so fast,
But TALGOL first, with hardy thwack,
Twice bruis'd his head, and twice his back.
But when his nut-brown sword was out,
With stomach huge he laid about,
Imprinting many a wound upon
His mortal foe, the truncheon.
The trusty cudgel did oppose
Itself against dead-doing blows,
To guard its leader from fell bane,
And then reveng'd itself again.
And though the sword (some understood)
In force had much the odds of wood,
'Twas nothing so; both sides were ballanc't
So equal, none knew which was valiant'st:
For wood with Honour b'ing engag'd,
Is so implacably enrag'd,
Though iron hew and mangle sore,
Wood wounds and bruises Honour more.

And now both Knights were out of breath,
Tir'd in the hot pursuit of death;
While all the rest amaz'd stood still,
Expecting which should take or kill.
This HUDIBRAS observ'd; and fretting
Conquest should be so long a getting,
He drew up all his force into
One body, and that into one blow.
But TALGOL wisely avoided it
By cunning sleight; for had it hit,
The upper part of him the blow
Had slit as sure as that below.

Meanwhile th' incomparable COLON,
To aid his friend, began to fall on.
Him RALPH encounter'd, and straight grew
A dismal combat 'twixt them two:
Th' one arm'd with metal, th' other with wood;
This fit for bruise, and that for blood.
With many a stiff thwack, many a bang,
Hard crab-tree and old iron rang;
While none that saw them cou'd divine
To which side conquest would incline,
Until MAGNANO, who did envy
That two should with so many men vie,
By subtle stratagem of brain,
Perform'd what force could ne'er attain;
For he, by foul hap, having found
Where thistles grew on barren ground,
In haste he drew his weapon out,
And having cropp'd them from the root,
He clapp'd them underneath the tail
Of steed, with pricks as sharp as nail.
The angry beast did straight resent
The wrong done to his fundament;
Began to kick, and fling, and wince,
As if h' had been beside his sense,
Striving to disengage from thistle,
That gall'd him sorely under his tail:
Instead of which, he threw the pack
Of Squire and baggage from his back;
And blund'ring still with smarting rump,
He gave the Knight's steed such a thump
As made him reel. The Knight did stoop,
And sat on further side aslope.
This TALGOL viewing, who had now
By sleight escap'd the fatal blow,
He rally'd, and again fell to't;

For catching foe by nearer foot,
He lifted with such might and strength,
As would have hurl'd him thrice his length,
And dash'd his brains (if any) out:
But MARS, that still protects the stout,
In pudding-time came to his aid,
And under him the Bear convey'd;
The Bear, upon whose soft fur-gown
The Knight with all his weight fell down.
The friendly rug preserv'd the ground,
And headlong Knight, from bruise or wound;
Like feather-bed betwixt a wall
And heavy brunt of cannon-ball.
As Sancho on a blanket fell,
And had no hurt, our's far'd as well
In body; though his mighty spirit,
B'ing heavy, did not so well bear it,
The Bear was in a greater fright,
Beat down and worsted by the Knight.
He roar'd, and rak'd, and flung about,
To shake off bondage from his snout.
His wrath inflam'd, boil'd o'er, and from
His jaws of death he threw the foam:
Fury in stranger postures threw him,
And more than herald ever drew him.
He tore the earth which he had sav'd
From squelch of Knight, and storm'd and rav'd,
And vext the more because the harms
He felt were 'gainst the law of arms:
For men he always took to be
His friends, and dogs the enemy;
Who never so much hurt had done him,
As his own side did falling on him.
It griev'd him to the guts that they
For whom h' had fought so many a fray,
And serv'd with loss of blood so long,
Shou'd offer such inhuman wrong;
Wrong of unsoldier-like condition;
For which he flung down his commission;
And laid about him, till his nose
From thrall of ring and cord broke loose.
Soon as he felt himself enlarg'd,
Through thickest of his foes he charg'd,
And made way through th' amazed crew;
Some he o'erran, and some o'erthrew,
But took none; for by hasty flight
He strove t' escape pursuit of Knight;
From whom he fled with as much haste

And dread as he the rabble chas'd.
In haste he fled, and so did they;
Each and his fear a several way.

CROWDERO only kept the field;
Not stirring from the place he held;
Though beaten down and wounded sore,
I' th' fiddle, and a leg that bore
One side of him; not that of bone,
But much it's better, th' wooden one.
He spying HUDIBRAS lie strow'd
Upon the ground, like log of wood,
With fright of fall, supposed wound,
And loss of urine, in a swound,
In haste he snatch'd the wooden limb,
That hurt i' the ankle lay by him,
And fitting it for sudden fight,
Straight drew it up t' attack the Knight;
For getting up on stump and huckle,
He with the foe began to buckle;
Vowing to be reveng'd for breach
Of crowd and skin upon the wretch,
Sole author of all detriment
He and his fiddle underwent.

But RALPHO (who had now begun
T' adventure resurrection
From heavy squelch, and had got up
Upon his legs, with sprained crup)
Looking about, beheld pernicion
Approaching Knight from fell musician.
He snatch'd his whinyard up, that fled
When he was falling off his steed,
(As rats do from a falling house,)
To hide itself from rage of blows;
And, wing'd with speed and fury, flew
To rescue Knight from black and blew;
Which, e'er he cou'd atchieve, his sconce
The leg encounter'd twice and once;
And now 'twas rais'd to smite agen,
When RALPHO thrust himself between.
He took the blow upon his arm,
To shield the Knight from further harm;
And, joining wrath with force, bestow'd
On th' wooden member such a load,
That down it fell, and with it bore
CROWDERO, whom it propp'd before.
To him the Squire right nimbly run,

And setting conquering foot upon
His trunk, thus spoke: What desp'rate frenzy
Made thee (thou whelp of Sin!) to fancy
Thyself, and all that coward rabble,
T' encounter us in battle able?
How durst th', I say, oppose thy curship
'Gainst arms, authority, and worship?
And HUDIBRAS or me provoke,
Though all thy limbs, were heart of oke,
And th' other half of thee as good
To bear out blows, as that of wood?
Cou'd not the whipping-post prevail
With all its rhet'ric, nor the jail,
To keep from flaying scourge thy skin,
And ankle free from iron gin?
Which now thou shalt — But first our care
Must see how HUDIBRAS doth fare.
This said, he gently rais'd the Knight,
And set him on his bum upright.
To rouse him from lethargic dump,
He tweak'd his nose; with gentle thump
Knock'd on his breast, as if 't had been
To raise the spirits lodg'd within.
They, waken'd with the noise, did fly
From inward room to window eye,
And gently op'ning lid, the casement,
Look'd out, but yet with some amazement.
This gladded RALPHO much to see,
Who thus bespoke the Knight: quoth he,
Tweaking his nose, You are, great Sir,
A self-denying conqueror;
As high, victorious, and great,
As e'er fought for the Churches yet,
If you will give yourself but leave
To make out what y' already have;
That's victory. The foe, for dread
Of your nine-worthiness, is fled:
All, save CROWDERO, for whose sake
You did th' espous'd Cause undertake;
And he lies pris'ner at your feet,
To be dispos'd as you think meet;
Either for life, or death, or sale,
The gallows, or perpetual jail;
For one wink of your powerful eye
Must sentence him to live or die.
His fiddle is your proper purchase,
Won in the service of the Churches;
And by your doom must be allow'd

To be, or be no more, a crowd.
For though success did not confer
Just title on the conqueror;
Though dispensations were not strong
Conclusions, whether right or wrong,
Although out-goings did confirm,
And owning were but a mere term;
Yet as the wicked have no right
To th' creature, though usurp'd by might,
The property is in the Saint,
From whom th' injuriously detain 't;
Of him they hold their luxuries,
Their dogs, their horses, whores, and dice,
Their riots, revels, masks, delights,
Pimps, buffoons, fiddlers, parasites;
All which the Saints have title to,
And ought t' enjoy, if th' had their due.
What we take from them is no more
Than what was our's by right before;
For we are their true landlords still,
And they our tenants but at will.
At this the Knight began to rouze,
And by degrees grow valorous.
He star'd about, and seeing none
Of all his foes remain, but one,
He snatch'd his weapon, that lay near him,
And from the ground began to rear him;
Vowing to make CROWDERO pay
For all the rest that ran away.
But RALPHO now, in colder blood,
His fury mildly thus withstood:
Great Sir, quoth he, your mighty spirit
Is rais'd too high: this slave does merit
To be the hangman's bus'ness, sooner
Than from your hand to have the honour
Of his destruction. I, that am
A nothingness in deed and name
Did scorn to hurt his forfeit carcase,
Or ill intreat his fiddle or case:
Will you, great Sir, that glory blot
In cold blood which you gain'd in hot?
Will you employ your conqu'ring sword
To break a fiddle and your word?
For though I fought, and overcame,
And quarter gave, 'twas in your name.
For great commanders only own
What's prosperous by the soldier done.
To save, where you have pow'r to kill,

Argues your pow'r above your will;
And that your will and pow'r have less
Than both might have of selfishness.
This pow'r which, now alive, with dread
He trembles at, if he were dead,
Wou'd no more keep the slave in awe,
Than if you were a Knight of straw:
For death would then be his conqueror;
Not you, and free him from that terror.
If danger from his life accrue;
Or honour from his death, to you,
'Twere policy, and honour too,
To do as you resolv'd to do:
But, Sir, 'twou'd wrong your valour much,
To say it needs or fears a crutch.
Great conquerors greater glory gain
By foes in triumph led, than slain:
The laurels that adorn their brows
Are pull'd from living not dead boughs,
And living foes: the greatest fame
Of cripple slain can be but lame.
One half of him's already slain,
The other is not worth your pain;
Th' honour can but on one side light,
As worship did, when y' were dubb'd Knight.
Wherefore I think it better far
To keep him prisoner of war;
And let him fast in bonds abide,
At court of Justice to be try'd;
Where, if he appear so bold and crafty,
There may be danger in his safety.
If any member there dislike
His face, or to his beard have pique;
Or if his death will save or yield,
Revenge or fright, it is reveal'd.
Though he has quarter, ne'er the less
Y' have power to hang him when you please.
This has been often done by some
Of our great conqu'rors, you know whom;
And has by most of us been held
Wise Justice, and to some reveal'd.
For words and promises, that yoke
The conqueror, are quickly broke;
Like SAMPSON's cuffs, though by his own
Direction and advice put on.
For if we should fight for the CAUSE
By rules of military laws,
And only do what they call just,

The Cause would quickly fall to dust.
This we among ourselves may speak;
But to the wicked, or the weak,
We must be cautious to declare
Perfection-truths, such as these are.

This said, the high outrageous mettle
Of Knight began to cool and settle.
He lik'd the Squire's advice, and soon
Resolv'd to see the business done
And therefore charg'd him first to bind
CROWDERO'S hands on rump behind,
And to its former place and use,
The wooden member to reduce
But force it take an oath before,
Ne'er to bear arms against him more.

RALPHO dispatch'd with speedy haste,
And having ty'd CROWDERO fast,
He gave Sir Knight the end of cord,
To lead the captive of his sword
In triumph, whilst the steeds he caught,
And them to further service brought.
The Squire in state rode on before,
And on his nut-brown whinyard bore
The trophee-fiddle and the case,
Leaning on shoulder like a mace.
The Knight himself did after ride,
Leading CROWDERO by his side;
And tow'd him, if he lagg'd behind,
Like boat against the tide and wind.
Thus grave and solemn they march'd on,
Until quite thro' the town th' had gone;
At further end of which there stands
An ancient castle, that commands
Th' adjacent parts: in all the fabrick
You shall not see one stone nor a brick;
But all of wood; by pow'rful spell
Of magic made impregnable.
There's neither iron-bar nor gate,
Portcullis, chain, nor bolt, nor grate,
And yet men durance there abide,
In dungeon scarce three inches wide;
With roof so low, that under it
They never stand, but lie or sit;
And yet so foul, that whoso is in,
Is to the middle-leg in prison;
In circle magical conflu'd,

With walls of subtile air and wind,
Which none are able to break thorough,
Until they're freed by head of borough.
Thither arriv'd, th' advent'rous Knight
And bold Squire from their steeds alight
At th' outward wall, near which there stands
A bastile, built to imprison hands;
By strange enchantment made to fetter
The lesser parts and free the greater;
For though the body may creep through,
The hands in grate are fast enough:
And when a circle 'bout the wrist
Is made by beadle exorcist,
The body feels the spur and switch,
As if 'twere ridden post by witch
At twenty miles an hour pace,
And yet ne'er stirs out of the place.
On top of this there is a spire,
On which Sir Knight first bids the Squire
The fiddle and its spoils, the case,
In manner of a trophee place.
That done, they ope the trap-door gate,
And let CROWDERO down thereat;
CROWDERO making doleful face,
Like hermit poor in pensive place.
To dungeon they the wretch commit,
And the survivor of his feet
But th' other, that had broke the peace
And head of Knighthood, they release;
Though a delinquent false and forged,
Yet be'ing a stranger, he's enlarged;
While his comrade, that did no hurt,
Is clapp'd up fast in prison for't.
So Justice, while she winks at crimes,
Stumbles on innocence sometimes.

PART I

CANTO III

THE ARGUMENT

The scatter'd rout return and rally,
Surround the place; the Knight does sally,
And is made pris'ner: Then they seize
Th' inchanted fort by storm; release

Crowdero, and put the Squire in's place;
I should have first said Hudibras.

Ah me! what perils do environ
The man that meddles with cold iron!
What plaguy mischiefs and mishaps
Do dog him still with after-claps!
For though dame Fortune seem to smile
And leer upon him for a while,
She'll after shew him, in the nick
Of all his glories, a dog-trick.
This any man may sing or say,
I' th' ditty call'd, What if a Day?
For HUDIBRAS, who thought h' had won
The field, as certain as a gun;
And having routed the whole troop,
With victory was cock a-hoop;
Thinking h' had done enough to purchase
Thanksgiving-day among the Churches,
Wherein his mettle, and brave worth,
Might be explain'd by Holder-forth,
And register'd, by fame eternal,
In deathless pages of diurnal;
Found in few minutes, to his cost,
He did but count without his host;
And that a turn-stile is more certain
Than, in events of war, dame Fortune.

For now the late faint-hearted rout,
O'erthrown, and scatter'd round about,
Chas'd by the horror of their fear
From bloody fray of Knight and Bear,
(All but the dogs, who, in pursuit
Of the Knight's victory, stood to't,
And most ignobly fought to get
The honour of his blood and sweat,)
Seeing the coast was free and clear
O' th' conquer'd and the conqueror,
Took heart again, and fac'd about,
As if they meant to stand it out:
For by this time the routed Bear,
Attack'd by th' enemy i' th' rear,
Finding their number grew too great
For him to make a safe retreat,
Like a bold chieftain, fac'd about;
But wisely doubting to hold out,
Gave way to Fortune, and with haste

Fac'd the proud foe, and fled, and fac'd;
Retiring still, until he found
H' had got the advantage of the ground;
And then as valiantly made head
To check the foe, and forthwith fled;
Leaving no art untry'd, nor trick
Of warrior stout and politick,
Until, in spite of hot pursuit,
He gain'd a pass to hold dispute
On better terms, and stop the course
Of the proud foe. With all his force
He bravely charg'd, and for a while
Forc'd their whole body to recoil;
But still their numbers so increas'd,
He found himself at length oppress'd,
And all evasions, so uncertain,
To save himself for better fortune,
That he resolv'd, rather than yield,
To die with honour in the field,
And sell his hide and carcase at
A price as high and desperate
As e'er he could. This resolution
He forthwith put in execution,
And bravely threw himself among
The enemy i' th' greatest throng.
But what cou'd single valour do
Against so numerous a foe?
Yet much he did indeed, too much
To be believ'd, where th' odds were such.
But one against a multitude
Is more than mortal can make good.
For while one party he oppos'd,
His rear was suddenly inclos'd;
And no room left him for retreat,
Or fight against a foe so great.
For now the mastives, charging home,
To blows and handy gripes were come:
While manfully himself he bore,
And setting his right-foot before,
He rais'd himself, to shew how tall
His person was above them all.
This equal shame and envy stirr'd
In th' enemy, that one should beard
So many warriors, and so stout,
As he had done, and stav'd it out,
Disdaining to lay down his arms,
And yield on honourable terms.
Enraged thus, some in the rear

Attack'd him, and some ev'ry where,
Till down he fell; yet falling fought,
And, being down, still laid about;
As WIDDRINGTON, in doleful dumps,
Is said to light upon his stumps.

But all, alas! had been in vain,
And he inevitably slain,
If TRULLA and CERDON, in the nick,
To rescue him had not been quick;
For TRULLA, who was light of foot
As shafts which long-field Parthians shoot,
(But not so light as to be borne
Upon the ears of standing corn,
Or trip it o'er the water quicker
Than witches, when their staves they liquor,
As some report,) was got among
The foremost of the martial throng;
There pitying the vanquish'd Bear,
She call'd to CERDON, who stood near,
Viewing the bloody fight; to whom,
Shall we (quoth she) stand still hum-drum,
And see stout Bruin all alone,
By numbers basely overthrown?
Such feats already h' has atchiev'd,
In story not to be believ'd;
And 'twould to us be shame enough,
Not to attempt to fetch him off.
I would (quoth he) venture a limb
To second thee, and rescue him:
But then we must about it straight,
Or else our aid will come too late.
Quarter he scorns, he is so stout,
And therefore cannot long hold out.
This said, they wav'd their weapons round
About their heads, to clear the ground;
And joining forces, laid about
So fiercely, that th' amazed rout
Turn'd tale again, and straight begun,
As if the Devil drove, to run.
Meanwhile th' approach'd th' place where Bruin
Was now engag'd to mortal ruin.
The conqu'ring foe they soon assail'd;
First TRULLA stav'd, and CERDON tail'd,
Until their mastives loos'd their hold:
And yet, alas! do what they could,
The worsted Bear came off with store
Of bloody wounds, but all before:

For as ACHILLES, dipt in pond,
Was ANABAPTIZ'D free from wound,
Made proof against dead-doing steel
All over, but the Pagan heel;
So did our champion's arms defend
All of him, but the other end,
His head and ears, which, in the martial
Encounter, lost a leathern parcel
For as an Austrian Archduke once
Had one ear (which in ducatoons
Is half the coin) in battle par'd
Close to his head, so Bruin far'd;
But tugg'd and pull'd on th' other side,
Like scriv'ner newly crucify'd;
Or like the late corrected leathern
Ears of the Circumcised Brethren.
But gentle TRULLA into th' ring
He wore in's nose convey'd a string,
With which she march'd before, and led
The warrior to a grassy bed,
As authors write, in a cool shade,
Which eglantine and roses made;
Close by a softly murm'ring stream,
Where lovers us'd to loll and dream.
There leaving him to his repose,
Secured from pursuit of foes,
And wanting nothing but a song,
And a well-tun'd theorbo hung
Upon a bough, to ease the pain
His tugg'd ears suffer'd, with a strain,
They both drew up, to march in quest
Of his great leader and the rest.

For ORSIN (who was more renown'd
For stout maintaining of his ground
In standing fight, than for pursuit,
As being not so quick of foot)
Was not long able to keep pace
With others that pursu'd the chace;
But found himself left far behind,
Both out of heart and out of wind:
Griev'd to behold his Bear pursu'd
So basely by a multitude;
And like to fall, not by the prowess,
But numbers of his coward foes.
He rag'd, and kept as heavy a coil as
Stout HERCULES for loss of HYLAS;
Forcing the vallies to repeat

The accents of his sad regret.
He beat his breast, and tore his hair,
For loss of his dear Crony Bear;
That Eccho, from the hollow ground,
His doleful wailings did resound
More wistfully, by many times,
Than in small poets splay-foot rhimes
That make her, in their rueful stories
To answer to int'rogatories,
And most unconscionably depose
To things of which she nothing knows;
And when she has said all she can say,
'Tis wrested to the lover's fancy.
Quoth he, O whither, wicked Bruin
Art thou fled to my — Eccho, Ruin?
I thought th' hadst scorn'd to budge a step
For fear. (Quoth Eccho) Marry guep.
Am not I here to take thy part?
Then what has quelled thy stubborn heart?
Have these bones rattled, and this head
So often in thy quarrel bled?
Nor did I ever winch or grudge it,
For thy dear sake. (Quoth she) Mum budget
Think'st thou 'twill not be laid i' th' dish
Thou turn'dst thy back? Quoth Eccho, Fish.
To run from those t'hast overcome
Thus cowardly? Quoth Eccho, Mum.
But what a vengeance makes thee fly
From me too, as thine enemy?
Or if thou hast no thought of me,
Nor what I have endur'd for thee,
Yet shame and honour might prevail
To keep thee thus from turning tail:
For who would grudge to spend his blood in
His honour's cause? Quoth she, A puddin.
This said, his grief to anger turn'd,
Which in his manly stomach burn'd;
Thirst of revenge, and wrath, in place
Of sorrow, now began to blaze.
He vow'd the authors of his woe
Should equal vengeance undergo;
And with their bones and flesh pay dear
For what he suffer'd, and his Bear.
This b'ing resolv'd, with equal speed
And rage he hasted to proceed
To action straight, and giving o'er
To search for Bruin any more,
He went in quest of HUDIBRAS,

To find him out where-e'er he was;
And, if he were above ground, vow'd
He'd ferret him, lurk where be wou'd.

But scarce had he a furlong on
This resolute adventure gone,
When he encounter'd with that crew
Whom HUDIBRAS did late subdue.
Honour, revenge, contempt, and shame,
Did equally their breasts inflame.
'Mong these the fierce MAGNANO was,
And TALGOL, foe to HUDIBRAS;
CERDON and COLON, warriors stout,
As resolute, as ever fought;
Whom furious ORSIN thus bespoke:
Shall we (quoth be) thus basely brook
The vile affront that paltry ass,
And feeble scoundrel, HUDIBRAS,
With that more paltry ragamuffin,
RALPHO, with vapouring and huffing,
Have put upon us like tame cattle,
As if th' had routed us in battle?
For my part, it shall ne'er be said,
I for the washing gave my bead:
Nor did I turn my back for fear
O' th' rascals, but loss of my Bear,
Which now I'm like to undergo;
For whether those fell wounds, or no
He has receiv'd in fight, are mortal,
Is more than all my skill can foretell
Nor do I know what is become
Of him, more than the Pope of Rome.
But if I can but find them out
That caus'd it (as I shall, no doubt,
Where-e'er th' in hugger-mugger lurk)
I'll make them rue their handy-work;
And wish that they had rather dar'd
To pull the Devil by the beard.

Quoth CERDN, Noble ORSIN, th' hast
Great reason to do as thou say'st,
And so has ev'ry body here,
As well as thou hast, or thy Bear.
Others may do as they see good;
But if this twig be made of wood
That will hold tack, I'll make the fur
Fly 'bout the ears of that old cur;
And the other mungrel vermin, RALPH,

That brav'd us all in his behalf.
Thy Bear is safe, and out of peril,
Though lugg'd indeed, and wounded very ill;
Myself and TRULLA made a shift
To help him out at a dead lift;
And, having brought him bravely off,
Have left him where he's safe enough:
There let him rest; for if we stay,
The slaves may hap to get away.

This said, they all engag'd to join
Their forces in the same design;
And forthwith put themselves in search
Of HUDIBRAS upon their march.
Where leave we awhile, to tell
What the victorious knight befel.
For such, CROWDERO being fast
In dungeon shut, we left him last.
Triumphant laurels seem'd to grow
No where so green as on his brow;
Laden with which, as well as tir'd
With conquering toil, he now retir'd
Unto a neighb'ring castle by,
To rest his body, and apply
Fit med'cines to each glorious bruise
He got in fight, reds, blacks, and blues,
To mollify th' uneasy pang
Of ev'ry honourable bang,
Which b'ing by skilful midwife drest,
He laid him down to take his rest.
But all in vain. H' had got a hurt
O' th' inside, of a deadlier sort,
By CUPID made, who took his stand
Upon a Widow's jointure land,
(For he, in all his am'rous battels,
No 'dvantage finds like goods and chattels,)
Drew home his bow, and, aiming right,
Let fly an arrow at the Knight:
The shaft against a rib did glance,
And gall'd him in the purtenance.
But time had somewhat 'swag'd his pain,
After he found his suit in vain.
For that proud dame, for whom his soul
Was burnt in's belly like a coal,
(That belly which so oft did ake
And suffer griping for her sake,
Till purging comfits and ants-eggs
Had almost brought him off his legs,)

Us'd him so like a base rascallion,
That old Pyg — (what d'y' call him) malion,
That cut his mistress out of stone,
Had not so hard a-hearted one.
She had a thousand jadish tricks,
Worse than a mule that flings and kicks;
'Mong which one cross-grain'd freak she had,
As insolent as strange and mad;
She could love none, but only such
As scorn'd and hated her as much.
'Twas a strange riddle of a lady:
Not love, if any lov'd her! Hey dey!
So cowards never use their might,
But against such as will not fight;
So some diseases have been found
Only to seize upon the sound.
He that gets her by heart, must say her
The back way, like a witch's prayer.
Mean while the Knight had no small task
To compass what he durst not ask.
He loves, but dares not make the motion;
Her ignorance is his devotion:
Like caitiff vile, that, for misdeed,
Rides with his face to rump of steed,
Or rowing scull, he's fain to love,
Look one way, and another move;
Or like a tumbler, that does play
His game, and look another way,
Until he seize upon the cony;
Just so he does by matrimony:
But all in vain; her subtle snout
Did quickly wind his meaning out;
Which she return'd with too much scorn
To be by man of honour borne:
Yet much he bore, until the distress
He suffer'd from his spightful mistress
Did stir his stomach; and the pain
He had endur'd from her disdain,
Turn'd to regret so resolute,
That he resolv'd to wave his suit,
And either to renounce her quite,
Or for a while play least in sight.
This resolution b'ing put on,
He kept some months, and more had done;
But being brought so nigh by Fate,
The victory he atchiev'd so late
Did set his thoughts agog, and ope
A door to discontinu'd hope,

That seem'd to promise he might win
His dame too, now his hand was in;
And that his valour, and the honour
H' had newly gain'd, might work upon her.
These reasons made his mouth to water
With am'rous longings to be at her.

Quoth he, unto himself, Who knows,
But this brave conquest o'er my foes
May reach her heart, and make that stoop,
As I but now have forc'd the troop?
If nothing can oppugn love,
And virtue invious ways can prove,
What may he not confide to do
That brings both love and virtue too?
But thou bring'st valour too and wit;
Two things that seldom fail to hit.
Valour's a mouse-trap, wit a gin,
Which women oft are taken in.
Then, HUDIBRAS, why should'st thou fear
To be, that art a conqueror?
Fortune th' audacious doth juvare,
But lets the timidous miscarry.
Then while the honour thou hast got
Is spick and span new, piping hot,
Strike her up bravely, thou hadst best,
And trust thy fortune with the rest.
Such thoughts as these the Knight did keep,
More than his bangs or fleas, from sleep.
And as an owl, that in a barn
Sees a mouse creeping in the corn,
Sits still, and shuts his round blue eyes,
As if he slept, until he spies
The little beast within his reach,
Then starts, and seizes on the wretch;
So from his couch the Knight did start
To seize upon the widow's heart;
Crying with hasty tone, and hoarse,
RALPHO, dispatch; To Horse, To Horse.
And 'twas but time; for now the rout,
We left engag'd to seek him out,
By speedy marches, were advanc'd
Up to the fort, where he ensconc'd;
And all th' avenues had possest
About the place, from east to west.

That done, a while they made a halt,
To view the ground, and where t' assault:

Then call'd a council, which was best,
By siege or onslaught, to invest
The enemy; and 'twas agreed,
By storm and onslaught to proceed.
This b'ing resolv'd, in comely sort
They now drew up t' attack the fort;
When HUDIBRAS, about to enter
Upon another-gates adventure,
To RALPHO call'd aloud to arm,
Not dreaming of approaching storm.
Whether Dame Fortune, or the care
Of Angel bad or tutelar,
Did arm, or thrust him on a danger
To which he was an utter stranger;
That foresight might, or might not, blot
The glory he had newly got;
For to his shame it might be said,
They took him napping in his bed;
To them we leave it to expound,
That deal in sciences profound.

His courser scarce he had bestrid,
And RALPHO that on which he rid,
When setting ope the postern gate,
Which they thought best to sally at,
The foe appear'd, drawn up and drill'd,
Ready to charge them in the field.
This somewhat startled the bold Knight,
Surpriz'd with th' unexpected sight.
The bruises of his bones and flesh
The thought began to smart afresh;
Till recollecting wonted courage,
His fear was soon converted to rage,
And thus he spoke: The coward foe,
Whom we but now gave quarter to,
Look, yonder's rally'd, and appears
As if they had out-run their fears.
The glory we did lately get,
The Fates command us to repeat;
And to their wills we must succumb,
Quocunque trahunt, 'tis our doom.
This is the same numeric crew
Which we so lately did subdue;
The self-same individuals that
Did run as mice do from a cat,
When we courageously did wield
Our martial weapons in the field
To tug for victory; and when

We shall our shining blades agen
Brandish in terror o'er our heads,
They'll straight resume their wonted dreads.
Fear is an ague, that forsakes
And haunts by fits those whom it takes:
And they'll opine they feel the pain
And blows they felt to-day again.
Then let us boldly charge them home,
And make no doubt to overcome.

This said, his courage to inflame,
He call'd upon his mistress' name.
His pistol next he cock'd a-new,
And out his nut-brown whinyard drew;
And, placing RALPHO in the front,
Reserv'd himself to bear the brunt,
As expert warriors use: then ply'd
With iron heel his courser's side,
Conveying sympathetic speed
From heel of Knight to heel of Steed.

Mean while the foe, with equal rage
And speed, advancing to engage,
Both parties now were drawn so close,
Almost to come to handy-blows;
When ORSIN first let fly a stone
At RALPHO: not so huge a one
As that which DIOMED did maul
AENEAS on the bum withal
Yet big enough if rightly hurl'd,
T' have sent him to another world,
Whether above-ground, or below,
Which Saints Twice Dipt are destin'd to.
The danger startled the bold Squire,
And made him some few steps retire.
But HUDIBRAS advanc'd to's aid,
And rouz'd his spirits, half dismay'd.
He wisely doubting lest the shot
Of th' enemy, now growing hot,
Might at a distance gall, press'd close,
To come pell-mell to handy-blows,
And, that he might their aim decline,
Advanc'd still in an oblique line;
But prudently forbore to fire,
Till breast to breast he had got nigher,
As expert warriors use to do
When hand to hand they charge their foe.
This order the advent'rous Knight,

Most soldier-like, observ'd in fight,
When fortune (as she's wont) turn'd fickle,
And for the foe began to stickle.
The more shame for her Goody-ship,
To give so near a friend the slip.
For COLON, choosing out a stone,
Levell'd so right, it thump'd upon
His manly paunch with such a force,
As almost beat him off his horse.
He lost his whinyard, and the rein;
But, laying fast hold of the mane,
Preserv'd his seat; and as a goose
In death contracts his talons close,
So did the Knight, and with one claw
The trigger of his pistol draw.
The gun went off: and as it was
Still fatal to stout HUDIBRAS,
In all his feats of arms, when least
He dreamt of it, to prosper best,
So now he far'd: the shot, let fly
At random 'mong the enemy,
Pierc'd TALGOL's gaberdine, and grazing
Upon his shoulder, in the passing,
Lodg'd in MAGNANO's brass habergeon,
Who straight, A Surgeon, cry'd, A Surgeon.
He tumbled down, and, as he fell,
Did Murther, Murther, Murther, yell.
This startled their whole body so,
That if the Knight had not let go
His arms, but been in warlike plight,
H' had won (the second time) the fight;
As, if the Squire had but fall'n on,
He had inevitably done:
But he, diverted with the care
Or HUDIBRAS his hurt, forbare
To press th' advantage of his fortune
While danger did the rest dishearten:
For he with CERDON b'ing engag'd
In close encounter, they both wag'd
The fight so well, 'twas hard to say
Which side was like to get the day.
And now the busy work of death
Had tir'd them so, th' agreed to breath,
Preparing to renew the fight,
When the disaster of the Knight,
And th' other party, did divert
Their fell intent, and forc'd them part.
RALPHO press'd up to HUDIBRAS,

And CERDON where MAGNANO was;
Each striving to confirm his party
With stout encouragements, and hearty.

Quoth RALIHO, Courage, valiant Sir,
And let revenge and honour stir
Your spirits up: once we fall on,
The shatter'd foe begins to run:
For if but half so well you knew
To use your victory as subdue,
They durst not, after such a blow
As you have given them, face us now;
But from so formidable a soldier
Had fled like crows when they smell powder.
Thrice have they seen your sword aloft
Wav'd o'er their heads, and fled as oft.
But if you let them recollect
Their spirits, now dismay'd and checkt,
You'll have a harder game to play
Than yet y' have had to get the day.

Thus spoke the stout Squire; but was heard
By HUDIBRAS with small regard.
His thoughts were fuller of the bang
Be lately took than RALPH'S harangue;
To which he answer'd, Cruel Fate
Tells me thy counsel comes too late.
The knotted blood within my hose,
That from my wounded body flows,
With mortal crisis doth portend
My days to appropinque an end.
I am for action now unfit,
Either of fortitude or wit:
Fortune, my foe, begins to frown,
Resolv'd to pull my stomach down.
I am not apt, upon a wound,
Or trivial basting, to despond:
Yet I'd be loth my days to curtail:
For if I thought my wounds not mortal,
Or that we'd time enough as yet,
To make an hon'rable retreat,
'Twere the best course: but if they find
We fly, and leave our arms behind
For them to seize on, the dishonour,
And danger too, is such, I'll sooner
Stand to it boldly, and take quarter,
To let them see I am no starter.
In all the trade of war, no feat

Is nobler than a brave retreat:
For those that run away, and fly,
Take place at least of th' enemy.

This said, the Squire, with active speed
Dismounted from his bonny steed,
To seize the arms, which, by mischance,
Fell from the bold Knight in a trance.
These being found out, and restor'd
To HUDIBRAS their natural lord,
As a man may say, with might and main,
He hasted to get up again.
Thrice he assay'd to mount aloft,
But, by his weighty bum, as oft
He was pull'd back, till having found
Th' advantage of the rising ground,
Thither he led his warlike steed,
And having plac'd him right, with speed
Prepar'd again to scale the beast,
When ORSIN, who had newly drest
The bloody scar upon the shoulder
Of TALGOL with Promethean powder,
And now was searching for the shot
That laid MAGNANO on the spot,
Beheld the sturdy Squire aforesaid
Preparing to climb up his horse side.
He left his cure, and laying hold
Upon his arms, with courage bold,
Cry'd out, 'Tis now no time to dally,
The enemy begin to rally:
Let us, that are unhurt and whole,
Fall on, and happy man be's dole.

This said, like to a thunderbolt,
He flew with fury to th' assault,
Striving the enemy to attack
Before he reach'd his horse's back.
RALPHO was mounted now, and gotten
O'erthwart his beast with active vau'ting,
Wrigling his body to recover
His seat, and cast his right leg over,
When ORSIN, rushing in, bestow'd
On horse and man so heavy a load,
The beast was startled, and begun
To kick and fling like mad, and run,
Bearing the tough Squire like a sack,
Or stout king RICHARD, on his back,
'Till stumbling, he threw him down,

Sore bruis'd, and cast into a swoon.
Meanwhile the Knight began to rouze
The sparkles of his wonted prowess.
He thrust his hand into his hose,
And found, both by his eyes and nose,
'Twas only choler, and not blood,
That from his wounded body flow'd.
This, with the hazard of the Squire,
Inflam'd him with despightful ire.
Courageously he fac'd about.
And drew his other pistol out,
And now had half way bent the cock,
When CERDON gave so fierce a shock,
With sturdy truncheon, thwart his arm,
That down it fell, and did no harm;
Then stoutly pressing on with speed,
Assay'd to pull him off his steed.
The Knight his sword had only left,
With which he CERDON'S head had cleft,
Or at the least cropt off a limb,
But ORSIN came, and rescu'd him.
He, with his lance, attack'd the Knight
Upon his quarters opposite.
But as a barque, that in foul weather,
Toss'd by two adverse winds together,
Is bruis'd, and beaten to and fro,
And knows not which to turn him to;
So far'd the Knight between two foes,
And knew not which of them t'oppose;
Till ORSIN, charging with his lance
At HUDIBRAS, by spightful chance,
Hit CERDON such a bang, as stunn'd
And laid him flat upon the ground.
At this the Knight began to chear up,
And, raising up himself on stirrup,
Cry'd out, Victoria! Lie thou there,
And I shall straight dispatch another,
To bear thee company in death:
But first I'll halt a while, and breath:
As well he might; for ORSIN, griev'd
At th' wound that CERDON had receiv'd,
Ran to relieve him with his lore,
And cure the hurt he gave before.
Mean while the Knight had wheel'd about,
To breathe himself, and next find out
Th' advantage of the ground, where best
He might the ruffled foe infest.
This b'ing resolv'd, he spurr'd his steed,

To run at ORSIN with full speed,
While he was busy in the care
Of CERDON'S wound, and unaware:
But he was quick, and had already
Unto the part apply'd remedy:
And, seeing th' enemy prepar'd,
Drew up, and stood upon his guard.
Then, like a warrior right expert
And skilful in the martial art,
The subtle Knight straight made a halt,
And judg'd it best to stay th' assault,
Until he had reliev'd the Squire,
And then in order to retire;
Or, as occasion should invite,
With forces join'd renew the fight.
RALPHO, by this time disentranc'd,
Upon his bum himself advanc'd,
Though sorely bruis'd; his limbs all o'er
With ruthless bangs were stiff and sore.
Right fain he would have got upon
His feet again, to get him gone;
When HUDIBRAS to aid him came:

Quoth he (and call'd him by his name,)
Courage! the day at length is ours;
And we once more, as conquerors,
Have both the field and honour won:
The foe is profligate, and run.
I mean all such as can; for some
This hand hath sent to their long home;
And some lie sprawling on the ground,
With many a gash and bloody wound.
CAESAR himself could never say
He got two victories in a day,
As I have done, that can say, Twice I
In one day, Veni, Vidi, Vici.
The foe's so numerous, that we
Cannot so often vincere
As they perire, and yet enow
Be left to strike an after-blow;
Then, lest they rally, and once more
Put us to fight the bus'ness o'er,
Get up, and mount thy steed: Dispatch,
And let us both their motions watch.

Quoth RALPH, I should not, if I were
In case for action, now be here:
Nor have I turn'd my back, or hang'd

An arse, for fear of being bang'd.
It was for you I got these harms,
Advent'ring to fetch off your arms.
The blows and drubs I have receiv'd
Have bruis'd my body, and bereav'd
My limbs of strength. Unless you stoop,
And reach your hand to pull me up,
I shall lie here, and be a prey
To those who now are run away.

That thou shalt not, (quoth HUDIBRAS;)
We read, the ancients held it was
More honourable far, servare
Civem, than slay an adversary:
The one we oft to-day have done,
The other shall dispatch anon:
And though th' art of a diff'rent Church
I will not leave thee in the lurch.
This said, he jogg'd his good steed nigher,
And steer'd him gently toward the Squire;
Then bowing down his body, stretch'd
His hand out, and at RALPHO reach'd;
When TRULLA, whom he did not mind,
Charg'd him like lightening behind.
She had been long in search about
MAGNANO'S wound, to find it out;
But could find none, nor where the shot,
That had so startled him, was got
But having found the worst was past,
She fell to her own work at last,
The pillage of the prisoners,
Which in all feats of arms was hers;
And now to plunder RALPH she flew,
When HUDIBRAS his hard fate drew
To succour him; for, as he bow'd
To help him up, she laid a load
Of blows so heavy, and plac'd so well,
On t'other side, that down he fell.
Yield, scoundrel base, (quoth she,) or die:
Thy life is mine and liberty:
But if thou think'st I took thee tardy,
And dar'st presume to be so hardy,
To try thy fortune o'er a-fresh,
I'll wave my title to thy flesh,
Thy arms and baggage, now my right;
And if thou hast the heart to try't,
I'll lend thee back thyself a while,
And once more, for that carcass vile,

Fight upon tick. — Quoth HUDIBRAS,
Thou offer'st nobly, valiant lass,
And I shall take thee at thy word.
First let me rise and take my sword.
That sword which has so oft this day
Through squadrons of my foes made way,
And some to other worlds dispatch'd,
Now with a feeble spinster match'd,
Will blush with blood ignoble stain'd,
By which no honour's to be gain'd.
But if thou'lt take m' advice in this,
Consider whilst thou may'st, what 'tis
To interrupt a victor's course,
B' opposing such a trivial force:
For if with conquest I come off,
(And that I shall do sure enough,)
Quarter thou canst not have, nor grace,
By law of arms, in such a case;
Both which I now do offer freely.
I scorn (quoth she) thou coxcomb silly,
(Clapping her hand upon her breech,
To shew how much she priz'd his speech,)
Quarter or counsel from a foe
If thou can'st force me to it, do.
But lest it should again be said,
When I have once more won thy head,
I took thee napping, unprepar'd,
Arm, and betake thee to thy guard.

This said, she to her tackle fell,
And on the Knight let fall a peal
Of blows so fierce, and press'd so home,
That he retir'd, and follow'd's bum.
Stand to't (quoth she) or yield to mercy
It is not fighting arsie-versie
Shall serve thy turn. — This stirr'd his spleen
More than the danger he was in,
The blows he felt, or was to feel,
Although th' already made him reel.
Honour, despight; revenge and shame,
At once into his stomach came,
Which fir'd it so, he rais'd his arm
Above his head, and rain'd a storm
Of blows so terrible and thick,
As if he meant to hash her quick.
But she upon her truncheon took them,
And by oblique diversion broke them,
Waiting an opportunity

To pay all back with usury;
Which long she fail'd not of; for now
The Knight with one dead-doing blow
Resolving to decide the fight,
And she, with quick and cunning slight,
Avoiding it, the force and weight
He charged upon it was so great,
As almost sway'd him to the ground.
No sooner she th' advantage found,
But in she flew; and seconding
With home-made thrust the heavy swing,
She laid him flat upon his side;
And mounting on his trunk a-stride,
Quoth she, I told thee what would come
Of all thy vapouring, base scum.
Say, will the law of arms allow
I may have grace and quarter now?
Or wilt thou rather break thy word,
And stain thine honour than thy sword?
A man of war to damn his soul,
In basely breaking his parole
And when, before the fight, th' had'st vow'd
To give no quarter in cold blood
Now thou hast got me for a Tartar,
To make me 'gainst my will take quarter;
Why dost not put me to the sword,
But cowardly fly from thy word?

Quoth HUDIBRAS, The day's thine own:
Thou and thy Stars have cast me down:
My laurels are transplanted now,
And flourish on thy conqu'ring brow:
My loss of honour's great enough,
Thou need'st not brand it with a scoff:
Sarcasms may eclipse thine own,
But cannot blur my lost renown.
I am not now in Fortune's power;
He that is down can fall no lower.
The ancient heroes were illustrious
For being benign, and not blustrous,
Against a vanquish'd foe: their swords
Were sharp and trenchant, not their words;
And did in fight but cut work out
To employ their courtesies about.

Quoth she, Although thou hast deserv'd
Base slubberdegullion, to be serv'd
As thou did'st vow to deal with me,

If thou had'st got the victory
Yet I shall rather act a part
That suits my fame than thy desert.
Thy arms, thy liberty, beside
All that's on th' outside of thy hide,
Are mine by military law,
Of which I will not hate one straw:
The rest, thy life and limbs, once more,
Though doubly forfeit, I restore,

Quoth HUDIBRAS, It is too late
For me to treat or stipulate
What thou command'st, I must obey:
Yet those whom I expugn'd to-day
Of thine own party, I let go,
And gave them life and freedom too:
Both dogs and bear, upon their parole,
Whom I took pris'ners in this quarrel.

Quoth TRULLA, Whether thou or they
Let one another run away,
Concerns not me; but was't not thou
That gave CROWDERO quarter too?
CROWDERO, whom, in irons bound,
Thou basely threw'st into LOB'S Pound,
Where still he lies, and with regret
His gen'rous bowels rage and fret.
But now thy carcass shall redeem,
And serve to be exchang'd for him.

This said, the Knight did straight submit,
And laid his weapons at her feet.
Next he disrob'd his gaberdine,
And with it did himself resign.
She took it, and forthwith divesting
The mantle that she wore, said jesting,
Take that, and wear it for my sake
Then threw it o'er his sturdy back,
And as the FRENCH, we conquer'd once,
Now give us laws for pantaloons,
The length of breeches, and the gathers,
Port-cannons, perriwigs, and feathers;
Just so the proud insulting lass
Array'd and dighted HUDIBRAS.

Mean while the other champions, yerst
In hurry of the fight disperst,
Arriv'd, when TRULLA won the day,

To share in th' honour and the prey,
And out of HUDIBRAS his hide
With vengeance to be satisfy'd;
Which now they were about to pour
Upon him in a wooden show'r;
But TRULLA thrust herself between,
And striding o'er his back agen,
She brandish'd o'er her head his sword,
And vow'd they should not break her word;
Sh' had giv'n him quarter, and her blood
Or theirs should make that quarter good;
For she was bound by law of arms
To see him safe from further harms.
In dungeon deep CROWDERO, cast
By HUDIBRAS, as yet lay fast;
Where, to the hard and ruthless stones,
His great heart made perpetual moans:
Him she resolv'd that HUDIBRAS
Should ransom, and supply his place.

This stopt their fury, and the basting
Which toward HUDIBRAS was hasting.
They thought it was but just and right,
That what she had atchiev'd in fight,
She should dispose of how she pleas'd.
CROWDERO ought to be releas'd;
Nor could that any way be done
So well as this she pitch'd upon
For who a better could imagine
This therefore they resolv'd t'engage in.
The Knight and Squire first they made
Rise from the ground, where they were laid
Then mounted both upon their horses,
But with their faces to the arses,
ORSIN led HUDIBRAS's beast,
And TALGOL that which RALPHO prest,
Whom stout MAGNANO, valiant CERDON,
And COLON, waited as a guard on;
All ush'ring TRULLA in the rear,
With th' arms of either prisoner.
In this proud order and array
They put themselves upon their way,
Striving to reach th' enchanted castle,
Where stout CROWDERO in durance lay still.
Thither with greater speed than shows
And triumph over conquer'd foes
Do use t' allow, or than the bears
Or pageants borne before Lord-Mayors

Are wont to use, they soon arriv'd
In order, soldier-like contriv'd;
Still marching in a warlike posture,
As fit for battle as for muster.
The Knight and Squire they first unhorse,
And bending 'gainst the fort their force,
They all advanc'd, and round about
Begirt the magical redoubt.
MAGNAN led up in this adventure,
And made way for the rest to enter;
For he was skilful in black art.
No less than he that built the fort;
And with an iron mace laid flat
A breach, which straight all enter'd at,
And in the wooden dungeon found
CROWDERO laid upon the ground.
Him they release from durance base,
Restor'd t' his fiddle and his case,
And liberty, his thirsty rage
With luscious vengeance to asswage:
For he no sooner was at large,
But TRULLA straight brought on the charge,
And in the self-same limbo put
The Knight and Squire where he was shut;
Where leaving them in Hockley i' th' Hole,
Their bangs and durance to condole,
Confin'd and conjur'd into narrow
Enchanted mansion to know sorrow,
In the same order and array
Which they advanc'd, they march'd away.
But HUDIBRAS who scorn'd to stoop
To Fortune, or be said to droop,
Chear'd up himself with ends of verse,
And sayings of philosophers.

Quoth he, Th' one half of man, his mind,
Is, sui juris, unconfin'd,
And cannot be laid by the heels,
Whate'er the other moiety feels.
'Tis not restraint or liberty
That makes men prisoners or free;
But perturbations that possess
The mind, or aequanimities.
The whole world was not half so wide
To ALEXANDER, when he cry'd,
Because he had but one to subdue,
As was a paltry narrow tub to
DIOGENES; who is not said

(For aught that ever I could read)
To whine, put finger i' th' eye, and sob,
Because h' had ne'er another tub.
The ancients make two sev'ral kinds
Of prowess in heroic minds;
The active, and the passive valiant;
Both which are pari libra gallant:
For both to give blows, and to carry,
In fights are equinecessary
But in defeats, the passive stout
Are always found to stand it out
Most desp'rately, and to out-do
The active 'gainst the conqu'ring foe.
Tho' we with blacks and blues are suggill'd,
Or, as the vulgar say, are cudgell'd;
He that is valiant, and dares fight,
Though drubb'd, can lose no honour by't.
Honour's a lease for lives to come,
And cannot be extended from
The legal tenant: 'tis a chattel
Not to be forfeited in battel.
If he that in the field is slain,
Be in the bed of Honour lain,
He that is beaten, may be said
To lie in Honour's truckle-bed.
For as we see th' eclipsed sun
By mortals is more gaz'd upon,
Than when, adorn'd with all his light,
He shines in serene sky most bright:
So valour, in a low estate,
Is most admir'd and wonder'd at.

Quoth RALPH, How great I do not know
We may by being beaten grow;
But none, that see how here we sit,
Will judge us overgrown with wit.
As gifted brethren, preaching by
A carnal hour-glass, do imply,
Illumination can convey
Into them what they have to say,
But not how much; so well enough
Know you to charge, but not draw off:
For who, without a cap and bauble,
Having subdu'd a bear and rabble,
And might with honour have come off
Would put it to a second proof?
A politic exploit, right fit
For Presbyterian zeal and wit.

Quoth HUDIBRAS, That cuckow's tone,
RALPHO, thou always harp'st upon.
When thou at any thing would'st rail,
Thou mak'st Presbytery the scale
To take the height on't, and explain
To what degree it is prophane
Whats'ever will not with (thy what d'ye call)
Thy light jump right, thou call'st synodical;
As if Presbytery were the standard
To size whats'ever's to he slander'd.
Dost not remember how this day,
Thou to my beard wast bold to say,
That thou coud'st prove bear-baiting equal
With synods orthodox and legal?
Do if thou canst; for I deny't,
And dare thee to 't with all thy light.

Quoth RALPHO, Truly that is no
Hard matter for a man to do,
That has but any guts in 's brains,
And cou'd believe it worth his pains;
But since you dare and urge me to it,
You'll find I've light enough to do it.

Synods are mystical bear-gardens,
Where elders, deputies, church-wardens,
And other members of the court,
Manage the Babylonish sport;
For prolocutor, scribe, and bear-ward,
Do differ only in a mere word;
Both are but sev'ral synagogues
Of carnal men, and bears, and dogs:
Both antichristian assemblies,
To mischief bent far as in them lies:
Both stave and tail with fierce contests;
The one with men, the other beasts.
The diff'rence is, the one fights with
The tongue, the other with the teeth;
And that they bait but bears in this,
In th' other, souls and consciences;
Where Saints themselves are brought to stake
For gospel-light, and conscience sake;
Expos'd to Scribes and Presbyters,
Instead of mastive dogs and curs,
Than whom th' have less humanity;
For these at souls of men will fly.
This to the prophet did appear,

Who in a vision saw a bear,
Prefiguring the beastly rage
Of Church-rule in this latter age;
As is demonstrated at full
By him that baited the Pope's Bull.
Bears nat'rally are beasts of prey,
That live by rapine; so do they.
What are their orders, constitutions,
Church-censures, curses, absolutions,
But' sev'ral mystic chains they make,
To tie poor Christians to the stake,
And then set heathen officers,
Instead of dogs, about their ears?
For to prohibit and dispense;
To find out or to make offence;
Of Hell and Heaven to dispose;
To play with souls at fast and loose;
To set what characters they please,
And mulcts on sin or godliness;
Reduce the Church to gospel-order,
By rapine, sacrilege, and murder;
To make Presbytery supreme,
And Kings themselves submit to them;
And force all people, though against
Their consciences, to turn Saints;
Must prove a pretty thriving trade,
When Saints monopolists are made;
When pious frauds, and holy shifts,
Are dispensations and gifts,
Their godliness becomes mere ware,
And ev'ry Synod but a fair.
Synods are whelps of th' Inquisition,
A mungrel breed of like pernicion,
And growing up, became the sires
Of scribes, commissioners, and triers;
Whose bus'ness is, by cunning slight,
To cast a figure for mens' light;
To find, in lines of beard and face,
The physiognomy of grace;
And by the sound and twang of nose,
If all be sound within disclose,
Free from a crack or flaw of sinning,
As men try pipkins by the ringing;
By black caps underlaid with white,
Give certain guess at inward light.
Which serjeants at the gospel wear,
To make the spiritual calling clear;
The handkerchief about the neck

(Canonical cravat of SMECK,
From whom the institution came,
When Church and State they set on flame,
And worn by them as badges then
Of spiritual warfaring men)
Judge rightly if regeneration
Be of the newest cut in fashion.
Sure 'tis an orthodox opinion,
That grace is founded in dominion.
Great piety consists in pride;
To rule is to be sanctified:
To domineer, and to controul,
Both o'er the body and the soul,
Is the most perfect discipline
Of church-rule, and by right-divine.
Bell and the Dragon's chaplains were
More moderate than these by far:
For they (poor knaves) were glad to cheat,
To get their wives and children meat;
But these will not be fobb'd off so;
They must have wealth and power too,
Or else with blood and desolation
They'll tear it out o' th' heart o' th' nation.
Sure these themselves from primitive
And Heathen Priesthood do derive,
When butchers were the only Clerks,
Elders and Presbyters of Kirks;
Whose directory was to kill;
And some believe it is so still.
The only diff'rence is, that then
They slaughter'd only beasts, now men.
For then to sacrifice a bullock,
Or now and then a child to Moloch,
They count a vile abomination,
But not to slaughter a whole nation.
Presbytery does but translate
The Papacy to a free state;
A commonwealth of Popery,
Where ev'ry village is a See
As well as Rome, and must maintain
A Tithe-pig Metropolitan;
Where ev'ry Presbyter and Deacon
Commands the keys for cheese and bacon;
And ev'ry hamlet's governed
By's Holiness, the Church's Head;
More haughty and severe in's place,
Than GREGORY or BONIFACE.
Such Church must (surely) be a monster

With many heads: for if we conster
What in th' Apocalypse we find,
According to th' Apostle's mind,
'Tis that the Whore of Babylon
With many heads did ride upon;
Which heads denote the sinful tribe
Of Deacon, Priest, Lay-Elder, Scribe.

Lay-Elder, SIMEON to LEVI,
Whose little finger is as heavy
As loins of patriarchs, prince-prelate,
And bishop-secular. This zealot
Is of a mungrel, diverse kind;
Cleric before, and lay behind;
A lawless linsie-woolsie brother,
Half of one order, half another;
A creature of amphibious nature;
On land a beast, a fish in water;
That always preys on grace or sin;
A sheep without, a wolf within.
This fierce inquisitor has chief
Dominion over men's belief
And manners: can pronounce a Saint
Idolatrous or ignorant,
When superciliously he sifts
Through coarsest boulter others' gifts;
For all men live and judge amiss,
Whose talents jump not just with his.
He'll lay on gifts with hands, and place
On dullest noddle Light and Grace,
The manufacture of the Kirk.
Those pastors are but th' handy-work
Of his mechanic paws, instilling
Divinity in them by feeling;
From whence they start up Chosen Vessels,
Made by contact, as men get meazles.
So Cardinals, they say, do grope
At th' other end the new-made Pope.

Hold, hold, quoth HUDIBRAS; soft fire,
They say, does make sweet malt. Good Squire,
Festina lente, not too fast;
For haste (the proverb says) makes waste.
The quirks and cavils thou dost make
Are false, and built upon mistake:
And I shall bring you, with your pack
Of fallacies, t' elenchi back;
And put your arguments in mood

And figure to be understood.
I'll force you, by right ratiocination,
To leave your vitilitigation,
And make you keep to th' question close,
And argue dialecticos.

The question then, to state it first,
Is, Which is better, or which worst,
Synods or Bears? Bears I avow
To be the worst, and Synods thou.
But, to make good th' assertion,
Thou say'st th' are really all one.
If so, not worst; for if th' are idem
Why then, tantundem dat tantidem.
For if they are the same, by course,
Neither is better, neither worse.
But I deny they are the same,
More than a maggot and I am.
That both are animalia
I grant, but not rationalia:
For though they do agree in kind,
Specific difference we find;
And can no more make bears of these,
Than prove my horse is SOCRATES.
That Synods are bear-gardens too,
Thou dost affirm; but I say no:
And thus I prove it in a word;
Whats'ver assembly's not impow'r'd
To censure, curse, absolve, and ordain,
Can be no Synod: but bear-garden
Has no such pow'r; ergo, 'tis none:
And so thy sophistry's o'erthrown.

But yet we are beside the question
Which thou didst raise the first contest on;
For that was, Whether Bears are better
Than Synod-men? I say, Negatur.
That bears are beasts, and synods men,
Is held by all: they're better then:
For bears and dogs on four legs go,
As beasts, but Synod-men on two.
'Tis true, they all have teeth and nails;
But prove that Synod-men have tails;
Or that a rugged, shaggy fur
Grows o'er the hide of Presbyter;
Or that his snout and spacious ears
Do hold proportion with a bear's.
A bears a savage beast, of all

Most ugly and unnatural
Whelp'd without form, until the dam
Has lick'd it into shape and frame:
But all thy light can ne'er evict,
That ever Synod-man was lick'd;
Or brought to any other fashion,
Than his own will and inclination.
But thou dost further yet in this
Oppugn thyself and sense; that is,
Thou would'st have Presbyters to go
For bears and dogs, and bearwards too;
A strange chimera of beasts and men,
Made up of pieces heterogene;
Such as in nature never met
In eodem subjecto yet.
Thy other arguments are all
Supposures, hypothetical,
That do but beg, and we may chose
Either to grant them, or refuse.
Much thou hast said, which I know when
And where thou stol'st from other men,
Whereby 'tis plain thy Light and Gifts
Are all but plagiary shifts;
And is the same that Ranter said,
Who, arguing with me, broke my head,
And tore a handful of my beard:
The self-same cavils then I heard,
When, b'ing in hot dispute about
This controversy, we fell out
And what thou know'st I answer'd then,
Will serve to answer thee agen.

Quoth RALPHO, Nothing but th' abuse
Of human learning you produce;
Learning, that cobweb of the brain,
Profane, erroneous, and vain;
A trade of knowledge, as replete
As others are with fraud and cheat;
An art t'incumber gifts and wit,
And render both for nothing fit;
Makes Light unactive, dull, and troubled,
Like little DAVID in SAUL's doublet;
A cheat that scholars put upon
Other mens' reason and their own;
A fort of error, to ensconce
Absurdity and ignorance,
That renders all the avenues
To truth impervious and abstruse,

By making plain things, in debate,
By art, perplex'd, and intricate
For nothing goes for sense or light
That will not with old rules jump right:
As if rules were not in the schools
Deriv'd from truth, but truth from rules.
This pagan, heathenish invention
Is good for nothing but contention.
For as, in sword-and-buckler fight,
All blows do on the target light;
So when men argue, the great'st part
O' th' contests falls on terms of art,
Until the fustian stuff be spent,
And then they fall to th' argument.

Quoth HUDIBRAS Friend RALPH, thou hast
Out-run the constable at last:
For thou art fallen on a new
Dispute, as senseless as untrue,
But to the former opposite
And contrary as black to white;
Mere disparata; that concerning
Presbytery; this, human learning;
Two things s'averse, they never yet
But in thy rambling fancy met.
But I shall take a fit occasion
T' evince thee by ratiocination,
Some other time, in place more proper
Than this we're in; therefore let's stop here,
And rest our weary'd bones a-while,
Already tir'd with other toil.

PART II

CANTO I

THE ARGUMENT

The Knight by damnable Magician,
Being cast illegally in prison,
Love brings his Action on the Case.
And lays it upon Hudibras.
How he receives the Lady's Visit,
And cunningly solicits his Suite,
Which she defers; yet on Parole
Redeems him from th' inchanted Hole.

But now, t'observe a romantic method,
Let bloody steel a while be sheathed,
And all those harsh and rugged sounds
Of bastinadoes, cuts, and wounds,
Exchang'd to Love's more gentle stile,
To let our reader breathe a while;
In which, that we may be as brief as
Is possible, by way of preface,
Is't not enough to make one strange,
That some men's fancies should ne'er change,
But make all people do and say
The same things still the self-same way
Some writers make all ladies purloin'd,
And knights pursuing like a whirlwind
Others make all their knights, in fits
Of jealousy, to lose their wits;
Till drawing blood o'th' dames, like witches,
Th' are forthwith cur'd of their capriches.
Some always thrive in their amours
By pulling plaisters off their sores;
As cripples do to get an alms,
Just so do they, and win their dames.
Some force whole regions, in despight
O' geography, to change their site;
Make former times shake hands with latter,
And that which was before, come after.
But those that write in rhime, still make
The one verse for the other's sake;
For, one for sense, and one for rhime,
I think's sufficient at one time.

But we forget in what sad plight
We whilom left the captiv'd Knight
And pensive Squire, both bruis'd in body,
And conjur'd into safe custody.
Tir'd with dispute and speaking Latin,
As well as basting and bear-baiting,
And desperate of any course,
To free himself by wit or force,
His only solace was, that now
His dog-bolt fortune was so low,
That either it must quickly end
Or turn about again, and mend;
In which he found th' event, no less
Than other times beside his guess.

There is a tall long sided dame
(But wond'rous light,) ycleped Fame
That, like a thin camelion, boards
Herself on air, and eats her words;
Upon her shoulders wings she wears
Like hanging-sleeves, lin'd through with ears,
And eyes, and tongues, as poets list,
Made good by deep mythologist,
With these she through the welkin flies,
And sometimes carries truth, oft lies
With letters hung like eastern pigeons,
And Mercuries of furthest regions;
Diurnals writ for regulation
Of lying, to inform the nation;
And by their public use to bring down
The rate of whetstones in the kingdom.
About her neck a pacquet-male,
Fraught with advice, some fresh, some stale,
Of men that walk'd when they were dead,
And cows of monsters brought to bed;
Of hail-stones big as pullets eggs,
And puppies whelp'd with twice two legs;
A blazing star seen in the west,
By six or seven men at least.
Two trumpets she does sound at once,
But both of clean contrary tones;
But whether both with the same wind,
Or one before, and one behind,
We know not; only this can tell,
The one sounds vilely, th' other well;
And therefore vulgar authors name
Th' one Good, the other Evil, Fame.

This tattling gossip knew too well
What mischief HUDIBRAS befell.
And straight the spiteful tidings bears
Of all to th' unkind widow's ears.
DEMOCRITUS ne'er laugh'd so loud
To see bawds carted through the crowd,
Or funerals with stately pomp
March slowly on in solemn dump,
As she laugh'd out, until her back,
As well as sides, was like to crack.
She vow'd she would go see the sight,
And visit the distressed Knight;
To do the office of a neighbour,
And be a gossip at his labour;
And from his wooden jail, the stocks,

To set at large his fetter-locks;
And, by exchange, parole, or ransom,
To free him from th' enchanted mansion.
This b'ing resolv'd, she call'd for hood
And usher, implements abroad
Which ladies wear, beside a slender
Young waiting damsel to attend her;
All which appearing, on she went,
To find the Knight in limbo pent.
And 'twas not long before she found
Him, and the stout Squire, in the pound;
Both coupled in enchanted tether,
By further leg behind together
For as he sat upon his rump,
His head like one in doleful dump,
Between his knees, his hands apply'd
Unto his ears on either side;
And by him, in another hole,
Afflicted RALPHO, cheek by jowl;
She came upon him in his wooden
Magician's circle on the sudden,
As spirits do t' a conjurer,
When in their dreadful shapes th' appear.

No sooner did the Knight perceive her,
But straight he fell into a fever,
Inflam'd all over with disgrace,
To be seen by her in such a place;
Which made him hang his head, and scoul,
And wink, and goggle like an owl.
He felt his brains begin to swim,
When thus the dame accosted him:

This place (quoth she) they say's enchanted,
And with delinquent spirits haunted,
That here are ty'd in chains, and scourg'd,
Until their guilty crimes be purg'd.
Look, there are two of them appear,
Like persons I have seen somewhere.
Some have mistaken blocks and posts
For spectres, apparitions, ghosts,
With saucer eyes, and horns; and some
Have heard the Devil beat a drum:
But if our eyes are not false glasses,
That give a wrong account of faces,
That beard and I should be acquainted,
Before 'twas conjur'd or enchanted;
For though it be disfigur'd somewhat,

As if 't had lately been in combat,
It did belong to a worthy Knight
Howe'er this goblin has come by't.

When HUDIBRAS the Lady heard
Discoursing thus upon his beard,
And speak with such respect and honour,
Both of the beard and the beard's owner,
He thought it best to set as good
A face upon it as he cou'd,
And thus he spoke: Lady, your bright
And radiant eyes are in the right:
The beard's th' identic beard you knew,
The same numerically true:
Nor is it worn by fiend or elf,
But its proprietor himself.

O, heavens! quoth she, can that be true?
I do begin to fear 'tis you:
Not by your individual whiskers,
But by your dialect and discourse,
That never spoke to man or beast
In notions vulgarly exprest.
But what malignant star, alas
Has brought you both to this sad pass?

Quoth he, The fortune of the war,
Which I am less afflicted for,
Than to be seen with beard and face,
By you in such a homely case.
Quoth she, Those need not he asham'd
For being honorably maim'd,
If he that is in battle conquer'd,
Have any title to his own beard;
Though yours be sorely lugg'd and torn,
It does your visage more adorn
Than if 'twere prun'd, and starch'd, and lander'd,
And cut square by the Russian standard.
A torn beard's like a tatter'd ensign,
That's bravest which there are most rents in.
That petticoat about your shoulders
Does not so well become a souldier's;
And I'm afraid they are worse handled
Although i' th' rear; your beard the van led;
And those uneasy bruises make
My heart for company to ake,
To see so worshipful a friend
I' th' pillory set, at the wrong end.

Quoth HUDIBRAS, This thing call'd pain
Is (as the learned Stoicks maintain)
Not bad simpliciter, nor good,
But merely as 'tis understood.
Sense is deceitful, and may feign,
As well in counterfeiting pain
As other gross phenomenas,
In which it oft mistakes the case.
But since the immortal intellect
(That's free from error and defect,
Whose objects still persist the same)
Is free from outward bruise and maim,
Which nought external can expose
To gross material bangs or blows,
It follows, we can ne'er be sure,
Whether we pain or not endure;
And just so far are sore and griev'd,
As by the fancy is believ'd.
Some have been wounded with conceit,
And dy'd of mere opinion straight;
Others, tho' wounded sore in reason,
Felt no contusion, nor discretion.
A Saxon Duke did grow so fat,
That mice (as histories relate)
Eat grots and labyrinths to dwell in
His postick parts without his feeling:
Then how is't possible a kick
Should e'er reach that way to the quick?

Quoth she, I grant it is in vain.
For one that's basted to feel pain,
Because the pangs his bones endure
Contribute nothing to the cure:
Yet honor hurt, is wont to rage
With pain no med'cine can asswage.

Quoth he, That honour's very squeamish
That takes a basting for a blemish;
For what's more hon'rable than scars,
Or skin to tatters rent in wars?
Some have been beaten till they know
What wood a cudgel's of by th' blow;
Some kick'd until they can feel whether
A shoe be Spanish or neat's leather;
And yet have met, after long running,
With some whom they have taught that cunning.
The furthest way about t' o'ercome,

In the end does prove the nearest home.
By laws of learned duellists,
They that are bruis'd with wood or fists,
And think one beating may for once
Suffice, are cowards and pultroons:
But if they dare engage t' a second,
They're stout and gallant fellows reckon'd.

Th' old Romans freedom did bestow,
Our princes worship, with a blow.
King PYRRHUS cur'd his splenetic
And testy courtiers with a kick.
The NEGUS, when some mighty lord
Or potentate's to be restor'd
And pardon'd for some great offence,
With which be's willing to dispense,
First has him laid upon his belly,
Then beaten back and side to a jelly;
That done, he rises, humbly bows,
And gives thanks for the princely blows;
Departs not meanly proud, and boasting
Of this magnificent rib-roasting.
The beaten soldier proves most manful,
That, like his sword, endures the anvil,
And justly's held more formidable,
The more his valour's malleable:
But he that fears a bastinado
Will run away from his own shadow:
And though I'm now in durance fast,
By our own party basely cast,
Ransom, exchange, parole refus'd,
And worse than by the enemy us'd;
In close catasta shut, past hope
Of wit or valour to elope;
As beards the nearer that they tend
To th' earth still grow more reverend;
And cannons shoot the higher pitches,
The lower we let down their breeches;
I'll make this low dejected fate
Advance me to a greater height.

Quoth she, Y' have almost made me in love
With that which did my pity move.
Great wits and valours, like great states,
Do sometimes sink with their own weights:
Th' extremes of glory and of shame,
Like East and West, become the same:
No Indian Prince has to his palace

More foll'wers than a thief to th' gallows,
But if a beating seem so brave,
What glories must a whipping have
Such great atchievements cannot fail
To cast salt on a woman's tail:
For if I thought your nat'ral talent
Of passive courage were so gallant,
As you strain hard to have it thought,
I could grow amorous, and dote.

When HUDIBRAS this language heard,
He prick'd up's ears and strok'd his beard;
Thought he, this is the lucky hour;
Wines work when vines are in the flow'r;
This crisis then I'll set my rest on,
And put her boldly to the question.

Madam, what you wou'd seem to doubt,
Shall be to all the world made out,
How I've been drubb'd, and with what spirit
And magnanimity I bear it;
And if you doubt it to be true,
I'll stake myself down against you:
And if I fail in love or troth,
Be you the winner, and take both.

Quoth she, I've beard old cunning stagers
Say, fools for arguments use wagers;
And though I prais'd your valour, yet
I did not mean to baulk your wit;
Which, if you have, you must needs know
What I have told you before now,
And you b' experiment have prov'd,
I cannot love where I'm belov'd.

Quoth HUDIBRAS, 'tis a caprich
Beyond th' infliction of a witch;
So cheats to play with those still aim
That do not understand the game.
Love in your heart as icily burns
As fire in antique Roman urns,
To warm the dead, and vainly light
Those only that see nothing by't.
Have you not power to entertain,
And render love for love again;
As no man can draw in his breath
At once, and force out air beneath?
Or do you love yourself so much,

To bear all rivals else a grutch?
What fate can lay a greater curse
Than you upon yourself would force?
For wedlock without love, some say,
Is but a lock without a key.
It is a kind of rape to marry
One that neglects, or cares not for ye:
For what does make it ravishment,
But b'ing against the mind's consent?
A rape that is the more inhuman
For being acted by a woman.
Why are you fair, but to entice us
To love you, that you may despise us?
But though you cannot Love, you say,
Out of your own fanatick way,
Why should you not at least allow
Those that love you to do so too?
For, as you fly me, and pursue
Love more averse, so I do you;
And am by your own doctrine taught
To practise what you call a fau't.

Quoth she, If what you say is true,
You must fly me as I do you;
But 'tis not what we do, but say,
In love and preaching, that must sway.

Quoth he, To bid me not to love,
Is to forbid my pulse to move,
My beard to grow, my ears to prick up,
Or (when I'm in a fit) to hickup:
Command me to piss out the moon,
And 'twill as easily be done:
Love's power's too great to be withstood
By feeble human flesh and blood.
'Twas he that brought upon his knees
The hect'ring, kill-cow HERCULES;
Transform'd his leager-lion's skin
T' a petticoat, and made him spin;
Seiz'd on his club, and made it dwindle
T' a feeble distaff, and a spindle.
'Twas he that made emperors gallants
To their own sisters and their aunts;
Set popes and cardinals agog,
To play with pages at leap-frog.
'Twas he that gave our Senate purges,
And flux'd the House of many a burgess;
Made those that represent the nation

Submit, and suffer amputation;
And all the Grandees o' the Cabal
Adjourn to tubs at Spring and Fall.
He mounted Synod-Men, and rode 'em
To Dirty-Lane and Little Sodom;
Made 'em curvet like Spanish jenets,
And take the ring at Madam [Bennet's]
'Twas he that made Saint FRANCIS do
More than the Devil could tempt him to,
In cold and frosty weather, grow
Enamour'd of a wife of snow;
And though she were of rigid temper,
With melting flames accost and tempt her;
Which after in enjoyment quenching,
He hung a garland on his engine

Quoth she, If Love have these effects,
Why is it not forbid our sex?
Why is't not damn'd and interdicted,
For diabolical and wicked?
And sung, as out of tune, against,
As Turk and Pope are by the Saints?
I find I've greater reason for it,
Than I believ'd before t' abhor it.

Quoth HUDIBRAS, These sad effects
Spring from your Heathenish neglects
Of Love's great pow'r, which he returns
Upon yourselves with equal scorns;
And those who worthy lovers slight,
Plagues with prepost'rous appetite.
This made the beauteous Queen of Crete
To take a town-bull for her sweet,
And from her greatness stoop so low,
To be the rival of a cow:
Others to prostitute their great hearts,
To he baboons' and monkeys' sweet-hearts;
Some with the Dev'l himself in league grow,
By's representative a Negro.
'Twas this made vestal-maids love-sick,
And venture to be bury'd quick:
Some by their fathers, and their brothers,
To be made mistresses and mothers.
'Tis this that proudest dames enamours
On lacquies and valets des chambres;
Their haughty stomachs overcomes,
And makes 'em stoop to dirty grooms;
To slight the world, and to disparage

Claps, issue, infamy, and marriage.

Quoth she, These judgments are severe,
Yet such as I should rather bear,
Than trust men with their oaths, or prove
Their faith and secresy in love,

Says he, There is as weighty reason
For secresy in love as treason.
Love is a burglarer, a felon,
That at the windore-eyes does steal in
To rob the heart, and with his prey
Steals out again a closer way,
Which whosoever can discover,
He's sure (as he deserves) to suffer.
Love is a fire, that burns and sparkles
In men as nat'rally as in charcoals,
Which sooty chymists stop in holes
When out of wood they extract coals:
So lovers should their passions choak,
That, tho' they burn, they may not smoak.
'Tis like that sturdy thief that stole
And dragg'd beasts backwards into's hole:
So Love does lovers, and us men
Draws by the tails into his den,
That no impression may discover,
And trace t' his cave, the wary lover,
But if you doubt I should reveal
What you entrust me under seal.
I'll prove myself as close and virtuous
As your own secretary ALBERTUS.

Quoth she, I grant you may be close
In hiding what your aims propose.
Love-passions are like parables,
By which men still mean something else,
Though love be all the world's pretence,
Money's the mythologick sense;
The real substance of the shadow,
Which all address and courtship's made to.

Thought he, I understand your play,
And how to quit you your own way:
He that will win his dame, must do
As Love does when he bends his bow;
With one hand thrust the lady from,
And with the other pull her home.
I grant, quoth he, wealth is a great

Provocative to am'rous heat.
It is all philters, and high diet,
That makes love rampant, and to fly out:
'Tis beauty always in the flower,
That buds and blossoms at fourscore:
'Tis that by which the sun and moon
At their own weapons are out-done:
That makes Knights-Errant fall in trances,
And lay about 'em in romances:
'Tis virtue, wit, and worth, and all
That men divine and sacred call:
For what is worth in any thing,
But so much money as 'twill bring?
Or what, but riches is there known,
Which man can solely call his own
In which no creature goes his half;
Unless it be to squint and laugh?
I do confess, with goods and land,
I'd have a wife at second-hand;
And such you are. Nor is 't your person
My stomach's set so sharp and fierce on;
But 'tis (your better part) your riches,
That my enamour'd heart bewitches.
Let me your fortune but possess,
And settle your person how you please:
Or make it o'er in trust to th' Devil;
You'll find me reasonable and civil.

Quoth she, I like this plainness better
Than false mock-passion, speech, or letter,
Or any feat of qualm or sowning,
But hanging of yourself, or drowning.
Your only way with me to break
Your mind, is breaking of your neck;
For as when merchants break, o'erthrown,
Like nine-pins they strike others down,
So that would break my heart; which done,
My tempting fortune is your own,
These are but trifles: ev'ry lover
Will damn himself over and over,
And greater matters undertake
For a less worthy mistress' sake:
Yet th' are the only ways to prove
Th' unfeign'd realities of love:
For he that hangs, or beats out's brains,
The Devil's in him if he feigns.

Quoth HUDIBRAS, This way's too rough

For mere experiment and proof:
It is no jesting, trivial matter,
To swing t' th' air, or douce in Water,
And, like a water-witch, try love;
That's to destroy, and not to prove;
As if a man should be dissected
To find what part is disaffected.
Your better way is to make over,
In trust, your fortune to your lover.
Trust is a trial; if it break,
'Tis not so desp'rate as a neck.
Beside, th' experiment's more certain;
Men venture necks to gain a fortune:
The soldier does it ev'ry day.
(Eight to the week) for sixpence pay:
Your pettifoggers damn their souls,
To share with knaves in cheating fools:
And merchants, vent'ring through the main,
Slight pirates, rocks, and horns, for gain.
This is the way I advise you to:
Trust me, and see what I will do.

Quoth she, I should be loth to run
Myself all th' hazard, and you none;
Which must be done, unless some deed
Of your's aforesaid do precede.
Give but yourself one gentle swing
For trial, and I'll cut the string:
Or give that rev'rend head a maul,
Or two, or three, against a wall,
To shew you are a man of mettle,
And I'll engage myself to settle.

Quoth he, My head's not made of brass,
As Friar BACON'S noodle was;
Nor (like the Indian's skull) so tough
That, authors say, 'twas musket-proof,
As yet on any new adventure,
As it had need to be, to enter.
You see what bangs it has endur'd,
That would, before new feats, be cur'd.
But if that's all you stand upon,
Here, strike me luck, it shall be done.

Quoth she, The matter's not so far gone
As you suppose: Two words t' a bargain:
That may be done, and time enough,
When you have given downright proof;

And yet 'tis no fantastic pique
I have to love, nor coy dislike:
'Tis no implicit, nice aversion
T' your conversation, mein, or person,
But a just fear, lest you should prove
False and perfidious in love:,
For if I thought you could be true,
I could love twice as much as you.

Quoth he, My faith as adamanatine,
As chains of destiny, I'll maintain:
True as APOLLO ever spoke,
Or Oracle from heart of oak;
And if you'll give my flame but vent,
Now in close hugger-mugger pent,
And shine upon me but benignly,
With that one, and that other pigsney,
The sun and day shall sooner part,
Than love or you shake off my heart;
The sun, that shall no more dispense
His own but your bright influence.
I'll carve your name on barks of trees,
With true-loves-knots and flourishes,
That shall infuse eternal spring,
And everlasting flourishing:
Drink ev'ry letter on't in stum,
And make it brisk champaign become;
Where-e'er you tread, your foot shall set
The primrose and the violet:
All spices, perfumes, and sweet powders,
Shall borrow from your breath their odours:
Nature her charter shall renew,
And take all lives of things from you;
The world depend upon your eye,
And when you frown upon it, die:
Only our loves shall still survive,
New worlds and natures to out-live:
And, like to heralds' moons, remain
All crescents, without change or wane.

Hold, hold, quoth she; no more of this,
Sir Knight; you take your aim amiss:
For you will find it a hard chapter
To catch me with poetic rapture,
In which your mastery of art
Doth shew itself, and not your heart:
Nor will you raise in mine combustion
By dint of high heroic fustian.

She that with poetry is won,
Is but a desk to write upon;
And what men say of her, they mean
No more than on the thing they lean.
Some with Arabian spices strive
T' embalm her cruelly alive;
Or season her, as French cooks use
Their haut-gousts, bouillies, or ragousts:
Use her so barbarously ill,
To grind her lips upon a mill,
Until the facet doublet doth
Fit their rhimes rather than her mouth:
Her mouth compar'd to an oyster's, with
A row of pearl in't — stead of teeth.
Others make posies of her cheeks,
Where red and whitest colours mix;
In which the lily, and the rose,
For Indian lake and ceruse goes.
The sun and moon by her bright eyes
Eclips'd, and darken'd in the skies,
Are but black patches, that she wears,
Cut into suns, and moons, and stars:
By which astrologers as well,
As those in Heav'n above, can tell
What strange events they do foreshow
Unto her under-world below.
Her voice, the music of the spheres,
So loud, it deafens mortals ears;
As wise philosophers have thought;
And that's the cause we hear it not.
This has been done by some, who those
Th' ador'd in rhime, would kick in prose;
And in those ribbons would have hung
On which melodiously they sung;
That have the hard fate to write best
Of those still that deserve it least;
It matters not how false, or forc'd:
So the best things be said o' th' worst:
It goes for nothing when 'tis said;
Only the arrow's drawn to th' bead,
Whether it be a swan or goose
They level at: So shepherds use
To set the same mark on the hip
Both of their sound and rotten sheep:
For wits, that carry low or wide,
Must be aim'd higher, or beside
The mark, which else they ne'er come nigh,
But when they take their aim awry.

But I do wonder you should choose
This way t' attack me with your Muse,
As one cut out to pass your tricks on,
With fulhams of poetic fiction:
I rather hop'd I should no more
Hear from you o' th' gallanting score:
For hard dry-bastings us'd to prove
The readiest remedies of love;
Next a dry-diet: but if those fail,
Yet this uneasy loop-hol'd jail,
In which ye are hamper'd by the fetlock,
Cannot but put y' in mind of wedlock;
Wedlock, that's worse than any hole here,
If that may serve you for a cooler,
T' allay your mettle, all agog
Upon a wife, the heavi'r clog:
Or rather thank your gentler fate,
That for a bruis'd or broken pate,
Has freed you from those knobs that grow
Much harder on the marry'd brow:
But if no dread can cool your courage,
From vent'ring on that dragon, marriage,
Yet give me quarter, and advance
To nobler aims your puissance:
Level at beauty and at wit;
The fairest mark is easiest hit.

Quoth HUDIBRAS, I'm beforehand
In that already, with your command
For where does beauty and high wit
But in your constellation meet?

Quoth she, What does a match imply,
But likeness and equality?
I know you cannot think me fit
To be th' yoke-fellow of your wit;
Nor take one of so mean deserts,
To be the partner of your parts;
A grace which, if I cou'd believe,
I've not the conscience to receive.

That conscience, quoth HUDIBRAS,
Is mis-inform'd: I'll state the case
A man may be a legal donor,
Of any thing whereof he's owner,
And may confer it where he lists,
I' th' judgment of all casuists,
Then wit, and parts, and valour, may

Be ali'nated, and made away,
By those that are proprietors,
As I may give or sell my horse.

Quoth she, I grant the case is true
And proper 'twixt your horse and you;
But whether I may take as well
As you may give away or sell?
Buyers you know are bid beware;
And worse than thieves receivers are.
How shall I answer hue and cry,
For a roan gelding, twelve hands high,
All spurr'd and switch'd, a lock on's hoof,
A sorrel mane? Can I bring proof
Where, when, by whom, and what y' were sold for,
And in the open market toll'd for?
Or should I take you for a stray,
You must be kept a year and day
(Ere I can own you) here i' the pound,
Where, if y' are sought, you may be found
And in the mean time I must pay
For all your provender and hay.

Quoth he, It stands me much upon
T' enervate this objection,
And prove myself; by topic clear
No gelding, as you would infer.
Loss of virility's averr'd
To be the cause of loss of beard,
That does (like embryo in the womb)
Abortive on the chin become.
This first a woman did invent,
In envy of man's ornament;
SEMIRAMIS, of Babylon,
Who first of all cut men o' th' stone,
To mar their beards, and lay foundation
Of sow-geldering operation.
Look on this beard, and tell me whether
Eunuchs wear such, or geldings either?
Next it appears I am no horse;
That I can argue and discourse
Have but two legs, and ne'er a tail.

Quoth she, That nothing will avail
For some philosophers of late here,
Write, men have four legs by nature,
And that 'tis custom makes them go
Erron'ously upon but two;

As 'twas in Germany made good
B' a boy that lost himself in a wood,
And growing down to a man, was wont
With wolves upon all four to hunt.
As for your reasons drawn from tails,
We cannot say they're true or false,
Till you explain yourself, and show,
B' experiment, 'tis so or no.

Quoth he, If you'll join issue on't,
I'll give you satisfactory account;
So you will promise, if you lose,
To settle all, and be my spouse.

That never shall be done (quoth she)
To one that wants a tail, by me
For tails by nature sure were meant,
As well as beards, for ornament:
And though the vulgar count them homely,
In men or beast they are so comely,
So gentee, alamode, and handsome,
I'll never marry man that wants one;
And till you can demonstrate plain,
You have one equal to your mane,
I'll be torn piece-meal by a horse,
Ere I'll take you for better or worse.
The Prince of CAMBAY's daily food
Is asp, and basilisk, and toad;
Which makes him have so strong a breath,
Each night he stinks a queen to death;
Yet I shall rather lie in's arms
Than yours, on any other terms.

Quoth he, What nature can afford,
I shall produce, upon my word;
And if she ever gave that boon
To man, I'll prove that I have one
I mean by postulate illation,
When you shall offer just occasion:
But since y' have yet deny'd to give
My heart, your pris'ner, a reprieve,
But made it sink down to my heel,
Let that at least your pity feel;
And, for the sufferings of your martyr,
Give its poor entertainer quarter;
And, by discharge or main-prize, grant
Deliv'ry from this base restraint.

Quoth she, I grieve to see your leg
Stuck in a hole here like a peg;
And if I knew which way to do't
(Your honour safe) I'd let you out.
That Dames by jail-delivery
Of Errant-Knights have been set free,
When by enchantment they have been,
And sometimes for it too, laid in,
Is that which Knights are bound to do
By order, oath, and honour too:
For what are they renown'd, and famous else,
But aiding of distressed damosels?
But for a Lady no ways errant,
To free a Knight, we have no warrant
In any authentical romance,
Or classic author, yet of France;
And I'd be loth to have you break
An ancient custom for a freak,
Or innovation introduce
In place of things of antique use;
To free your heels by any course,
That might b' unwholesome to your spurs;
Which, if I should consent unto,
It is not in my pow'r to do;
For 'tis a service must be done ye
With solemn previous ceremony;
Which always has been us'd t' untie
The charms of those who here do lie
For as the ancients heretofore
To Honour's Temple had no door,
But that which thorough Virtue's lay,
So from this dungeon there's no way
To honour'd freedom, but by passing
That other virtuous school of lashing,
Where Knights are kept in narrow lists,
With wooden lockets 'bout their wrists;
In which they for a while are tenants,
And for their Ladies suffer penance:
Whipping, that's Virtue's governess,
Tutress of arts and sciences;
That mends the gross mistakes of Nature,
And puts new life into dull matter;
That lays foundation for renown,
And all the honours of the gown.
This suffer'd, they are set at large,
And freed with hon'rable discharge.
Then in their robes the penitentials
Are straight presented with credentials,

And in their way attended on
By magistrates of ev'ry town;
And, all respect and charges paid,
They're to their ancient seats convey'd.
Now if you'll venture, for my sake,
To try the toughness of your back,
And suffer (as the rest have done)
The laying of a whipping on,
(And may you prosper in your suit,
As you with equal vigour do't,)
I here engage myself to loose ye,
And free your heels from Caperdewsie.
But since our sex's modesty
Will not allow I should be by,
Bring me, on oath, a fair account,
And honour too, when you have done't,
And I'll admit you to the place
You claim as due in my good grace.
If matrimony and hanging go
By dest'ny, why not whipping too?
What med'cine else can cure the fits
Of lovers when they lose their wits?
Love is a boy by poets stil'd;
Then spare the rod and spoil the child.
A Persian emp'ror whipp'd his grannam
The sea, his mother VENUS came on;
And hence some rev'rend men approve
Of rosemary in making love.
As skilful coopers hoop their tubs
With Lydian and with Phrygian dubs,
Why may not whipping have as good
A grace, perform'd in time and mood,
With comely movement, and by art,
Raise passion in a lady's heart?
It is an easier way to make
Love by, than that which many take.
Who would not rather suffer whipping,
Than swallow toasts of bits of ribbon?
Make wicked verses, treats, and faces,
And spell names over with beer-glasses
Be under vows to hang and die
Love's sacrifice, and all a lie?
With china-oranges and tarts
And whinning plays, lay baits for hearts?
Bribe chamber-maids with love and money,
To break no roguish jests upon ye?
For lilies limn'd on cheeks, and roses,
With painted perfumes, hazard noses?

Or, vent'ring to be brisk and wanton,
Do penance in a paper lanthorn?
All this you may compound for now,
By suffering what I offer you;
Which is no more than has been done
By Knights for Ladies long agone.
Did not the great LA MANCHA do so
For the INFANTA DEL TOBOSO?
Did not th' illustrious Bassa make
Himself a slave for Misse's sake?
And with bull's pizzle, for her love,
Was taw 'd as gentle as a glove?
Was not young FLORIO sent (to cool
His flame for BIANCAFIORE) to school,
Where pedant made his pathic bum
For her sake suffer martyrdom?
Did not a certain lady whip
Of late her husband's own Lordship?
And though a grandee of the House,
Claw'd him with fundamental blows
Ty'd him stark naked to a bed-post,
And firk'd his hide, as if sh' had rid post
And after, in the sessions-court,
Where whipping's judg'd, had honour for't?
This swear you will perform, and then
I'll set you from th' inchanted den,
And the magician's circle clear.

Quoth he, I do profess and swear,
And will perform what you enjoin,
Or may I never see you mine.
Amen, (quoth she;) then turn'd about,
And bid her Esquire let him out.
But ere an artist could be found
T' undo the charms another bound,
The sun grew low, and left the skies,
Put down (some write) by ladies eyes,
The moon pull'd off her veil of light
That hides her face by day from sight,
(Mysterious veil, of brightness made,
That's both her lustre and her shade,)
And in the lanthorn of the night
With shining horns hung out her light;
For darkness is the proper sphere,
Where all false glories use t' appear.
The twinkling stars began to muster,
And glitter with their borrow'd lustre,
While sleep the weary 'd world reliev'd,

By counterfeiting death reviv'd;
His whipping penance till the morn
Our vot'ry thought it best t' adjourn,
And not to carry on a work
Of such importance in the dark,
With erring haste, but rather stay,
And do't in th' open face of day;
And in the mean time go in quest
Of next retreat to take his rest.

PART II

CANTO II

THE ARGUMENT

The Knight and Squire, in hot dispute,
Within an ace of falling out,
Are parted with a sudden fright
Of strange alarm, and stranger sight;
With which adventuring to stickle,
They're sent away in nasty pickle.

'Tis strange how some mens' tempers suit
(Like bawd and brandy) with dispute,
That for their own opinions stand last
Only to have them claw'd and canvast;
That keep their consciences in cases,
As fiddlers do their crowds and bases,
Ne'er to be us'd, but when they're bent
To play a fit for argument;
Make true and false, unjust and just,
Of no use but to be discust;
Dispute, and set a paradox
Like a straight boot upon the stocks,
And stretch it more unmercifully
Than HELMONT, MONTAIGN, WHITE, or TULLY,
So th' ancient Stoicks, in their porch,
With fierce dispute maintain'd their church;
Beat out their brains in fight and study,
To prove that Virtue is a Body;
That Bonum is an Animal,
Made good with stout polemic brawl;
in which some hundreds on the place
Were slain outright; and many a face

Retrench'd of nose, and eyes, and beard,
To maintain what their sect averr'd;
All which the Knight and Squire, in wrath,
Had like t' have suffered for their faith,
Each striving to make good his own,
As by the sequel shall be shown.

The Sun had long since, in the lap
Of THETIS, taken out his nap,
And, like a lobster boil'd, the morn
From black to red began to turn,
When HUDIBRAS, whom thoughts and aking,
'Twixt sleeping kept all night and waking,
Began to rub his drowsy eyes,
And from his couch prepar'd to rise,
Resolving to dispatch the deed
He vow'd to do with trusty speed.
But first, with knocking loud, and bawling,
He rouz'd the Squire, in truckle lolling;
And, after many circumstances,
Which vulgar authors, in romances,
Do use to spend their time and wits on,
To make impertinent description,
They got (with much ado) to horse,
And to the Castle bent their course,
In which he to the Dame before
To suffer whipping duly swore;
Where now arriv'd, and half unharnest,
To carry on the work in earnest,
He stopp'd, and paus'd upon the sudden,
And with a serious forehead plodding,
Sprung a new scruple his head,
Which first he scratch'd, and after said —
Whether it be direct infringing
An oath, if I should wave this swingeing,
And what I've sworn to bear, forbear,
And so b' equivocation swear,
Or whether it be a lesser sin
To be forsworn than act the thing,
Are deep and subtle points, which must,
T' inform my conscience, be discust;
In which to err a tittle may
To errors infinite make way;
And therefore I desire to know
Thy judgment e'er we further go.

Quoth Ralpho, Since you do enjoin't,
I shall enlarge upon the point;

And, for my own part, do not doubt
Th' affirmative may be made out,
But first, to state the case aright,
For best advantage of our light,
And thus 'tis: Whether 't be a sin
To claw and curry your own skin,
Greater or less, than to forbear,
And that you are forsworn, forswear.
But first, o' th' first: The inward man,
And outward, like a clan and clan,
Have always been at daggers-drawing,
And one another clapper-clawing.
Not that they really cuff, or fence,
But in a Spiritual Mystick sense;
Which to mistake, and make 'em squabble
In literal fray's abominable.
'Tis heathenish, in frequent use
With Pagans and apostate Jews,
To offer sacrifice of bridewells,
Like modern Indians to their idols;
And mongrel Christians of our times,
That expiate less with greater crimes,
And call the foul abomination,
Contrition and mortification.
Is 't not enough we're bruis'd and kicked
With sinful members of the wicked,
Our vessels, that are sanctify'd,
Prophan'd and curry'd back and side,
But we must claw ourselves with shameful
And heathen stripes, by their example;
Which (were there nothing to forbid it)
Is impious because they did it;
This, therefore, may be justly reckon'd
A heinous sin. Now to the second
That Saints may claim a dispensation
To swear and forswear, on occasion,
I doubt not but it will appear
With pregnant light: the point is clear.
Oaths are but words, and words but wind;
Too feeble implements to bind;
And hold with deeds proportion so
As shadows to a substance do.
Then when they strive for place, 'tis fit
The weaker vessel should submit.
Although your Church be opposite
To ours as Black Friars are to White,
In rule and order, yet I grant,
You are a Reformado Saint;

And what the Saints do claim as due,
You may pretend a title to:
But Saints whom oaths and vows oblige,
Know little of their privilege;
Further (I mean) than carrying on
Some self-advantage of their own:
For if the Dev'l, to serve his turn,
Can tell troth, why the Saints should scorn,
When it serves theirs, to swear and lye;
I think there's little reason why:
Else h' has a greater pow'r than they,
Which 't were impiety to say.
W' are not commanded to forbear
Indefinitely at all to swear;
But to swear idly, and in vain,
Without self-interest or gain
For breaking of an oath, and lying,
Is but a kind of self-denying;
A Saint-like virtue: and from hence
Some have broke oaths by Providence
Some, to the glory of the Lord,
Perjur'd themselves, and broke their word;
And this the constant rule and practice
Of all our late Apostles acts is.
Was not the cause at first begun
With perjury, and carried on?
Was there an oath the Godly took,
But in due time and place they broke?
Did we not bring our oaths in first,
Before our plate, to have them burst,
And cast in fitter models for
The present use of Church and War?
Did not our Worthies of the House,
Before they broke the peace, break vows?
For having freed us first from both
Th' Allegiance and Supremacy Oath,
Did they not next compel the Nation
To take and break the Protestation?
To swear, and after to recant
The solemn League and Covenant?
To take th' Engagement, and disclaim it,
Enforc'd by those who first did frame it
Did they not swear, at first, to fight
For the KING'S Safety and his Right,
And after march'd to find him out,
And charg'd him home with horse and foot;
But yet still had the confidence
To swear it was in his defence

Did they not swear to live and die
With Essex, and straight laid him by?

If that were all, for some have swore
As false as they, if th' did no more,
Did they not swear to maintain Law,
In which that swearing made a flaw?
For Protestant Religion vow,
That did that vowing disallow?
For Privilege of Parliament,
In which that swearing made a rent?
And since, of all the three, not one
Is left in being, 'tis well known.
Did they not swear, in express words,
To prop and back the House of Lords,
And after turn'd out the whole House-full
Of Peers, as dang'rous and unusefull?
So CROMWELL, with deep oaths and vows,
Swore all the Commons out o' th' House;
Vow'd that the red-coats would disband,
Ay, marry wou'd they, at their command;
And troll'd them on, and swore, and swore,
Till th' army turn'd them out of door.
This tells us plainly what they thought,
That oaths and swearing go for nought,
And that by them th' were only meant
To serve for an expedient.
What was the Public Faith found out for,
But to slur men of what they fought for
The Public Faith, which ev'ry one
Is bound t' observe, yet kept by none;
And if that go for nothing, why
Should Private Faith have such a tye?
Oaths were not purpos'd more than law,
To keep the good and just in awe,
But to confine the bad and sinful,
Like moral cattle, in a pinfold.
A Saint's of th' Heav'nly Realm a Peer;
And as no Peer is bound to swear,
But on the Gospel of his Honour,
Of which he may dispose as owner,
It follows, though the thing be forgery,
And false th' affirm, it is no perjury,
But a mere ceremony, and a breach
Of nothing, but a form of speech;
And goes for no more when 'tis took,
Than mere saluting of the book.
Suppose the Scriptures are of force,

They're but commissions of course,
And Saints have freedom to digress,
And vary from 'em, as they please;
Or mis-interpret them, by private
Instructions, to all aims they drive at.
Then why should we ourselves abridge
And curtail our own privilege?
Quakers (that, like to lanthorns, bear
Their light within 'em) will not swear
Their gospel is an accidence,
By which they construe conscience,
And hold no sin so deeply red,
As that of breaking Priscian's head;
(The head and founder of their order,)
That stirring Hat's held worse than murder.
These thinking th' are oblig'd to troth
In swearing, will not take an oath
Like mules, who, if th' have not their will
To keep their own pace, stand stock-still:
But they are weak, and little know
What free-born consciences may do.
'Tis the temptation of the Devil
That makes all human actions evil
For Saints may do the same things by
The Spirit, in sincerity,
Which other men are tempted to,
And at the Devil's instance do
And yet the actions be contrary,
Just as the Saints and Wicked vary.
For as on land there is no beast,
But in some fish at sea's exprest,
So in the Wicked there's no Vice,
Of which the Saints have not a spice;
And yet that thing that's pious in
The one, in th' other is a sin.
Is't not ridiculous, and nonsense,
A Saint should be a slave to conscience,
That ought to be above such fancies,
As far as above ordinances?
She's of the wicked, as I guess,
B' her looks, her language, and her dress:
And though, like constables, we search,
For false wares, one another's Church,
Yet all of us hold this for true,
No Faith is to the wicked due;
For truth is precious and divine;
Too rich a pearl for carnal swine,

Quoth HUDIBRAS, All this is true;
Yet 'tis not fit that all men knew,
Those mysteries and revelations,
And therefore topical evasions
Of subtle turns and shifts of sense,
Serve best with th' wicked for pretence,
Such as the learned Jesuits use,
And Presbyterians for excuse
Against the Protestants, when th' happen
To find their Churches taken napping:
As thus: A breach of oath is duple,
And either way admits a scruple,
And may be, ex parte of the maker
More criminal than th' injur'd taker;
For he that strains too far a vow,
Will break it, like an o'er-bent bow:
And he that made, and forc'd it, broke it,
Not he that for convenience took it.
A broken oath is, quatenus oath,
As sound t' all purposes of troth,
As broken laws are ne'er the worse;
Nay, till th' are broken have no force.
What's justice to a man, or laws,
That never comes within their claws
They have no pow'r, but to admonish:
Cannot controul, coerce, or punish,
Until they're broken, and then touch
Those only that do make 'em such.
Beside, no engagement is allow'd
By men in prison made for good;
For when they're set at liberty,
They're from th' engagement too set free.
The rabbins write, when any Jew
Did make to God, or man, a vow,
Which afterward he found untoward,
And stubborn to be kept, or too hard,
Any three other Jews o' th' nation,
Might free him from the obligation
And have not two saints pow'r to use
A greater privilege than three Jews?
The court of conscience, which in man
Should be supreme and sovereign,
Is't fit should be subordinate
To ev'ry petty court i' the state,
And have less power than the lesser,
To deal with perjury at pleasure?
Have its proceedings disallow'd, or
Allow'd, at fancy of Pye-Powder?

Tell all it does, or does not know,
For swearing ex officio?
Be forc'd t' impeach a broken hedge,
And pigs unring'd at Vis. Franc. Pledge?
Discover thieves, and bawds, recusants,
Priests, witches, eves-droppers, and nuisance:
Tell who did play at games unlawful,
And who fill'd pots of ale but half-full
And have no pow'r at all, nor shift,
To help itself at a dead lift
Why should not conscience have vacation
As well as other courts o' th' nation
Have equal power to adjourn,
Appoint appearance and return;
And make as nice distinction serve
To split a case, as those that carve,
Invoking cuckolds' names, hit joints;
Why should not tricks as slight do points
Is not th' High-Court of Justice sworn
To judge that law that serves their turn,
Make their own jealousies high-treason,
And fix 'm whomsoe'er they please on?
Cannot the learned counsel there
Make laws in any shape appear?
Mould 'em as witches do their clay,
When they make pictures to destroy
And vex 'em into any form
That fits their purpose to do harm?
Rack 'em until they do confess,
Impeach of treason whom they please,
And most perfidiously condemn
Those that engag'd their lives for them?
And yet do nothing in their own sense,
But what they ought by oath and conscience?
Can they not juggle, and, with slight
Conveyance, play with wrong and right;
And sell their blasts of wind as dear
As Lapland witches bottled air?
Will not fear, favour, bribe and grudge
The same case sev'ral ways adjudge?
As seamen, with the self-same gale,
Will sev'ral different courses sail?
As when the sea breaks o'er its bounds,
And overflows the level grounds,
Those banks and dams, that, like a screen,
Did keep it out, now keep it in;
So when tyrannic usurpation
Invades the freedom of a nation,

The laws o' th' land, that were intended
To keep it out, are made defend it.
Does not in chanc'ry ev'ry man swear
What makes best for him in his answer?
Is not the winding up witnesses
And nicking more than half the bus'ness?
For witnesses, like watches, go
Just as they're set, too fast or slow;
And where in conscience they're strait-lac'd,
'Tis ten to one that side is cast.
Do not your juries give their verdict
As if they felt the cause, not heard it?
And as they please, make matter of fact
Run all on one side, as they're pack't?
Nature has made man's breast no windores,
To publish what he does within doors,
Nor what dark secrets there inhabit,
Unless his own rash folly blab it.
If oaths can do a man no good
In his own bus'ness, why they shou'd
In other matters do him hurt,
I think there's little reason for't.
He that imposes an oath, makes it,
Not he that for convenience takes it:
Then how can any man be said
To break an oath he never made?
These reasons may, perhaps, look oddly
To th' Wicked, though th' evince the Godly;
But if they will not serve to clear
My honour, I am ne'er the near.
Honour is like that glassy bubble
That finds philosophers such trouble,
Whose least part crack't, the whole does fly,
And wits are crack'd to find out why.

Quoth RALPHO, Honour's but a word
To swear by only in a Lord:
In other men 'tis but a huff,
To vapour with instead of proof;
That, like a wen, looks big and swells,
Is senseless, and just nothing else.

Let it (quoth he) be what it will,
It has the world's opinion still.
But as men are not wise that run
The slightest hazard they may shun,
There may a medium be found out
To clear to all the world the doubt;

And that is, if a man may do't,
By proxy whipt, or substitute.

Though nice and dark the point appear,
(Quoth RALPH) it may hold up and clear.
That sinners may supply the place
Of suff'ring Saints is a plain case.
Justice gives sentence many times
On one man for another's crimes.

Our brethren of NEW ENGLAND use
Choice malefactors to excuse,
And hang the guiltless in their stead,
Of whom the Churches have less need;
As lately 't happen'd: In a town
There liv'd a cobler, and but one,
That out of doctrine could cut use,
And mend men's lives as well as shoes,
This precious brother having slain,
In time of peace, an Indian,
(Not out of malice, but mere zeal,
Because he was an Infidel,)
The mighty TOTTIPOTTYMOY
Sent to our elders an envoy,
Complaining sorely of the breach
Of league held forth by brother Patch
Against the articles in force
Between both Churches, his and ours
For which he crav'd the Saints to render
Into his hands or hang th' offender
But they maturely having weigh'd,
They had no more but him o' th' trade,
(A man that serv'd them in a double
Capacity, to teach and cobble,)
Resolv'd to spare him; yet, to do
The Indian Hoghgan Moghgan too
Impartial justice, in his stead did
Hang an old Weaver, that was bed-rid.
Then wherefore way not you be skipp'd,
And in your room another whipp'd?
For all Philosophers, but the Sceptick,
Hold whipping may be sympathetick.

It is enough, quoth HUDIBRAS,
Thou hast resolv'd and clear'd the case
And canst, in conscience, not refuse
From thy own doctrine to raise use.
I know thou wilt not (for my sake)

Be tender-conscienc'd of thy back.
Then strip thee off thy carnal jerking,
And give thy outward-fellow a ferking;
For when thy vessel is new hoop'd,
All leaks of sinning will be stopp'd.

Quoth RALPHO, You mistake the matter;
For in all scruples of this nature,
No man includes himself, nor turns
The point upon his own concerns.
As no man of his own self catches
The itch, or amorous French aches
So no man does himself convince,
By his own doctrine, of his sins
And though all cry down self, none means
His ownself in a literal sense.
Beside, it is not only foppish,
But vile, idolatrous and Popish,
For one man, out of his own skin,
To ferk and whip another's sin;
As pedants out of school-boys' breeches
Do claw and curry their own itches.
But in this case it is prophane,
And sinful too, because in vain;
For we must take our oaths upon it,
You did the deed, when I have done it.

Quoth HUDIBRAS, That's answer'd soon
Give us the whip, we'll lay it on.

Quoth RALPHO, That we may swear true,
'Twere properer that I whipp'd you
For when with your consent 'tis done,
The act is really your own.

Quoth HUDIBRAS, It is in vain
(I see) to argue 'gainst the grain;
Or, like the stars, incline men to
What they're averse themselves to do:
For when disputes are weary'd out,
'Tis interest still resolves the doubt
But since no reason can confute ye,
I'll try to force you to your duty
For so it is, howe'er you mince it;
As ere we part, I shall evince it
And curry (if you stand out) whether
You will or no, your stubborn leather.
Canst thou refuse to hear thy part

I' th' publick work, base as thou art?
To higgle thus for a few blows,
To gain thy Knight an op'lent spouse
Whose wealth his bowels yearn to purchase,
Merely for th' interest of the Churches;
And when he has it in his claws,
Will not be hide-bound to the Cause?
Nor shalt thou find him a Curmudgin,
If thou dispatch it without grudging.
If not, resolve, before we go,
That you and I must pull a crow.

Y' had best (quoth RALPHO) as the ancients
Say wisely, Have a care o' th' main chance,
And look before you ere you leap;
For as you sow, y' are like to reap:
And were y' as good as George-a-Green,
I shall make bold to turn agen
Nor am I doubtful of the issue
In a just quarrel, and mine is so.
Is't fitting for a man of honour
To whip the Saints, like Bishop Bonner?
A Knight t' usurp the beadle's office,
For which y' are like to raise brave trophies.
But I advise you (not for fear,
But for your own sake) to forbear;
And for the Churches, which may chance,
From hence, to spring a variance;
And raise among themselves new scruples,
Whom common danger hardly couples.
Remember how, in arms and politicks,
We still have worsted all your holy tricks;
Trepann'd your party with intrigue,
And took your grandees down a peg;
New modell'd th' army, and cashier'd
All that to legion SMEC adher'd;
Made a mere utensil o' your Church,
And after left it in the lurch
A scaffold to build up our own,
And, when w' had done with't, pull'd it down
Capoch'd your Rabbins of the Synod,
And snap'd their Canons with a why-not;
(Grave Synod Men, that were rever'd
For solid face and depth of beard;)
Their classic model prov'd a maggot,
Their direct'ry an Indian Pagod;
And drown'd their discipline like a kitten,
On which they'd been so long a sitting;

Decry'd it as a holy cheat,
Grown out of date, and obsolete;
And all the Saints of the first grass
As casting foals of Balaam's ass.

At this the Knight grew high in chafe,
And staring furiously on RALPH,
He trembled, and look'd pale with ire
Like ashes first, then red as fire.
Have I (quoth he) been ta'en in fight,
And for so many moons lain by't,
And, when all other means did fail,
Have been exchang'd for tubs of ale?
Not but they thought me worth a ransome
Much more consid'rable and handsome,
But for their own sakes, and for fear
They were not safe when I was there
Now to be baffled by a scoundrel,
An upstart sect'ry, and a mungrel;
Such as breed out of peccant humours,
Of our own Church, like wens or tumours,
And, like a maggot in a sore,
Would that which gave it life devour;
It never shall be done or said;
With that he seiz'd upon his blade;
And RALPHO too, as quick and bold,
Upon his basket-hilt laid hold,
With equal readiness prcpar'd
To draw, and stand upon his guard;
When both were parted on the sudden,
 With hideous clamour, and a loud one
As if all sorts of noise had been
Contracted into one loud din;
Or that some member to be chosen,
Had got the odds above a thousand,
And by the greatness of its noise,
Prov'd fittest for his country's choice.
This strange surprisal put the Knight
And wrathful Squire into a fright;
And though they stood prepar'd, with fatal
Impetuous rancour to join battel,
Both thought it was the wisest course
To wave the fight and mount to horse,
And to secure by swift retreating,
Themselves from danger of worse beating.
Yet neither of them would disparage,
By utt'ring of his mind, his courage,
Which made them stoutly keep their ground,

With horror and disdain wind-bound.

And now the cause of all their fear
By slow degrees approach'd so near,
They might distinguish different noise
Of horns, and pans, and dogs, and boys,
And kettle-drums, whose sullen dub
Sounds like the hooping of a tub.
But when the sight appear'd in view,
They found it was an antique show;
A triumph, that, for pomp and state,
Did proudest Romans emulate:
For as the aldermen of Rome
Their foes at training overcome,
And not enlarging territory,
(As some mistaken write in Story,)
Being mounted, in their best array,
Upon a carr, and who but they!
And follow'd with a world of tall-lads,
That merry ditties troll'd, and ballads,
Did ride with many a good-morrow,
Crying, Hey for our Town! through the Borough
So when this triumph drew so nigh
They might particulars descry,
They never saw two things so pat,
In all respects, as this and that.
First, he that led the cavalcade,
Wore a sow-gelder's flagellate,
On which he blew as strong a levet
As well-fee'd lawyer on his breviate,
When over one another's heads
They charge (three ranks at once) like Swedes,
Next pans and kettle, of all keys,
From trebles down to double base;
And after them, upon a nag,
That might pass for a forehand stag,
A cornet rode, and on his staff
A smock display'd did proudly wave.
Then bagpipes of the loudest drones,
With snuffling broken-winded tones,
Whose blasts of air, in pockets shut
Sound filthier than from the gut,
And make a viler noise than swine
In windy weather, when they whine.
Next one upon a pair of panniers,
Full fraught with that which for good manners
Shall here be nameless, mixt with grains,
Which he dispens'd among the swains,

And busily upon the crowd
At random round about bestow'd.
Then, mounted on a horned horse,
One bore a gauntlet and gilt spurs,
Ty'd to the pummel of a long sword
He held reverst, the point turn'd downward,
Next after, on a raw-bon'd steed,
The conqueror's standard-bearer rid,
And bore aloft before the champion
A petticoat display'd, and rampant
Near whom the Amazon triumphant
Bestrid her beast, and on the rump on't
Sat face to tail, and bum to bum,
The warrior whilom overcome;
Arm'd with a spindle and a distaff,
Which, as he rode, she made him twist off;
And when he loiter'd, o'er her shoulder
Chastis'd the reformado soldier.
Before the dame, and round about,
March'd whifflers and staffiers on foot,
With lackies, grooms, valets, and pages,
In fit and proper equipages;
Of whom some torches bore, some links,
Before the proud virago minx,
That was both Madam and a Don,
Like NERO'S SPORUS, or POPE JOAN;
And at fit periods the whole rout
Set up their throats with clamorous shout.
The Knight, transported, and the Squire,
Put up their weapons, and their ire;
And HUDIBRAS, who us'd to ponder
On such sights with judicious wonder,
Could hold no longer to impart
His animadversions, for his heart.

Quoth he, In all my life, till now,
I ne'er saw so prophane a show.
It is a Paganish invention, —
Which heathen writers often mention:
And he who made it had read GOODWIN,
Or Ross, or CAELIUS RHODOGINE,
With all the Grecians, SPEEDS and STOWS,
That best describe those ancient shows;
And has observ'd all fit decorums
We find describ'd by old historians:
For as the Roman conqueror,
That put an end to foreign war,
Ent'ring the town in triumph for it,

Bore a slave with him, in his chariot;
So this insulting female brave,
Carries behind her here a slave:
And as the ancients long ago,
When they in field defy'd the foe,
Hung out their mantles della guerre,
So her proud standard-bearer here
Waves on his spear, in dreadful manner,
A Tyrian-petticoat for banner:
Next links and torches, heretofore
Still borne before the emperor.
And as, in antique triumphs, eggs
Were borne for mystical intrigues,
There's one with truncheon, like a ladle,
That carries eggs too, fresh or addle;
And still at random, as he goes,
Among the rabble-rout bestows.

Quoth Ralpho, You mistake the matter;
For all th' antiquity you smatter,
Is but a riding, us'd of course
When the grey mare's the better horse;
When o'er the breeches greedy women
Fight to extend their vast dominion;
And in the cause impatient Grizel
Has drubb'd her Husband with bull's pizzle,
And brought him under Covert-Baron,
To turn her vassal with a murrain;
When wives their sexes shift, like hares,
And ride their husbands like night-mares,
And they in mortal battle vanquish'd,
Are of their charter disenfranchis'd
And by the right of war, like gills,
Condemn'd to distaff, horns, and wheels:
For when men by their wives are cow'd,
Their horns of course are understood

Quoth HUDIBRAS thou still giv'st sentence
Impertinently, and against sense.
Tis not the least disparagement
To be defeated by th' event,
Nor to be beaten by main force;
That does not make a man the worse,
Although his shoulders with battoon
Be claw'd and cudgel'd to some tune.
A taylor's 'prentice has no hard
Measure that's bang'd with a true yard:
But to turn tail, or run away,

And without blows give up the day,
Or to surrender ere th' assault,
That's no man's fortune, but his fault,
And renders men of honour less
Than all th' adversity of success;
And only unto such this shew
Of horns and petticoats is due.
There is a lesser profanation,
Like that the Romans call'd ovation:
For as ovation was allow'd
For conquest purchas'd without blood,
So men decree these lesser shows
For victory gotten without blows,
By dint of sharp hard words, which some
Give battle with, and overcome.
These mounted in a chair-curule,
Which moderns call a cucking-stool,
March proudly to the river's side,
And o'er the waves in triumph ride;
Like Dukes of VENICE, who are said
The Adriatick Sea to wed;
And have a gentler wife than those
For whom the State decrees those shows,
But both are heathenish, and come
From th' whores of Babylon and Rome;
And by the Saints should be withstood,
As Antichristian and lewd;
And as such, should now contribute
Our utmost struggling to prohibit.

This said, they both advanc'd, and rode
A dog-trot through the bawling crowd,
T'attack the leader, and still prest,
Till they approach'd him breast to breast
Then HUDIBRAS, with face and hand,
Made signs for silence; which obtain'd,
What means (quoth he) this Devil's precession
With men of orthodox profession?
'Tis ethnic and idolatrous,
From heathenism deriv'd to us,
Does not the Whore of Babylon ride
Upon her horned beast astride
Like this proud dame, who either is
A type of her, or she of this?
Are things of superstitious function
Fit to be us'd in Gospel Sun-shine?
It is an Antichristian opera,
Much us'd in midnight times of Popery,

Of running after self-inventions
Of wicked and profane intentions;
To scandalize that sex for scolding,
To whom the Saints are so beholden.
Women, who were our first Apostles
Without whose aid we had been lost else;
Women, that left no stone unturn'd
In which the Cause might he concern'd;
Brought in their children's' spoons and whistles,
To purchase swords, carbines, and pistols;
Their husbands, cullies, and sweet-hearts,
To take the Saints and Churches' parts;
Drew several gifted Brethren in,
That for the Bishops would have been,
And fix'd 'em constant to the party,
With motives powerful and hearty;
Their husbands robb'd, and made hard shifts
T'administer unto their gifts
All they cou'd rap, and rend, and pilfer,
To scraps and ends of gold and silver;
Rubb'd down the Teachers, tir'd and spent
With holding forth for Parliament,
Pamper'd and edify'd their zeal
With marrow-puddings many a meal;
And led them, with store of meat,
On controverted points to eat;
And cram'd 'em, till their guts did ake,
With cawdle, custard, and plum-cake:
What have they done, or what left undone,
That might advance the Cause at London?
March'd rank and file, with drum and ensign,
T'intrench the city for defence in
Rais'd rampiers with their own soft hands,
To put the enemy to stands;
From ladies down to oyster-wenches,
Labour'd like pioneers in trenches;
Fell to their pick-axes, and tools,
And help'd the men to dig like moles?
Have not the handmaids of the city
Chose of their members a committee,
For raising of a common purse
Out of their wages to raise horse?
And do they not as triers sit,
To judge what officers are fit
Have they —? At that an egg let fly,
Hit him directly o'er the eye,
And running down his cheek, besmear'd,
With orange tawny slime, his beard;

But beard and slime being of one hue,
The wound the less appear'd in view.
Then he that on the panniers rode,
Let fly on th' other side a load,
And, quickly charg'd again, gave fully
In RALPHO'S face another volley.
The Knight was startled with the smell,
And for his sword began to feel;
And RALPHO, smother'd with the stink,
Grasp'd his; when one, that bore a link,
O' th' sudden clapp'd his flaming cudgel,
Like linstock, to the horse's touch-hole;
And straight another, with his flambeaux,
Gave RALPHO'S o'er the eye a damn'd blow.
The beasts began to kick and fling,
And forc'd the rout to make a ring,
Through which they quickly broke their way,
And brought them off from further fray;
And though disorder'd in retreat,
Each of them stoutly kept his seat
For quitting both their swords and reins,
They grasp'd with all their strength the manes,
And, to avoid the foe's pursuit,
With spurring put their cattle to't;
And till all four were out of wind,
And danger too, ne'er look'd behind.
After th' had paus'd a while, supplying
Their spirits, spent with fight and flying,
And HUDIBRAS recruited force
Of lungs, for action or discourse,

Quoth he, That man is sure to lose
That fouls his hands with dirty foes:
For where no honour's to be gain'd,
'Tis thrown away in b'ing maintain'd.
'Twas ill for us we had to do
With so dishonourable a foe:
For though the law of arms doth bar
The use of venom'd shot in war,
Yet, by the nauseous smell, and noisome,
Their case-shot savours strong of poison;
And doubtless have been chew'd with teeth
Of some that had a stinking breath;
Else, when we put it to the push,
They have not giv'n us such a brush.
But as those pultroons, that fling dirt,
Do but defile, but cannot hurt,
So all the honour they have won,

Or we have lost, is much as one,
'Twas well we made so resolute
And brave retreat without pursuit;
For if we had not, we had sped
Much worse, to be in triumph led;
Than which the ancients held no state
Of man's life more unfortunate.
But if this bold adventure e'er
Do chance to reach the widow's ear,
It may, b'ing destin'd to assert
Her sex's honour, reach her heart:
And as such homely treats (they say)
Portend good fortune, so this may.
VESPASIAN being daub'd with dirt,
Was destin'd to the empire for't;
And from a Scavenger did come
To be a mighty Prince in Rome
And why may not this foul address
Presage in love the same success
Then let us straight, to cleanse our wounds,
Advance in quest of nearest ponds,
And after (as we first design'd)
Swear I've perform'd what she enjoin'd.

PART II

CANTO III

THE ARGUMENT

The Knight, with various Doubts possest,
To win the Lady goes in quest
Of Sidrophel, the Rosy-Crucian,
To know the Dest'nies' Resolution;
With whom being met, they both chop Logick
About the Science Astrologick,
Till falling from Dispute to Fight,
The Conj'rer's worsted by the Knight.

Doubtless the pleasure is as great
Of being cheated as to cheat;
As lookers-on feel most delight,
That least perceive a jugler's slight;
And still the less they understand,
The more th' admire his slight of hand.

Some with a noise, and greasy light,
Are snapt, as men catch larks by night;
Ensnar'd and hamper'd by the soul,
As nooses by their legs catch fowl
Some with a med'cine, and receipt,
Are drawn to nibble at the bait;
And tho' it be a two-foot trout,
'Tis with a single hair pull'd out.

Others believe no voice t' an organ
So sweet as lawyer's in his bar-gown,
Until with subtle cobweb-cheats
Th'are catch'd in knotted law, like nets;
In which, when once they are imbrangled,
The more they stir, the more they're tangled;
And while their purses can dispute,
There's no end of th' immortal suit.

Others still gape t' anticipate
The cabinet-designs of fate;
Apply to wizards, to foresee
What shall and what shall never be;
And, as those vultures do forebode,
Believe events prove bad or good:
A flam more senseless than the roguery
Of old aruspicy and aug'ry.
That out of garbages of cattle
Presag'd th' events of truce or battle;
From flight of birds, or chickens pecking,
Success of great'st attempts would reckon:
Though cheats, yet more intelligible
Than those that with the stars do fribble.
This HUDIBRAS by proof found true,
As in due time and place we'll shew:
For he, with beard and face made clean,
B'ing mounted on his steed agen,
(And RALPHO got a cock-horse too
Upon his beast, with much ado)
Advanc'd on for the Widow's house,
To acquit himself, and pay his vows;
When various thoughts began to bustle,
And with his inward man to justle
He thought what danger might accrue
If she should find he swore untrue;
Or if his squire or he should fail,
And not be punctual in their tale:
It might at once the ruin prove

Both of his honour, faith, and love.
But if he should forbear to go,
She might conclude h'had broke his vow;
And that he durst not now for-shame
Appear in court to try his claim.
This was the pen'worth of his thought,
To pass time and uneasy trot.

Quoth he, In all my past adventures
I ne'er was set so on the tenters;
Or taken tardy with dilemma,
That ev'ry way I turn does hem me,
And with inextricable doubt
Besets my puzzled wits about:
For tho' the dame has been my bail,
To free me from enchanted jail,
Yet as a dog, committed close
For some offence, by chance breaks loose,
And quits his clog, but all in vain,
He still draws after him his chain;
So, though my ankle she has quitted,
My heart continues still committed;
And like a bail'd and main-priz'd lover,
Altho' at large, I am bound over;
And when I shall appear in court,
To plead my cause, and answer for't,
Unless the judge do partial prove,
What will become of me and love?
For if in our account we vary,
Or but in circumstance miscarry;
Or if she put me to strict proof,
And make me pull my doublet off,
To shew, by evident record
Writ on my skin, I've kept my Word;
How can I e'er expect to have her,
Having demurr'd onto her favour?
But faith, and love, and honour lost,.
Shall be reduc'd t' a Knight o' th' Post.
Beside, that stripping may prevent
What I'm to prove by argument,
And justify I have a tail
And that way, too, my proof may fail.
Oh that I cou'd enucleate,
And solve the problems of my fate
Or find, by necromantick art,
How far the dest'nies take my part
For if I were not more than certain
To win and wear her, and her fortune,

I'd go no farther in his courtship,
To hazard soul, estate, and worship
For though an oath obliges not
Where any thing is to be got,
(As thou last prov'd) yet 'tis profane,
And sinful, when men swear in vain.

Quoth RALPH, Not far from hence doth dwell
A cunning man, hight SIDROPHEL,
That deals in destiny's dark counsels,
And sage opinions of the Moon sells;
To whom all people, far and near,
On deep importances repair;
When brass and pewter hap to stray,
And linen slinks out of the way;
When geese and pullen are seduc'd,
And sows of sucking-pigs are chows'd;
When cattle feel indisposition,
And need th' opinion of physician;
When murrain reigns in hogs or sheep.
And chickens languish of the pip;
When yeast and outward means do fail,
And have no pow'r to work on ale:
When butter does refuse to come,
And love proves cross and humoursome:
To him with questions, and with urine,
They for discov'ry flock, or curing.

Quoth HUDIBRAS, This SIDROPHEL
I've heard of, and should like it well,
If thou canst prove the Saints have freedom
To go to Sorc'rers when they need 'em.

Says RALPHO, There's no doubt of that
Whose principles I quoted late,
Prove that the Godly may alledge
For any thing their Privilege;
And to the Dev'l himself may go,
If they have motives thereunto.
For, as there is a war between
The Dev'l and them, it is no sin,
If they by subtle stratagem
Make use of him, as he does them.
Has not this present Parliament
A Ledger to the Devil sent,
Fully impowr'd to treat about
Finding revolted witches out
And has not he, within a year,

Hang'd threescore of 'em in one shire?
Some only for not being drown'd,
And some for sitting above ground,
Whole days and nights, upon their breeches,
And feeling pain, were hang'd for witches.
And some for putting knavish tricks
Upon green geese and turky-chicks,
And pigs, that suddenly deceast
Of griefs unnat'ral, as he guest;
Who after prov'd himself a witch
And made a rod for his own breech.
Did not the Devil appear to MARTIN
LUTHER in Germany for certain;
And wou'd have gull'd him with a trick,
But Martin was too politick?
Did he not help the Dutch to purge
At ANTWERP their Cathedral Church?
Sing catches to the Saints at MASCON,
And tell them all they came to ask him
Appear'd in divers shapes to KELLY,
And speak i' th' Nun of LOUDON's belly?
Meet with the Parliament's Committee
At WOODSTOCK on a pers'nal treaty?
At SARUM take a cavalier
I' th' Cause's service prisoner
As WITHERS, in immortal rhime,
Has register'd to after-time!
Do not nor great Reformers use
This SIDROPHEL to forebode news?
To write of victories next year,
And castles taken yet i' th' air
Of battles fought at sea, and ships
Sank two years hence, the last eclipse?
A total overthrow giv'n the King
In Cornwall, horse and foot, next Spring!
And has not he point-blank foretold
Whats'e'er the Close Committee would?
Made Mars and Saturn for the Cause
The moon for Fundamental Laws?
The Ram, the Bull, and Goat declare
Against the Book of Common-Pray'r?
The Scorpion take the Protestation,
And Bear engage for Reformation?
Made all the Royal Stars recant,
Compound and take the Covenant?

Quoth HUDIBRAS, The case is clear,
The Saints may 'mploy a Conjurer,

As thou hast prov'd it by their practice;
No argument like matter of fact is;
And we are best of all led to
Men's principles by what they do.
Then let us straight advance in quest
Of this profound Gymnosophist
And as the Fates and he advise,
Pursue or wave this enterprise,

This said, he turn'd about his steed,
And eftsoons on th' adventure rid;
Where leave we him and RALPH a while,
And to the Conjurer turn our stile,
To let our reader understand
What's useful of him before-hand.

He had been long t'wards mathematicks,
Optics, philosophy, and staticks,
Magick, horoscopy, astrology,
And was old dog at physiology
But as a dog that turns the spit
Bestirs himself, and plies his feet,
To climb the wheel, but all in vain,
His own weight brings him down again,
And still he's in the self-same place
Where at his setting out h was
So in the circle of the arts
Did he advance his nat'ral parts,
Till falling back still, for retreat,
He fell to juggle, cant, and cheat:
For as those fowls that live in water
Are never wet, he did but smatter:
Whate'er he labour'd to appear,
His understanding still was clear
Yet none a deeper knowledge boasted,
Since old HODGE-BACON and BOB GROSTED.
Th' Intelligible World he knew,
And all men dream on't to be true;
That in this world there's not a wart
That has not there a counterpart;
Nor can there on the face of ground
An individual beard be found,
That has not, in that foreign nation,
A fellow of the self-same fashion
So cut, so colour'd, and so curl'd,
As those are in th' Inferior World.
H' had read DEE's Prefaces before,
The DEV'L, and EUCLID, o'er and o'er;

And all the intrigues 'twixt him and KELLY,
LESCUS and th' EMPEROR, wou'd tell ye;
But with the Moon was more familiar
Than e'er was almanack well-willer;
Her secrets understood so clear,
That some believ'd he had been there;
Knew when she was in the fittest mood
For cutting corns, or letting blood;
When for anointing scabs or itches,
Or to the bum applying leeches;
When sows and bitches may be spay'd,
And in what sign best cyder's made:
Whether the wane be, or increase,
Best to set garlick, or sow pease:
Who first found out the Man i' th' Moon,
That to the ancients was unknown;
How many dukes, and earls, and peers,
Are in the planetary spheres;
Their airy empire and command,
Their sev'ral strengths by sea and land;
What factions th' have, and what they drive at
In public vogue, or what in private;
With what designs and interests
Each party manages contests.
He made an instrument to know
If the Moon shine at full or no;
That wou'd as soon as e'er she shone, straight
Whether 'twere day or night demonstrate;
Tell what her d'meter t' an inch is,
And prove that she's not made of green cheese.
It wou'd demonstrate, that the Man in
The Moon's a Sea Mediterranean;
And that it is no dog nor bitch,
That stands behind him at his breech,
But a huge Caspian Sea, or lake,
With arms, which men for legs mistake;
How large a gulph his tail composes,
And what a goodly bay his nose is;
How many German leagues by th' scale
Cape Snout's from Promontory Tail.
He made a planetary gin,
Which rats would run their own heads in,
And cause on purpose to be taken,
Without th' expence of cheese or bacon.
With lute-strings he would counterfeit
Maggots that crawl on dish of meat:
Quote moles and spots on any place
O' th' body, by the index face:

Detect lost maiden-heads by sneezing,
Or breaking wind of dames, or pissing;
Cure warts and corns with application
Of med'cines to th' imagination;
Fright agues into dogs, and scare
With rhimes the tooth-ach and catarrh;
Chace evil spirits away by dint
Of cickle, horse-shoe, hollow-flint;
Spit fire out of a walnut-shell,
Which made the Roman slaves rebel;
And fire a mine in China here
With sympathetic gunpowder.
He knew whats'ever's to be known,
But much more than he knew would own;
What med'cine 'twas that PARACELSUS
Could make a man with, as he tells us;
What figur'd slates are best to make
On watry surface duck or drake;
What bowling-stones, in running race
Upon a board, have swiftest pace;
Whether a pulse beat in the black
List of a dappled louse's back;
If systole or diastole move
Quickest when he's in wrath or love
When two of them do run a race,
Whether they gallop, trot, or pace:
How many scores a flea will jump,
Of his own length, from head to rump;
Which SOCRATES and CHAEREPHON,
In vain, assay'd so long agon;
Whether his snout a perfect nose is,
And not an elephant's proboscis
How many diff'rent specieses
Of maggots breed in rotten cheese
And which are next of kin to those
Engender'd in a chandler's nose;
Or those not seen, but understood,
That live in vinegar and wood.

A paultry wretch he had, half-starv'd,
That him in place of Zany serv'd.
Hight WHACHUM, bred to dash and draw,
Not wine, but more unwholesome law
To make 'twixt words and lines huge gaps,
Wide as meridians in maps;
To squander paper, and spare ink,
And cheat men of their words, some think.
From this, by merited degrees,

He'd to more high advancement rise;
To be an under-conjurer,
A journeyman astrologer.
His business was to pump and wheedle,
And men with their own keys unriddle;
And make them to themselves give answers,
For which they pay the necromancers;
To fetch and carry intelligence,
Of whom, and what, and where, and whence,
And all discoveries disperse
Among th' whole pack of conjurers
What cut-purses have left with them
For the right owners to redeem;
And what they dare not vent find out,
To gain themselves and th' art repute;
Draw figures, schemes, and horoscopes,
Of Newgate, Bridewell, brokers' shops,
Of thieves ascendant in the cart;
And find out all by rules of art;
Which way a serving-man, that's run
With cloaths or money away, is gone:
Who pick'd a fob at holding forth;
And where a watch, for half the worth,
May be redeem'd; or stolen plate
Restor'd at conscionable rate.
Beside all this, he serv'd his master
In quality of poetaster;
And rhimes appropriate could make
To ev'ry month i' th almanack
What terms begin and end could tell,
With their returns, in doggerel;
When the exchequer opes and shuts,
And sowgelder with safety cuts
When men may eat and drink their fill,
And when be temp'rate, if they will;
When use and when abstain from vice,
Figs, grapes, phlebotomy, and spice.
And as in prison mean rogues beat
Hemp for the service of the great,
So WHACHUM beats his dirty brains,
T' advance his master's fame and gains
And, like the Devil's oracles,
Put into doggrel rhimes his spells,
Which, over ev'ry month's blank page
I' th' almanack, strange bilks presage.
He would an elegy compose
On maggots squeez'd out of his nose;
In lyrick numbers write an ode on

His mistress, eating a black-pudden:
And when Imprison'd air escap'd her,
It puft him with poetic rapture.
His sonnets charm'd th' attentive crowd,
By wide-mouth'd mortal troll'd aloud,
That 'circl'd with his long-ear'd guests,
Like ORPHEUS look'd among the beasts.
A carman's horse could not pass by,
But stood ty'd up to poetry:
No porter's burthen pass'd along,
But serv'd for burthen to his song:
Each window like a pill'ry appears,
With heads thrust through, nail'd by the ears
All trades run in as to the sight
Of monsters, or their dear delight
The gallow tree, when cutting purse
Breeds bus'ness for heroic verse,
Which none does hear, but would have hung
T' have been the theme of such a song.

Those two together long had liv'd,
In mansion prudently contriv'd;
Where neither tree nor house could bar
The free detection of a star
And nigh an ancient obelisk
Was rais'd by him, found out by FISK,
On which was a written not in words,
But hieroglyphic mute of birds,
Many rare pithy saws concerning
The worth of astrologic learning.
From top of this there hung a rope,
To a which he fasten'd telescope;
The spectacles with which the stars
He reads in smallest characters.
It happen'd as a boy, one night,
Did fly his tarsel of a kite,
The strangest long-wing'd hawk that flies,
That, like a bird of Paradise,
Or herald's martlet, has no legs,
Nor hatches young ones, nor lays eggs;
His train was six yards long, milk-white,
At th' end of which there hung a light,
Inclos'd in lanthorn, made of paper,
That far off like a star did appear.
This SIDROPHEL by chance espy'd,
And with amazement staring wide,
Bless us! quoth he, what dreadful wonder
Is that appears in heaven yonder?

A comet, and without a beard!
Or star that ne'er before appear'd!
I'm certain 'tis not in the scrowl
Of all those beasts, and fish, and fowl,
With which, like Indian plantations,
The learned stock the constellations
Nor those that draw for signs have bin
To th' houses where the planets inn.
It must be supernatural,
Unless it be that cannon-ball
That, shot i' th' air point-blank upright,
Was borne to that prodigious height,
That learn'd Philosophers maintain,
It ne'er came backwards down again;
But in the airy region yet
Hangs like the body of MAHOMET
For if it be above the shade
That by the earth's round bulk is made,
'Tis probable it may from far
Appear no bullet, but a star.

This said, he to his engine flew,
Plac'd near at hand, in open view,
And rais'd it 'till it levell'd right
Against the glow-worm tail of kite,
Then peeping thro', Bless us! (quoth he)
It is a planet, now I see
And, if I err not, by his proper
Figure, that's like tobacco-stopper,
It should be Saturn. Yes, 'tis clear
'Tis Saturn; but what makes him there?
He's got between the Dragon's Tail
And farther Leg behind o' th' Whale.
Pray heav'n divert the fatal omen,
For 'tis a prodigy not common;
And can no less than the world's end,
Or Nature's funeral, portend.

With that he fell again to pry.
Thro' perspective more wistfully,
When by mischance the fatal string,
That kept the tow'ring fowl on wing,
Breaking, down fell the star. Well shot,
Quoth WHACHUM, who right wisely thought
H' had levell'd at a star, and hit it
But SIDROPHEL, more subtle-witted,
Cry'd out, What horrible and fearful
Portent is this, to see a star fall?

It threatens nature, and the doom
Will not be long before It come
When stars do fail, 'tis plain enough,
The day of judgment's not far off;
As lately 'twas reveal'd to SEDGWICK,
And some of us find out by magick.
Then since the time we have to live
In this world's shorten'd, let us strive
To make our best advantage of it,
And pay our losses with our profit.

This feat fell out not long before
The Knight, upon the forenam'd score,
In quest of SIDROPHEL advancing,
Was now in prospect of the mansion
Whom he discov'ring, turn'd his glass,
And found far off, 'twas HUDIBRAS.

WHACHUM, (quoth he), look yonder, some
To try or use our art are come
The one's the learned Knight: seek out,
And pump 'em what they come about.
WHACHUM advanc'd, with all submissness,
T' accost em, but much more their bus'ness.
He held a stirrup, while the Knight
From leathern bare-bones did alight
And taking from his hand the bridle,
Approach'd the dark Squire to unriddle.
He gave him first the time o' th' day,
And welcom'd him, as he might say:
He ask'd him whence he came, and whither
Their bus'ness lay? Quoth RALPHO, Hither.
Did you not lose? Quoth RALPHO, Nay.
Quoth WHACHUM, Sir, I meant your way!
Your Knight — Quoth RALPHO, Is a lover,
And pains intolerable doth suffer:
For lovers' hearts are not their own hearts,
Nor lights, nor lungs, and so forth downwards.
What time, (quoth RALPHO), Sir? — Too long
Three years it off and on has hung. —
Quoth he, I meant what time o'the day 'tis. —
Quoth RALPHO, Between seven and eight 'tis.
Why then, (quoth Whachum) my small art
Tells me, the dame has a hard heart,
Or great estate. — Quoth RALPH, A jointer,
Which makes him have so hot a mind t'her.
Mean while the Knight was making water,
Before he fell upon the matter;

Which having done, the Wizard steps in,
To give him suitable reception
But kept his bus'ness at a bay
Till WHACHUM put him in the way;
Who having now, by RALPHO's light.
Expounded th' errand of the Knight,
And what he came to know, drew near,
To whisper in the Conj'rer's ear,
Which he prevented thus: What was't,
Quoth he, that I was saying last,
Before these gentlemen arriv'd?
Quoth WHACHUM, Venus you retriev'd,
In opposition with Mars,
And no benigne friendly stars
T' allay the effect. — Quoth Wizard, So
In Virgo? Ha! — Quoth WHACHUM, No.
Has Saturn nothing to do in it?
One-tenth of's circle to a minute.
'Tis well, quoth he. — Sir, you'll excuse
This rudeness I am forc'd to use
It is a scheme and face of Heaven,
As the aspects are dispos'd this even,
I was contemplating upon
When you arriv'd; but now I've done,

Quoth HUDIBRAS, If I appear
Unseasonable in coming here
At such a tone, to interrupt,
Your speculations, which I hop'd
Assistance from, and come to use,
'T is fit that I ask your excuse.
By no means, Sir, quoth SIDROPHEL;
The stars your coming did foretel:
I did expect you here, and knew,
Before you spake, your bus'ness too.

Quoth HUDIBRAS, Make that appear,
And I shall credit whatsoe'er
You tell me after on your word,
Howe'er unlikely, or absurd.

You are in love, Sir, with a widow,
Quoth he, that does not greatly heed you,
And for three years has rid your wit
And passion without drawing bit:
And now your bus'ness is to know,
If you shall carry her or no.

Quoth HUDIBRAS, You're in the right;
But how the Devil you came by't
I can't imagine; for the Stars,
I'm sure, can tell no more than a horse;
Nor can their aspects (though you pore
Your eyes out on 'em) tell you more
Than th' oracle of sieve and sheers,
That turns as certain as the spheres:
But if the Devil's of your counsel,
Much may be done my noble Donzel;
And 'tis on his account I come,
To know from you my fatal doom.

Quoth SIDROPHEL, If you Suppose,
Sir Knight, that I am one of those,
I might suspect, and take the alarm,
Your bus'ness is but to inform;
But if it be, 'tis ne'er the near;
You have a wrong sow by the ear;
For I assure you, for my part,
I only deal by rules of art,
Such as are lawful, and judge by
Conclusions of Astrology:
But for the Dev'l, know nothing by him;
But only this, that I defy him.

Quoth he, Whatever others deem ye,
I understand your metonymy:
Your words of second-hand intention,
When things by wrongful names you mention;
The mystick sense of all your terms,
That are, indeed, but magick charms
To raise the Devil, and mean one thing,
And that is down-right conjuring;
And in itself more warrantable,
Than cheat, or canting to a rabble,
Or putting tricks upon the Moon,
Which by confed'racy are done.
Your ancient conjurers were wont
To make her from her sphere dismount.
And to their incantations stoop:
They scorn'd to pore thro' telescope,
Or idly play at bo-peep with her,
To find out cloudy or fair weather,
Which ev'ry almanack can tell,
Perhaps, as learnedly and well,
As you yourself — Then, friend, I doubt
You go the furthest way about.

Your modern Indian magician
Makes but a hole in th' earth to piss in,
And straight resolves all questions by't,
And seldom fails to be i'th' right.
The Rosy-Crucian way's more sure
To bring the Devil to the lure;
Each of 'em has a sev'ral gin
To catch intelligences in.
Some by the nose with fumes trepan 'em,
As DUNSTAN did the Devil's grannam;
Others, with characters and words,
Catch 'em, as men in nets do birds;
And some with symbols, signs, and tricks,
Engrav'd with planetary nicks,
With their own influences will fetch 'em
Down from their orbs, arrest, and catch 'em;
Make 'em depose and answer to
All questions e're they let them go.
 BUMBASTUS kept a Devil's bird
Shut in the pummel of his sword,
That taught him all the cunning pranks
Of past and future mountebanks.
KELLY did all his feats upon
The Devil's looking-glass, a stone;
Where playing with him at bo-peep,
He solv'd all problems ne'er so deep.
AGRIPPA kept a Stygian pug,
I' th' garb and habit of a dog,
That was his tutor, and the cur
Read to th' occult philosopher,
And taught him subt'ly to maintain
All other sciences are vain.

To this, quoth SIDROPHELLO, Sir,
AGRIPPA was no conjurer,
Nor PARACELSUS, no, nor BEHMEN;
Nor was the dog a Cacodaemon,
But a true dog, that would shew tricks
For th' emperor, and leap o'er sticks;
Would fetch and carry; was more civil
Than other dogs, but yet no Devil;
And whatsoe'er he's said to do,
He went the self-same way we go.
As for the Rosy-Cross Philosophers,
Whom you will have to be but sorcerers,
What they pretend to is no more,
Than TRISMEGISTUS did before,
PYTHAGORAS, old ZOROASTER,

And APOLLONIUS their master;
To whom they do confess they owe
All that they do, and all they know.

Quoth HUDIBRAS, Alas! what is't t' us,
Whether 'twas said by TRISMEGISTUS,
If it be nonsense, false, or mystick,
Or not intelligible, or sophistick?
'Tis not antiquity, nor author,
That makes Truth Truth, altho' Times daughter;
'Twas he that put her in the pit
Before he pull'd her out of it;
And as he eats his sons, just so
He feeds upon his daughters too.
Nor does it follow, 'cause a herald,
Can make a gentleman, scarce a year old,
To be descended of a race
Of ancient kings in a small space,
That we should all opinions hold
Authentic that we can make old.

Quoth SIDROPHEL, It is no part
Of prudence to cry down an art,
And what it may perform deny,
Because you understand not why
(As AVERHOIS play'd but a mean trick
To damn our whole art for eccentrick:)
For Who knows all that knowledge contains
Men dwell not on the tops of mountains,
But on their sides, or rising's seat
So 'tis with knowledge's vast height.
Do not the hist'ries of all ages
Relate miraculous presages,
Of strange turns in the world's affairs,
Foreseen b' Astrologers, Soothsayers,
Chaldeans, learn'd Genethliacks,
And some that have writ almanacks?
The MEDIA N emp'ror dreamt his daughter
Had pist all ASIA under water,
And that a vine, sprung from her haunches,
O'erspread his empire with its branches:
And did not soothsayers expound it,
As after by th' event he found it?
When CAESAR in the senate fell,
Did not the sun eclips'd foretel,
And, in resentment of his slaughter,
Look'd pale for almost a year after?
AUGUSTUS having, b' oversight,

Put on his left shoe 'fore his right,
Had like to have been slain that day
By soldiers mutin'ing for pay.
Are there not myriads of this sort,
Which stories of all times report?
Is it not ominous in all countries
When crows and ravens croak upon trees?
The Roman senate, when within
The city walls an owl was seen
Did cause their clergy, with lustrations,
(Our Synod calls humiliations),
The round-fac'd prodigy t'avert
From doing town or country hurt
And if an owl have so much pow'r,
Why should not planets have much more,
That in a region far above
Inferior fowls of the air move,
And should see further, and foreknow
More than their augury below?
Though that once serv'd the polity
Of mighty states to govern by
And this is what we take in hand
By pow'rful art to understand
Which, how we have perform'd, all ages
Can speak th' events of our presages
Have we not lately, in the Moon,
Found a New World, to the Old unknown?
Discover'd sea and land, COLUMBUS
And MAGELLAN cou'd never compass?
Made mountains with our tubes appear,
And cattle grazing on 'em there?

Quoth HUDIBRAS, You lie so ope,
That I, without a telescope,
Can mind your tricks out, and descry
Where you tell truth, and where you lye:
For ANAXAGORAS, long agon,
Saw hills, as well as you, i' th' Moon;
And held the Sun was but a piece
Of red-hot ir'n, as big as Greece;
Believ'd the Heav'ns were made of stone,
Because the Sun had voided one;
And, rather than he would recant
Th' opinion, suffer'd banishment.

But what, alas! is it to us,
Whether i' th' Moon men thus or thus
Do eat their Porridge, cut their corns,

Or whether they have tails or horns?
What trade from thence can you advance,
But what we nearer have from France?
What can our travellers bring home,
That is not to be learnt at Rome?
What politicks, or strange opinions,
That are not in our own dominions?
What science can he brought from thence,
In which we do not here commence?
What revelations, or religions,
That are not in our native regions?
Are sweating lanthorns, or screen-fans,
Made better there than th' are in France?
Or do they teach to sing and play
O' th' gittar there a newer way?
Can they make plays there, that shall fit
The public humour, with less wit?
Write wittier dances, quainter shows,
Or fight with more ingenious blows?
Or does the man i' th' moon look big,
And wear a huger perriwig,
Shew in his gait or face more tricks,
Than our own native lunaticks?
And if w' out-do him here at home,
What good of your design can come?
As wind i' th' hypocondries pent,
Is but a blast if downward sent,
But if it upward chance to fly,
Becomes new Light and Prophecy
So when your speculations tend
Above their just and useful end,
Although they promise strange and great
Discoveries of things far set,
They are but idle dreams and fancies,
And savour strongly of the ganzas.
Tell me but what's the natural cause,
Why on a sign no painter draws
The full moon ever, but the half;
Resolve that with your JACOB's staff;
Or why wolves raise a hubbub at her,
And dogs howl when she shines in water;
And I shall freely give my vote,
You may know something more remote.

At this deep SIDROPHEL look'd wise,
And staring round with owl-like eyes,
He put his face into a posture
Of sapience, and began to bluster:

For having three times shook his head
To stir his wit up, thus he said
Art has no mortal enemies,
Next ignorance, but owls and geese;
Those consecrated geese in orders,
That to the Capitol were warders;
And being then upon patrol,
With noise alone beat off the Gaul:
Or those Athenian Sceptic owls,
That will not credit their own souls;
Or any science understand,
Beyond the reach of eye or hand;
But meas'ring all things by their own
Knowledge, hold nothing's to be known
Those wholesale criticks, that in coffee-
Houses cry down all philosophy,
And will not know upon what ground
In nature we our doctrine found,
Altho' with pregnant evidence
We can demonstrate it to sense,
As I just now have done to you,
Foretelling what you came to know.
Were the stars only made to light
Robbers and burglarers by night?
To wait on drunkards, thieves, gold-finders,
And lovers solacing behind doors,
Or giving one another pledges
Of matrimony under hedges?
Or witches simpling, and on gibbets
Cutting from malefactors snippets?
Or from the pillory tips of ears
Of Rebel-Saints and perjurers?
Only to stand by, and look on,
But not know what is said or done?
Is there a constellation there,
That was not born and bred up here?
And therefore cannot be to learn
In any inferior concern.
Were they not, during all their lives,
Most of 'em pirates, whores and thieves;
And is it like they have not still
In their old practices some skill
Is there a planet that by birth
Does not derive its house from earth?
And therefore probably must know,
What is and hath been done below.
Who made the Balance, or whence came
The Bull, the Lion, and the Ram?

Did not we here the Argo rig,
Make BERENICE's periwig?
Whose liv'ry does the Coachman wear?
Or who made Cassiopeia's chair?
And therefore, as they came from hence,
With us may hold intelligence.
PLATO deny'd the world can be
Govern'd without geometree,
(For money b'ing the common scale
Of things by measure, weight, and tale,
In all th' affairs of Church and State,
'Tis both the balance and the weight;)
Then much less can it be without
Divine Astrology made out;
That puts the other down in worth,
As far as Heav'n's above the earth.

These reasons (quoth the Knight) I grant
Are something more significant
Than any that the learned use
Upon this subject to produce;
And yet th' are far from satisfactory,
T' establish and keep up your factory.
Th' Egyptians say, the Sun has twice
Shifted his setting and his rise
Twice has he risen in the west,
As many times set in the east;
But whether that be true or no,
The Dev'l any of you know.
Some hold the heavens like a top,
And kept by circulation. up;
And, were't not for their wheeling round,
They'd instantly fall to the ground:
As sage EMPEDOCLES of old,
And from him modern authors hold.
PLATO believ'd the Sun and Moon
Below all other Planets run.
Some MERCURY, some VENUS, seat
Above the Sun himself in height.
The learned SCALIGER complain'd,
Gainst what COPERNICUS maintain'd,
That, in twelve hundred years and odd,
The Sun had left its ancient road,
And nearer to time earth is come
'Bove fifty thousand miles from home:
Swore 'twas a most notorious flam;
And he that had so little shame
To vent such fopperies abroad,

Deserv'd to have his rump well claw'd;
Which Monsieur BODIN hearing, swore
That he deserv'd the rod much more,
That durst upon a truth give doom;
He knew less than the Pope of Rome.
CARDAN believ'd great states depend
Upon the tip o' th' Bear's tail's end;
That, as she whisk'd it t'wards the Sun,
Strow'd mighty empires up and down;
Which others say must needs be false,
Because your true bears have no tails.
Some say the Zodiack Constellations
Have long since chang'd their antique stations
Above a sign, and prove the same
In Taurus now once in the Ram;
Affirm the trigons chop'd and chang'd,
The wat'ry with the fiery rang'd:
Then how can their effects still hold
To be the same they were of old?
This, though the art were true, would make
Our modern soothsayers mistake:
And in one cause they tell more lies,
In figures and nativities,
Than th' old Chaldean conjurers
In so many hundred thousand years
Beside their nonsense in translating,
For want of accidence and Latin,
Like Idus, and Calendae, Englisht
The quarter-days by skilful linguist;
And yet with canting, sleight and, cheat,
'Twill serve their turn to do the feat;
Make fools believe in their foreseeing
Of things before they are in being
To swallow gudgeons ere th' are catch'd;
And count their chickens ere th' are hatch'd
Make them the constellations prompt,
And give 'em back their own accompt
But still the best to him that gives
The best price for't, or best believes.
Some towns and cities, some, for brevity,
Have cast the 'versal world's nativity,
And made the infant-stars confess,
Like fools or children, what they please.
Some calculate the hidden fates
Of monkeys, puppy-dogs, and cats
Some running-nags and fighting cocks,
Some love, trade, law-suits, and the pox;
Some take a measure of the lives

Of fathers, mothers, husbands, wives;
Make opposition, trine, and quartile,
Tell who is barren, and who fertile;
As if the planet's first aspect
The tender infant did infect
In soul and body, and instill
All future good, and future ill;
Which, in their dark fatalities lurking,
At destin'd periods fall a working;
And break out, like the hidden seeds
Of long diseases, into deeds,
In friendships, enmities, and strife,
And all the emergencies of life.
No sooner does he peep into
The world, but he has done his do;
Catch'd all diseases, took all physick
That cures or kills a man that is sick;
Marry'd his punctual dose of wives;
Is cuckolded, and breaks or thrives.
There's but the twinkling of a star
Between a man of peace and war;
A thief and justice, fool and knave,
A huffing officer and a slave;
A crafty lawyer and a pick-pocket,
A great philosopher and a blockhead;
A formal preacher and a player,
A learn'd physician and manslayer.
As if men from the stars did suck
Old age, diseases, and ill-luck,
Wit, folly, honour, virtue, vice,
Trade, travel, women, claps, and dice;
And draw, with the first air they breathe,
Battle and murder, sudden death.
Are not these fine commodities
To be imported from the skies,
And vended here amongst the rabble,
For staple goods and warrantable?
Like money by the Druids borrow'd,
In th' other world to be restor'd?

Quoth SIDROPHEL, To let you know
You wrong the art, and artists too,
Since arguments are lost on those
That do our principles oppose,
I will (although I've done't before)
Demonstrate to your sense once more,
And draw a figure, that shall tell you
What you, perhaps, forget befel you,

By way of horary inspection,
Which some account our worst erection.
With that he circles draws, and squares,
With cyphers, astral characters;
Then looks 'em o'er, to und'erstand 'em,
Although set down hob-nab, at random.
Quoth he, This scheme of th' heavens set,
Discovers how in fight you met
At Kingston with a may-pole idol,
And that y' were bang'd both back and side well;
And though you overcame the bear,
The dogs beat you at Brentford fair;
Where sturdy butchers broke your noddle,
And handled you like a fop-doodle.

Quoth HUDIBRAS, I now perceive
You are no conj'rer, by your leave;
That paultry story is untrue,
And forg'd to cheat such gulls as you.

Not true? quoth he; howe'er you vapour,
I can what I affirm make appear.
WHACHUM shall justify't t' your face,
And prove he was upon the place.
He play'd the Saltinbancho's part,
Transform'd t' a Frenchman by my art
He stole your cloak, and pick'd your pocket,
Chows'd and caldes'd ye like a blockhead:
And what you lost I can produce,
If you deny it, here i' th' house.

Quoth HUDIBRAS, I do believe
That argument's demonstrative.
RALPHO, bear witness; and go fetch us
A constable to seize the wretches
For though th' are both false knaves and cheats,
Impostors, jugglers, counterfeits,
I'll make them serve for perpendiculars
As true as e'er were us'd by bricklayers.
They're guilty, by their own confessions,
Of felony, and at the sessions,
Upon the bench, I will so handle 'em,
That the vibration of this pendulum
Shalt make all taylors yards of one
Unanimous opinion,
A thing he long has vapour'd of,
But now shall wake it out of proof.

Quoth SIDROPHEL, I do not doubt
To find friends that will bear me out,
Nor have I hazarded my art,
And neck, so long on the state's part,
To be expos'd i' th' end to suffer
By such a braggadocio huffer.

Huffer! quoth HUDIBRAS: this sword
Shall down thy false throat craw that word.
RALPHO, make haste, and call an officer,
To apprehend this Stygian sophister,
Meanwhile I'll hold 'em at a bay,
Lest he and WHACHUM run away.

But SIDROPHEL who, from the aspect
Of HUDIBRAS did now erect
A figure worse portenting far
Than that of a malignant star,
Believ'd it now the fittest moment
To shun the danger that might come on't,
While HUDIBRAS was all alone,
And he and WHACHUM, two to one.
This being resolv'd, he spy'd, by chance,
Behind the door, an iron lance,
That many a sturdy limb had gor'd,
And legs, and loins, and shoulders bor'd:
He snatch'd it up, and made a pass,
To make his way through HUDIBRAS.
WHACHUM had got a fire-fork,
With which he vow'd to do his work.
But HUDIBRAS was well prepar'd,
And stoutly stood upon his guard:
He put by SIDROPHELLO'S thrust,
And in right manfully he rusht;   I
The weapon from his gripe he wrung,
And laid him on the earth along.
WHACHUM his sea-coal prong threw by,
And basely turn'd his back to fly
But HUDIBRAS gave him a twitch
As quick as light'ning in the breech,
Just in the place where honour's lodg'd,
As wise philosophers have judg'd;
Because a kick in that place more
Hurts honour than deep wounds before.

Quoth HUDIBRAS, The stars determine
You are my prisoners, base vermine!
Could they not tell you so as well

As what I came to know foretell?
By this what cheats you are we find,
That in your own concerns are blind.
Your lives are now at my dispose,
To be redeem'd by fine or blows:
But who his honour wou'd defile,
To take or sell two lives so vile?
I'll give you quarter; but your pillage,
The conq'ring warrior's crop and tillage,
Which with his sword he reaps and plows,
That's mine, the law of arms allows.

This said, in haste, in haste he fell
To rummaging of SIDROPHEL.
First, he expounded both his pockets,
And found a watch, with rings and lockets,
Which had been left with him t' erect
A figure for, and so detect;
A copper-plate, with almanacks
Engrav'd upon't; with other knacks,
Of BOOKER's LILLY's, SARAH JIMMERS',
And blank-schemes to discover nimmers;
A moon-dial, with Napier's bones,
And sev'ral constellation stones,
Engrav'd in planetary hours,
That over mortals had strange powers
To make 'em thrive in law or trade,
And stab or poison to evade;
In wit or wisdom to improve,
And be victorious in love,
WHACHUM had neither cross nor pile;
His plunder was not worth the while;
All which the conq'rer did discompt,
To pay for curing of his rump.
But SIDROPHEL, as full of tricks
As Rota-men of politicks,
Straight cast about to over-reach
Th' unwary conqu'ror with a fetch,
And make him clad (at least) to quit
His victory, and fly the pit,
Before the Secular Prince of Darkness
Arriv'd to seize upon his carcass?
And as a fox, with hot pursuit
Chac'd thro' a warren, casts about
To save his credit, and among
Dead vermin on a gallows hung,
And while the dogs run underneath,
Escap'd (by counterfeiting death)

Not out of cunning, but a train
Of atoms justling in his brain,
As learn'd philosophers give out,
So SIDROPHELLO cast about,
And fell to's wonted trade again,
To feign himself in earnest slain:
First stretch'd out one leg, than another,
And seeming in his breath to smother
A broken sigh; quoth he, Where am I,
Alive or dead? or which way came I,
Through so immense a space so soon
But now I thought myself in th' Moon
And that a monster with huge whiskers,
More formidable than a Switzer's,
My body through and through had drill'd,
And WHACHUM by my side had kill'd:
Had cross-examin'd both our hose,
And plunder'd all we had to lose.
Look, there he is; I see him now,
And feel the place I am run through:
And there lies WHACHUM by my side
Stone dead, and in his own blood dy'd.
Oh! Oh! with that he fetch'd a groan,
And fell again into a swoon;
Shut both his eyes, and stopp'd his breath,
And to the life out-acted death;
That HUDIBRAS, to all appearing,
Believ'd him to be dead as herring.
He held it now no longer safe
To tarry the return of RALPH,
But rather leave him in the lurch:
Thought he, he has abus'd our Church,
Refus'd to give himself one firk
To carry on the publick work;
Despis'd our Synod-men like dirt,
And made their discipline his sport;
Divulg'd the secrets of their classes,
And their conventions prov'd high places;
Disparag'd their tythe-pigs as Pagan,
And set at nought their cheese and bacon;
Rail'd at their Covenant, and jeer'd
Their rev'rend parsons to my beard:
For all which scandals, to be quit
At once, this juncture falls out fit,
I'll make him henceforth to beware,
And tempt my fury, if he dare.
He must at least hold up his hand,
By twelve freeholders to be scann'd;

Who, by their skill in palmistry,
Will quickly read his destiny;
And make him glad to read his lesson,
Or take a turn for it at the session;
Unless his Light and Gifts prove truer
Then ever yet they did, I'm sure;
For if he scape with whipping now,
'Tis more than he can hope to do;
And that will disengage my conscience
Of th' obligation in his own sense,
I'll make him now by force abide
What he by gentle means deny'd,
To give my honour satisfaction,
And right the Brethren in the action.
This being resolv'd, with equal speed
And conduct he approach'd his steed,
And with activity unwont,
Assay'd the lofty beast to mount;
Which once atchiev'd, he spurr'd his palfrey,
To get from th' enemy, and RALPH, free
Left dangers, fears, and foes behind,
And beat, at least three lengths, the wind.

AN HEROICAL EPISTLE OF HUDIBRAS TO SIDROPHEL

Ecce Iterum Crispinus.—-

WELL! SIDROPHEL, though 'tis in vain
To tamper with your crazy brain,
Without trepanning of your skull
As often as the moon's at full
'Tis not amiss, e're y' are giv'n o'er,
To try one desp'rate med'cine more
For where your case can be no worse,
The desp'rat'st is the wisest course.
Is't possible that you, whose ears
Are of the tribe of Issachar's,
And might (with equal reason) either,
For merit, or extent of leather,
With WILLIAM PRYN'S, before they were
Retrench'd and crucify'd, compare,
Shou'd yet be deaf against a noise
So roaring as the publick voice
That speaks your virtues free, and loud,
And openly, in ev'ry crowd,
As, loud as one that sings his part

T' a wheel-barrow or turnip-cart,
Or your new nick-nam'd old invention
To cry green-hastings with an engine;
(As if the vehemence had stunn'd,
And turn your drum-heads with the sound;)
And 'cause your folly's now no news,
But overgrown, and out of use,
Persuade yourself there's no such matter,
But that 'tis vanish'd out of nature;
When folly, as it grows in years,
The more extravagant appears;
For who but you could be possest
With so much ignorance, and beast,
That neither all mens' scorn and hate,
Nor being laugh'd and pointed at,
Nor bray'd so often in a mortar,
Can teach you wholesome sense and nurture;
But (like a reprobate) what course
Soever's us'd, grow worse and worse
Can no transfusion of the blood,
That makes fools cattle, do you good?
Nor putting pigs t' a bitch to nurse,
To turn 'em into mungrel-curs,
Put you into a way, at least,
To make yourself a better beast?
Can all your critical intrigues
Of trying sound from rotten eggs;
Your several new-found remedies
Of curing wounds and scabs in trees;
Your arts of flexing them for claps,
And purging their infected saps;
Recov'ring shankers, crystallines,
And nodes and botches in their rinds,
Have no effect to operate
Upon that duller block, your pate?
But still it must be lewdly bent
To tempt your own due punishment;
And, like your whymsy'd chariots, draw,
The boys to course you without law;
As if the art you have so long
Profess'd, of making old dogs young,
In you had virtue to renew
Not only youth, but childhood too.
Can you that understand all books,
By judging only with your looks,
Resolve all problems with your face,
As others do with B's and A's;
Unriddle all that mankind knows

With solid bending of your brows;
All arts and sciences advance,
With screwing of your countenance,
And, with a penetrating eye,
Into th' abstrusest learning pry?
Know more of any trade b' a hint;
Than those that have been bred up in't;
And yet have no art, true or false,
To help your own bad naturals;
But still, the more you strive t' appear,
Are found to be the wretcheder
For fools are known by looking wise,
As men find woodcocks by their eyes.
Hence 'tis that 'cause y' have gain'd o' th' college
A quarter share (at most) of knowledge,
And brought in none, but spent repute,
Y' assume a pow'r as absolute
To judge, and censure, and controll,
As if you were the sole Sir Poll;
And saucily pretend to know
More than your dividend comes to.
You'll find the thing will not be done
With ignorance and face alone
No, though y' have purchas'd to your name,
In history, so great a fame;
That now your talents, so well
For having all belief out-grown,
That ev'ry strange prodigious tale
Is measur'd by your German scale;
By which the virtuosi try
The magnitude of ev'ry lye,
Cast up to what it does amount,
And place the bigg'st to your account?
That all those stories that are laid
Too truly to you, and those made,
Are now still charg'd upon your score,
And lesser authors nam'd no more.
Alas! that faculty betrays
Those soonest it designs to raise;
And all your vain renown will spoil,
As guns o'ercharg'd the more recoil.
Though he that has but impudence,
To all things has a fair pretence;
And put among his wants but shame,
To all the world may lay his claim:
Though you have try'd that nothing's borne
With greater ease than public scorn,
That all affronts do still give place

To your impenetrable face,
That makes your way through all affairs,
As pigs through hedges creep with theirs;
Yet as 'tis counterfeit, and brass,
You must not think 'twill always pass;
For all impostors, when they're known,
Are past their labour, and undone.
And all the best that can befal
An artificial natural,
Is that which madmen find as soon
As once they're broke loose from the moon,
And, proof against her influence,
Relapse to e'er so little sense,
To turn stark fools, and subjects fit
For sport of boys, and rabble-wit.

PART III

CANTO I

THE ARGUMENT

The Knight and Squire resolve, at once,
The one the other to renounce.
They both approach the Lady's Bower;
The Squire t'inform, the Knight to woo her.
She treats them with a Masquerade,
By Furies and Hobgoblins made;
From which the Squire conveys the Knight,
And steals him from himself, by Night.

'Tis true, no lover has that pow'r
T' enforce a desperate amour,
As he that has two strings t' his bow,
And burns for love and money too;
For then he's brave and resolute,
Disdains to render in his suit,
Has all his flames and raptures double,
And hangs or drowns with half the trouble,
While those who sillily pursue,
The simple, downright way, and true,
Make as unlucky applications,
And steer against the stream their passions.
Some forge their mistresses of stars,
And when the ladies prove averse,

And more untoward to be won
Than by CALIGULA the Moon,
Cry out upon the stars, for doing
Ill offices to cross their wooing;
When only by themselves they're hindred,
For trusting those they made her kindred;
And still, the harsher and hide-bounder
The damsels prove, become the fonder.
For what mad lover ever dy'd
To gain a soft and gentle bride?
Or for a lady tender-hearted,
In purling streams or hemp departed?
Leap'd headlong int' Elysium,
Through th' windows of a dazzling room?
But for some cross, ill-natur'd dame,
The am'rous fly burnt in his flame.
This to the Knight could be no news,
With all mankind so much in use;
Who therefore took the wiser course,
To make the most of his amours,
Resolv'd to try all sorts of ways,
As follows in due time and place

No sooner was the bloody fight,
Between the Wizard, and the Knight,
With all th' appurtenances, over,
But he relaps'd again t' a lover;
As he was always wont to do,
When h' had discomfited a foe
And us'd the only antique philters,
Deriv'd from old heroic tilters.
But now triumphant, and victorious,
He held th' atchievement was too glorious
For such a conqueror to meddle
With petty constable or beadle,
Or fly for refuge to the Hostess
Of th' Inns of Court and Chancery, Justice,
Who might, perhaps reduce his cause
To th' ordeal trial of the laws,
Where none escape, but such as branded
With red-hot irons have past bare-handed;
And, if they cannot read one verse
I' th' Psalms, must sing it, and that's worse.
He therefore judging it below him,
To tempt a shame the Devil might owe him,
Resolv'd to leave the Squire for bail
And mainprize for him to the gaol,
To answer, with his vessel, all,

That might disastrously befall;
And thought it now the fittest juncture
To give the Lady a rencounter,
T' acquaint her 'with his expedition,
And conquest o'er the fierce Magician;
Describe the manner of the fray,
And show the spoils he brought away,
His bloody scourging aggravate,
The number of his blows, and weight,
All which might probably succeed,
And gain belief h' had done the deed,
Which he resolv'd t' enforce, and spare
No pawning of his soul to swear,
But, rather than produce his back,
To set his conscience on the rack,
And in pursuance of his urging
Of articles perform'd and scourging,
And all things else, his part,
Demand deliv'ry of her heart,
Her goods, and chattels, and good graces,
And person up to his embraces.
Thought he, the ancient errant knights
Won all their ladies hearts in fights;
And cut whole giants into fritters,
To put them into amorous twitters
Whose stubborn bowels scorn'd to yield
Until their gallants were half kill'd
But when their bones were drub'd so sore
They durst not woo one combat more,
The ladies hearts began to melt,
Subdu'd by blows their lovers felt.
So Spanish heroes, with their lances,
At once wound bulls and ladies' fancies;
And he acquires the noblest spouse
That widows greatest herds of cows:
Then what may I expect to do,
Wh' have quell'd so vast a buffalo?

Mean while, the Squire was on his way
The Knight's late orders to obey;
Who sent him for a strong detachment
Of beadles, constables, and watchmen,
T' attack the cunning-man fur plunder,
Committed falsely on his lumber;
When he, who had so lately sack'd
The enemy, had done the fact;
Had rifled all his pokes and fobs
Of gimcracks, whims, and jiggumbobs,

When he, by hook or crook, had gather'd,
And for his own inventions father'd
And when they should, at gaol delivery,
Unriddle one another's thievery,
Both might have evidence enough,
To render neither halter proof.
He thought it desperate to tarry,
And venture to be accessary
But rather wisely slip his fetters,
And leave them for the Knight, his betters.
He call'd to mind th' unjust, foul play
He wou'd have offer'd him that day,
To make him curry his own hide,
Which no beast ever did beside,
Without all possible evasion,
But of the riding dispensation;
And therefore much about the hour
The Knight (for reasons told before)
Resolv'd to leave them to the fury
Of Justice, and an unpack'd Jury,
The Squire concurr'd t' abandon him,
And serve him in the self-same trim;
T' acquaint the Lady what h' had done,
And what he meant to carry on;
What project 'twas he went about,
When SIDROPHEL and he fell out;
His firm and stedfast Resolution,
To swear her to an execution;
To pawn his inward ears to marry her,
And bribe the Devil himself to carry her;
In which both dealt, as if they meant
Their Party-Saints to represent,
Who never fail'd upon their sharing
In any prosperous arms-bearing
To lay themselves out to supplant
Each other Cousin-German Saint.
But, ere the Knight could do his part,
The Squire had got so much the start,
H' had to the Lady done his errand,
And told her all his tricks afore-hand.
Just as he finish'd his report,
The Knight alighted in the court;
And having ty'd his beast t' a pale,
And taking time for both to stale,
He put his band and beard in order,
The sprucer to accost and board her;
And now began t' approach the door,
When she, wh' had spy'd him out before

Convey'd th' informer out of sight,
And went to entertain the Knight
With whom encount'ring, after longees
Of humble and submissive congees,
And all due ceremonies paid,
He strok'd his beard, and thus he said:

Madam, I do, as is my duty,
Honour the shadow of your shoe-tye;
And now am come to bring your ear
A present you'll be glad to hear:
At least I hope so: the thing's done,
Or may I never see the sun;
For which I humbly now demand
Performance at your gentle hand
And that you'd please to do your part,
As I have done mine, to my smart.

With that he shrugg'd his sturdy back
As if he felt his shoulders ake.

But she, who well enough knew what
(Before he spoke) he would be at,
Pretended not to apprehend
The mystery of what he mean'd;.
And therefore wish'd him to expound
His dark expressions, less profound.

Madam, quoth he, I come to prove
How much I've suffer'd for your love,
Which (like your votary) to win,
I have not spar'd my tatter'd skin
And for those meritorious lashes,
To claim your favour and good graces.

Quoth she, I do remember once
I freed you from th' inchanted sconce;
And that you promis'd, for that favour,
To bind your back to good behaviour,
And, for my sake and service, vow'd
To lay upon't a heavy load,
And what 'twould bear t' a scruple prove,
As other Knights do oft make love
Which, whether you have done or no,
Concerns yourself, not me, to know.
But if you have, I shall confess,
Y' are honester than I could guess.

Quoth he, if you suspect my troth,
I cannot prove it but by oath;
And if you make a question on't,
I'll pawn my soul that I have done't;
And he that makes his soul his surety,
I think, does give the best security.

Quoth she, Some say, the soul's secure
Against distress and forfeiture
Is free from action, and exempt
From execution and contempt;
And to be summon'd to appear
In th' other world's illegal here;
And therefore few make any account
Int' what incumbrances they run't
For most men carry things so even
Between this World, and Hell, and Heaven,
Without the least offence to either,
They freely deal in all together;
And equally abhor to quit
This world for both or both for it;
And when they pawn and damn their souls,
They are but pris'ners on paroles.

For that (quoth he) 'tis rational,
Th' may be accountable in all:
For when there is that intercourse
Between divine and human pow'rs,
That all that we determine here
Commands obedience every where,
When penalties may be commuted
For fines or ears, and executed
It follows, nothing binds so fast
As souls in pawn and mortgage past
For oaths are th' only tests and seals
Of right and wrong, and true and false,
And there's no other way to try
The doubts of law and justice by.

(Quoth she) What is it you would swear
There's no believing till I hear
For, till they're understood all tales
(Like nonsense) are not true nor false.

(Quoth he) When I resolv'd t' obey
What you commanded th' other day,
And to perform my exercise,
(As schools are wont) for your fair eyes,

T' avoid all scruples in the case,
I went to do't upon the place.
But as the Castle is inchanted
By SIDROPHEL the Witch and haunted
By evil spirits, as you know,
Who took my Squire and me for two,
Before I'd hardly time to lay
My weapons by, and disarray
I heard a formidable noise,
Loud as the Stentrophonick voice,
That roar'd far off, Dispatch and strip,
I'm ready with th' infernal whip,
That shall divest thy ribs from skin,
To expiate thy ling'ring sin.
Th' hast broken perfidiously thy oath,
And not perform'd thy plighted troth;
But spar'd thy renegado back,
Where th' hadst so great a prize at stake;
Which now the fates have order'd me
For penance and revenge to flea,
Unless thou presently make haste:
Time is, time was: And there it ceas'd.
With which, though startled, I confess,
Yet th' horror of the thing was less
Than th' other dismal apprehension
Of interruption or prevention;
And therefore, snatching up the rod,
I laid upon my back a load;
Resolv'd to spare no flesh and blood,
To make my word and honour good;
Till tir'd, and making truce at length,
For new recruits of breath and strength,
I felt the blows still ply'd as fast
As th' had been by lovers plac'd,
In raptures of platonick lashing,
And chaste contemplative bardashing;
When facing hastily about,
To stand upon my guard and scout,
I found th' infernal Cunning-man,
And th' under-witch, his CALIBAN,
With scourges (like the Furies) arm'd,
That on my outward quarters storm'd.
In haste I snatch'd my weapon up,
And gave their hellish rage a stop;
Call'd thrice upon your name, and fell
Courageously on SIDROPHEL;
Who, now transform'd himself a bear,
Began to roar aloud, and tear;

When I as furiously press'd on,
My weapon down his throat to run;
Laid hold on him; but he broke loose,
And turn'd himself into a goose;
Div'd under water, in a pond,
To hide himself from being found.
In vain I sought him; but, as soon
As I perceiv'd him fled and gone,
Prepar'd with equal haste and rage,
His Under-sorcerer t' engage.
But bravely scorning to defile
My sword with feeble blood and vile,
I judg'd it better from a quick-
Set hedge to cut a knotted stick,
With which I furiously laid on
Till, in a harsh and doleful tone,
It roar'd, O hold for pity, Sir
I am too great a sufferer,
Abus'd, as you have been, b' a witch,
But conjur'd into a worse caprich;
Who sends me out on many a jaunt,
Old houses in the night to haunt,
For opportunities t' improve
Designs of thievery or love;
With drugs convey'd in drink or meat,
All teats of witches counterfeit;
Kill pigs and geese with powder'd glass,
And make it for enchantment pass;
With cow-itch meazle like a leper,
And choak with fumes of guiney pepper;
Make leachers and their punks with dewtry,
Commit fantastical advowtry;
Bewitch Hermetick-men to run
Stark staring mad with manicon;
Believe mechanick Virtuosi
Can raise 'em mountains in POTOSI;
And, sillier than the antick fools,
Take treasure for a heap of coals:
Seek out for plants with signatures,
To quack of universal cures:
With figures ground on panes of glass
Make people on their heads to pass;
And mighty heaps of coin increase,
Reflected from a single piece,
To draw in fools, whose nat'ral itches
Incline perpetually to witches;
And keep me in continual fears,
And danger of my neck and ears;

When less delinquents have been scourg'd,
And hemp on wooden anvil forg'd,
Which others for cravats have worn
About their necks, and took a turn.

I pity'd the sad punishment
The wretched caitiff underwent,
And left my drubbing of his bones,
Too great an honour for pultrones;
For Knights are bound to feel no blows
From paultry and unequal foes,
Who, when they slash, and cut to pieces,
Do all with civilest addresses:
Their horses never give a blow,
But when they make a leg, and bow.
I therefore spar'd his flesh, and prest him
About the witch with many a. question.

Quoth he, For many years he drove
A kind of broking-trade in love;
Employ'd in all th' intrigues, and trust
Of feeble, speculative lust:
Procurer to th' extravagancy,
And crazy ribaldry of fancy,
By those the Devil had forsook,
As things below him to provoke.
But b'ing a virtuoso, able
To smatter, quack, and cant, and dabble,
He held his talent most adroit
For any mystical exploit;
As others of his tribe had done,
And rais'd their prices three to one:
For one predicting pimp has th' odds
Of chauldrons of plain downright bawds.
But as an elf (the Devil's valet)
Is not so slight a thing to get;
For those that do his bus'ness best,
In hell are us'd the ruggedest;
Before so meriting a person
Cou'd get a grant, but in reversion,
He serv'd two prenticeships, and longer,
I' th' myst'ry of a lady-monger.
For (as some write) a witch's ghost,
As soon as from the body loos'd,
Becomes a puney-imp itself
And is another witch's elf.
He, after searching far and near,
At length found one in LANCASHIRE

With whom he bargain'd before-hand,
And, after hanging, entertained;
Since which h' has play'd a thousand feats,
And practis'd all mechanick cheats,
Transform'd himself to th' ugly shapes
Of wolves and bears, baboons and apes,
Which he has vary'd more than witches,
Or Pharaoh's wizards cou'd their switches;
And all with whom h' has had to do,
Turn'd to as monstrous figures too.
Witness myself, whom h' has abus'd,
And to this beastly shape reduc'd,
By feeding me on beans and pease,
He crams in nasty crevices,
And turns to comfits by his arts,
To make me relish for disserts,
And one by one, with shame and fear,
Lick up the candy'd provender.
Beside — But as h' was running on,
To tell what other feats h' had done,
The Lady stopt his full career,
And told him now 'twas time to hear
If half those things (said she) be true —
They're all, (quoth he,) I swear by you.
Why then (said she,) That SIDROPHEL
Has damn'd himself to th' pit of Hell;
Who, mounted on a broom, the nag
And hackney of a Lapland hag,
In quest of you came hither post,
Within an hour (I'm sure) at most;
Who told me all you swear and say,
Quite contrary another way;
Vow'd that you came to him to know
If you should carry me or no;
And would have hir'd him, and his imps,
To be your match-makers and pimps,
T' engage the Devil on. your side,
And steal (like PROSERPINE) your bride.
But he, disdaining to embrace.
So filthy a design and base,
You fell to vapouring and huffing
And drew upon him like a ruffin;
Surpriz'd him meanly, unprepar'd,
Before h' had time to mount his guard;
And left him dead upon the ground,
With many a bruise and desperate wound:
Swore you had broke and robb'd his house,
And stole his talismanique louse,

And all his new-found old inventions;.
With flat felonious intentions;
Which he could bring out where he had,
And what he bought them for, and paid.
His flea, his morpion, and punese,
H' had gotten for his proper ease,
And all perfect minutes made,
By th' ablest artist of the trade;
Which (he could prove it) since he lost,
He has been eaten up almost;
And all together might amount
To many hundreds on account;
For which h' had got sufficient warrant
To seize the malefactors errant,
Without capacity of bail,
But of a cart's or horse's tail;
And did not doubt to bring the wretches
To serve for pendulums to watches;
Which, modern virtuosos say,
Incline to hanging every way.
Beside, he swore, and swore 'twas true,
That, e're he went in quest of you,
He set a figure to discover
If you were fled to RYE or DOVER;
And found it clear, that, to betray
Yourselves and me, you fled this way;
And that he was upon pursuit,
To take you somewhere hereabout.
He vow' d he had intelligence
Of all that past before and since;
And found that, e'er you came to him,.
Y' had been engaging life and limb
About a case of tender conscience,
Where both abounded in your own sense:
Till RALPHO, by his light and grace,
Had clear'd all scruples in the case;
And prov'd that you might swear and own
Whatever's by the wicked done,
For which, most basely to requite
The service of his gifts and light,
You strove to oblige him, by main force,
To scourge his ribs instead of yours;
But that he stood upon his guard,
And all your vapouring out-dar'd;
For which, between you both, the feat
Has never been perform'd as yet.

While thus the Lady talk'd, the Knight

Turn'd th' outside of his eyes to white;
(As men of inward light are wont
To turn their opticks in upon 't)
He wonder'd how she came to know
What he had done, and meant to do;
Held up his affidavit-hand,
As if h' had been to be arraign'd;
Cast t'wards the door a look,
In dread of SIDROPHEL, and spoke:

Madam, if but one word be true
Of all the Wizard has told you,
Or but one single circumstance
In all th' apocryphal romance,
May dreadful earthquakes swallow down
This vessel, that is all your own;
Or may the heavens fall, and cover
These reliques of your constant lover.

You have provided well, quoth she,
(I thank you) for yourself and me,
And shown your presbyterian wits
Jump punctual with the Jesuits;
A most compendious way, and civil,
At once to cheat the world, the Devil,
And Heaven and Hell, yourselves, and those
On whom you vainly think t' impose.
Why then (quoth he) may Hell surprize —
That trick (said she) will not pass twice:
I've learn'd how far I'm to believe
Your pinning oaths upon your sleeve.
But there's a better way of clearing
What you would prove than downright swearing:
For if you have perform'd the feat,
The blows are visible as yet,
Enough to serve for satisfaction
Of nicest scruples in the action:
And if you can produce those knobs,
Although they're but the witch's drubs,
I'll pass them all upon account,
As if your natural self had done't
Provided that they pass th' opinion
Of able juries of old women
Who, us'd to judge all matter of facts
For bellies, may do so for backs,

Madam, (quoth he,) your love's a million;
To do is less than to be willing,

As I am, were it in my power,
T' obey, what you command, and more:
But for performing what you bid,
I thank you as much as if I did.
You know I ought to have a care
To keep my wounds from taking air:
For wounds in those that are all heart,
Are dangerous in any part.

I find (quoth she) my goods and chattels
Are like to prove but mere drawn battels;
For still the longer we contend,
We are but farther off the end.
But granting now we should agree,
What is it you expect from me?
Your plighted faith (quoth he) and word
You past in heaven on record,
Where all contracts, to have and t' hold,
Are everlastingly enroll'd:
And if 'tis counted treason here
To raze records, 'tis much more there.
Quoth she, There are no bargains driv'n,
Or marriages clapp'd up, in Heav'n,
And that's the reason, as some guess,
There is no heav'n in marriages;
Two things that naturally press
Too narrowly to be at ease.
Their bus'ness there is only love,
Which marriage is not like t' improve:
Love, that's too generous to abide
To be against its nature ty'd;
Or where 'tis of itself inclin'd,
It breaks loose when it is confin'd;
And like the soul, it's harbourer.
Debarr'd the freedom of the air,
Disdains against its will to stay,
But struggles out, and flies away;
And therefore never can comply
To endure the matrimonial tie,
That binds the female and the male,
Where th' one is but the other's bail;
Like Roman gaolers, when they slept,
Chain'd to the prisoners they kept
Of which the true and faithfull'st lover
Gives best security to suffer.
Marriage is but a beast, some say,
That carries double in foul way;
And therefore 'tis not to b' admir'd,

It should so suddenly be tir'd;
A bargain at a venture made,
Between two partners in a trade;
(For what's inferr'd by t' have and t' hold,
But something past away, and sold?)
That as it makes but one of two,
Reduces all things else as low;
And, at the best, is but a mart
Between the one and th' other part,
That on the marriage-day is paid,
Or hour of death, the bet is laid;
And all the rest of better or worse,
Both are but losers out of purse.
For when upon their ungot heirs
Th' entail themselves, and all that's theirs,
What blinder bargain e'er was driv'n,
Or wager laid at six and seven?
To pass themselves away, and turn
Their childrens' tenants e're they're born?
Beg one another idiot
To guardians, e'er they are begot;
Or ever shall, perhaps, by th' one,
Who's bound to vouch 'em for his own,
Though got b' implicit generation,
And gen'ral club of all the nation;
For which she's fortify'd no less
Than all the island, with four seas;
Exacts the tribute of her dower,
in ready insolence and power;
And makes him pass away to have
And hold, to her, himself, her slave,
More wretched than an ancient villain,
Condemn'd to drudgery and tilling;
While all he does upon the by,
She is not bound to justify,
Nor at her proper cost and charge
Maintain the feats he does at large.
Such hideous sots were those obedient
Old vassals to their ladies regent;
To give the cheats the eldest hand
In foul play by the laws o' th' land;
For which so many a legal cuckold
Has been run down in courts and truckeld:
A law that most unjustly yokes
All Johns of Stiles to Joans of Nokes,
Without distinction of degree,
Condition, age, or quality:
Admits no power of revocation,

Nor valuable consideration,
Nor writ of error, nor reverse
Of Judgment past, for better or worse:
Will not allow the priviledges
That beggars challenge under hedges,
Who, when they're griev'd, can make dead horses
Their spiritual judges of divorces;
While nothing else but Rem in Re
Can set the proudest wretches free;
A slavery beyond enduring,
But that 'tis of their own procuring.
As spiders never seek the fly,
But leave him, of himself, t' apply
So men are by themselves employ'd,
To quit the freedom they enjoy'd,
And run their necks into a noose,
They'd break 'em after, to break loose;
As some whom Death would not depart,
Have done the feat themselves by art;
Like Indian widows, gone to bed
In flaming curtains to the dead;
And men as often dangled for't,
And yet will never leave the sport.
Nor do the ladies want excuse
For all the stratagems they use
To gain the advantage of the set,
And lurch the amorous rook and cheat
For as the Pythagorean soul
Runs through all beasts, and fish and fowl,
And has a smack of ev'ry one,
So love does, and has ever done;
And therefore, though 'tis ne'er so fond,
Takes strangely to the vagabond.
'Tis but an ague that's reverst,
Whose hot fit takes the patient first,
That after burns with cold as much
As ir'n in GREENLAND does the touch;
Melts in the furnace of desire
Like glass, that's but the ice of fire;
And when his heat of fancy's over,
Becomes as hard and frail a lover.
For when he's with love-powder laden,
And prim'd and cock'd by Miss or Madam,
The smallest sparkle of an eye
Gives fire to his artillery;
And off the loud oaths go; but while
They're in the very act, recoil.
Hence 'tis so few dare take their chance

Without a sep'rate maintenance;
And widows, who have try'd one lover,
Trust none again, 'till th' have made over;
Or if they do, before they marry,
The foxes weigh the geese they carry;
And e're they venture o'er a stream,
Know how to size themselves and them;
Whence wittiest ladies always choose
To undertake the heaviest goose
For now the world is grown so wary,
That few of either sex dare marry,
But rather trust on tick t' amours,
The cross and pile for better or worse;
A mode that is held honourable,
As well as French, and fashionable:
For when it falls out for the best,
Where both are incommoded least,
In soul and body two unite,
To make up one hermaphrodite,
Still amorous, and fond, and billing,
Like PHILIP and MARY on a shilling,
Th' have more punctilios and capriches
Between the petticoat and breeches,
More petulant extravagances,
Than poets make 'em in romances.
Though when their heroes 'spouse the dames,
We hear no more charms and flames:
For then their late attracts decline,
And turn as eager as prick'd wine;
And all their catterwauling tricks,
In earnest to as jealous piques;
Which the ancients wisely signify'd,
By th' yellow mantos of the bride:
For jealousy is but a kind
Of clap and grincam of the mind,
The natural effects of love,
As other flames and aches prove;
But all the mischief is, the doubt
On whose account they first broke out.
For though Chineses go to bed,
And lie in, in their ladies stead,
And for the pains they took before,
Are nurs'd and pamper'd to do more
Our green men do it worse, when th' hap
To fail in labour of a clap
Both lay the child to one another:
But who's the father, who the mother,
'Tis hard to say in multitudes,

Or who imported the French goods.
But health and sickness b'ing all one,
Which both engag'd before to own,
And are not with their bodies bound
To worship, only when they're sound,
Both give and take their equal shares
Of all they suffer by false wares:
A fate no lover can divert
With all his caution, wit, and art.
For 'tis in vain to think to guess
At women by appearances,
That paint and patch their imperfections
Of intellectual complexions,
And daub their tempers o'er with washes
As artificial as their faces;
Wear under vizard-masks their talents
And mother-wits before their gallants,
Until they're hamper'd in the noose,
Too fast to dream of breaking loose;
When all the flaws they strove to hide
Are made unready with the bride,
That with her wedding-clothes undresses
Her complaisance and gentilesses,
Tries all her arts to take upon her
The government from th' easy owner;
Until the wretch is glad to wave
His lawful right, and turn her slave;
Find all his having, and his holding,
Reduc'd t' eternal noise and scolding;
The conjugal petard, that tears
Down all portcullises of ears,
And make the volley of one tongue
For all their leathern shields too strong
When only arm'd with noise and nails,
The female silk-worms ride the males,
Transform 'em into rams and goats,
Like Sirens, with their charming notes;
Sweet as a screech-owl's serenade,
Or those enchanting murmurs made
By th' husband mandrake and the wife,
Both bury'd (like themselves) alive.

Quoth he, These reasons are but strains
Of wanton, over-heated brains
Which ralliers, in their wit, or drink,
Do rather wheedle with than think
Man was not man in paradise,
Until he was created twice,

And had his better half, his bride,
Carv'd from the original, his side,
T' amend his natural defects,
And perfect his recruited sex;
Inlarge his breed at once, and lessen
The pains and labour of increasing,
By changing them for other cares,
As by his dry'd-up paps appears.
His body, that stupendous frame,
Of all the world the anagram
Is of two equal parts compact,
In shape and symmetry exact,
Of which the left and female side
Is to the manly right a bride;
Both join'd together with such art,
That nothing else but death can part.
Those heav'nly attracts of yours, your eyes,
And face, that all the world surprize,
That dazzle all that look upon ye,
And scorch all other ladies tawny,
Those ravishing and charming graces
Are all made up of two half faces,
That in a mathematick line,
Like those in other heavens, join,
Of which if either grew alone,
T' would fright as much to look upon:
And so would that sweet bud your lip,
Without the other's fellowship.
Our noblest senses act by pairs;
Two eyes to see; to hear, two ears;
Th' intelligencers of the mind,
To wait upon the soul design'd,
But those that serve the body alone,
Are single, and confin'd to one.
The world is but two parts, that meet
And close at th' equinoctial fit;
And so are all the works of nature,
Stamp'd with her signature on matter,
Which all her creatures, to a leaf,
Or smallest blade of grass receive;
All which sufficiently declare,
How entirely marriage is her care,
The only method that she uses
In all the wonders she produces:
And those that take their rules from her,
Can never be deceiv'd, nor err.
For what secures the civil life,
But pawns of children, and a wife?

That lie like hostages at stake,
To pay for all men undertake;
To whom it is as necessary
As to be born and breathe, to marry;
So universal all mankind,
In nothing else, is of one mind.
For in what stupid age, or nation,
Was marriage ever out of fashion?
Unless among the Amazons,
Or cloister'd friars, and vestal nuns;
Or Stoicks, who to bar the freaks
And loose excesses of the sex,
Prepost'rously wou'd have all women
Turn'd up to all the world in common.
Though men would find such mortal feuds,
In sharing of their publick goods,
'Twould put them to more charge of lives,
Than they're supply'd with now by wives;
Until they graze, and wear their clothes,
As beasts do, of their native growths:
For simple wearing of their horns
Will not suffice to serve their turns.
For what can we pretend t' inherit,
Unless the marriage-deed will bear it?
Could claim no right, to lands or rents,
But for our parents' settlements;
Had been but younger sons o' th' earth,
Debarr'd it all, but for our birth.
What honours or estates of peers,
Cou'd be preserv'd but by their heirs
And what security maintains
Their right and title, but the banes?
What crowns could be hereditary,
If greatest monarchs did not marry.
And with their consorts consummate
Their weightiest interests of state?
For all the amours of princes are
But guarantees of peace or war,
Or what but marriage has a charm
The rage of empires to disarm,
Make blood and desolation cease,
And fire and sword unite in peace,
When all their fierce contest for forage
Conclude in articles of marriage?
Nor does the genial bed provide
Less for the int'rests of the bride;
Who else had not the least pretence
T' as much as due benevolence;

Could no more title take upon her
To virtue, quality, and honour.
Than ladies-errant, unconfin'd,
And feme-coverts t' all mankind
All women would be of one piece,
The virtuous matron and the miss;
The nymphs of chaste Diana's train,
The same with those in LEWKNER's Lane;
But for the difference marriage makes
'Twixt wives and ladies of the lakes;
Besides the joys of place and birth,
The sex's paradise on earth;
A privilege so sacred held,
That none will to their mothers yield;
But rather than not go before,
Abandon Heaven at the door.
And if th' indulgent law allows
A greater freedom to the spouse,
The reason is, because the wife
Runs greater hazards of her life;
Is trusted with the form and matter
Of all mankind by careful nature;
Where man brings nothing but the stuff
She frames the wond'rous fabric of;
Who therefore, in a streight, may freely
Demand the clergy of her belly,
And make it save her the same way
It seldom misses to betray;
Unless both parties wisely enter
Into the liturgy indenture,
And though some fits of small contest
Sometimes fall out among the best,
That is no more than ev'ry lover
Does from his hackney-lady suffer;
That makes no breach of faith and love,
But rather (sometimes) serves t' improve.
For as in running, ev'ry pace
Is but between two legs a race,
In which both do their uttermost
To get before, and win the post,
Yet when they're at their race's ends,
They're still as kind and constant friends,
And, to relieve their weariness,
By turns give one another ease;
So all those false alarms of strife
Between the husband and the wife,
And little quarrels, often prove
To be but new recruits of love;

When those wh' are always kind or coy,
In time must either tire or cloy.
Nor are their loudest clamours more,
Than as they're relish'd, sweet or sour;
Like musick, that proves bad or good;
According as 'tis understood.
In all amours, a lover burns
With frowns as well as smiles by turns;
And hearts have been as aft with sullen
As charming looks surpriz'd and stolen.
Then why should more bewitching clamour
Some lovers not as much enamour?
For discords make the sweetest airs
And curses are a kind of pray'rs;
Too slight alloys for all those grand
Felicities by marriage gain'd.
For nothing else has pow'r to settle
Th' interests of love perpetual;
An act and deed, that that makes one heart
Becomes another's counter-part,
And passes fines on faith and love,
Inroll'd and register'd above,
To seal the slippery knots of vows,
Which nothing else but death can loose.
And what security's too strong,
To guard that gentle heart from wrong,
That to its friend is glad to pass
Itself away, and all it has;
And, like an anchorite, gives over
This world for th' heaven of lover?
I grant (quoth she) there are some few
Who take that course, and find it true
But millions whom the same does sentence
To heav'n b' another way — repentance.
Love's arrows are but shot at rovers;
Though all they hit, they turn to lovers;
And all the weighty consequents
Depend upon more blind events,
Than gamesters, when they play a set
With greatest cunning at piquet,
Put out with caution, but take in
They know not what, unsight, unseen,
For what do lovers, when they're fast
In one another's arms embrac't,
But strive to plunder, and convey
Each other, like a prize, away?
To change the property of selves,
As sucking children are by elves?

And if they use their persons so,
What will they to their fortunes do?
Their fortunes! the perpetual aims
Of all their extasies and flames.
For when the money's on the book,
And, All my worldly goods — but spoke,
(The formal livery and seisin
That puts a lover in possession,)
To that alone the bridegroom's wedded;
The bride a flam, that's superseded.
To that their faith is still made good,
And all the oaths to us they vow'd:
For when we once resign our pow'rs,
W' have nothing left we can call ours:
Our money's now become the Miss
Of all your lives and services;
And we forsaken, and postpon'd;
But bawds to what before we own'd;
Which, as it made y' at first gallant us,
So now hires others to supplant us,
Until 'tis all turn'd out of doors,
(As we had been) for new amours;
For what did ever heiress yet
By being born to lordships get?
When the more lady sh' is of manours,
She's but expos'd to more trepanners,
Pays for their projects and designs,
And for her own destruction fines;
And does but tempt them with her riches,
To use her as the Dev'l does witches;
Who takes it for a special grace
To be their cully for a space,
That when the time's expir'd, the drazels
For ever may become his vassals:
So she, bewitch'd by rooks and spirits,
Betrays herself, and all sh' inherits;
Is bought and sold, like stolen goods,
By pimps, and match-makers, and bawds,
Until they force her to convey,
And steal the thief himself away.
These are the everlasting fruits
Of all your passionate love-suits,
Th' effects of all your amorous fancies
To portions and inheritances;
Your love-sick rapture for fruition
Of dowry, jointure, and tuition;
To which you make address and courtship;
Ad with your bodies strive to worship,

That th' infants' fortunes may partake
Of love too, for the mother's sake.
For these you play at purposes,
And love your love's with A's and B's:
For these at Beste and L'Ombre woo,
And play for love and money too;
Strive who shall be the ablest man
At right gallanting of a fan;
And who the most genteelly bred
At sucking of a vizard-head;
How best t' accost us in all quarters;
T' our question — and — command new Garters
And solidly discourse upon
All sorts of dresses, Pro and Con.
For there's no mystery nor trade,
But in the art of love is made:
And when you have more debts to pay
Than Michaelmas and Lady-Day,
And no way possible to do't,
But love and oaths, and restless suit,
To us y' apply to pay the scores
Of all your cully'd, past amours;
Act o'er your flames and darts again,
And charge us with your wounds and pain;
Which others influences long since
Have charm'd your noses with and shins;
For which the surgeon is unpaid,
And like to be, without our aid.
Lord! what an am'rous thing is want!
How debts and mortgages inchant!
What graces must that lady have
That can from executions save!
What charms that can reverse extent,
And null decree and exigent!
What magical attracts and graces,
That can redeem from Scire facias!
From bonds and statutes can discharge,
And from contempts of courts enlarge!
These are the highest excellencies
Of all your true or false pretences:
And you would damn yourselves, and swear
As much t' an hostess dowager,
Grown fat and pursy by retail
Of pots of beer and bottled ale;
And find her fitter for your turn;
For fat is wondrous apt to burn;
Who at your flames would soon take fire,
Relent, and melt to your desire,

And like a candle in the socket,
Dissolve her graces int' your pocket.

By this time 'twas grown dark and late,
When they heard a knocking at the gate,
Laid on in haste with such a powder,
The blows grew louder still and louder;
Which HUDIBRAS, as if th' had been
Bestow'd as freely on his skin,
Expounding, by his inward light,
Or rather more prophetick fright,
To be the Wizard, come to search,
And take him napping in the lurch
Turn'd pale as ashes or a clout;
But why or wherefore is a doubt
For men will tremble, and turn paler,
With too much or too little valour.
His heart laid on, as if it try'd
To force a passage through his side,
Impatient (as he vow'd) to wait 'em,
But in a fury to fly at 'em;
And therefore beat, and laid about,
To find a cranny to creep out.
But she, who saw in what a taking
The Knight was by his furious quaking,
Undaunted cry'd, Courage, Sir Knight;
Know, I'm resolv'd to break no rite
Of hospitality t' a stranger;
But, to secure you out of danger,
Will here myself stand sentinel,
To guard this pass 'gainst SIDROPHEL.
Women, you know, do seldom fail
To make the stoutest men turn tail;
And bravely scorn to turn their backs
Upon the desp'ratest attacks.
At this the Knight grew resolute
As IRONSIDE and HARDIKNUTE
His fortitude began to rally,
And out he cry'd aloud to sally.
But she besought him to convey
His courage rather out o' th' way,
And lodge in ambush on the floor,
Or fortify'd behind a door;
That if the enemy shou'd enter,
He might relieve her in th' adventure.

Mean while they knock'd against the door
As fierce as at the gate before,

Which made the Renegado Knight
Relapse again t' his former fright.
He thought it desperate to stay
Till th' enemy had forc'd his way,
But rather post himself, to serve
The lady, for a fresh reserve
His duty was not to dispute,
But what sh' had order'd execute;
Which he resolv'd in haste t' obey,
And therefore stoutly march'd away;
And all h' encounter'd fell upon,
Though in the dark, and all alone;
Till fear, that braver feats performs
Than ever courage dar'd in arms,
Had drawn him up before a pass
To stand upon his guard, and face:
This he courageously invaded,
And having enter'd, barricado'd,
Insconc'd himself as formidable
As could be underneath a table,
Where he lay down in ambush close,
T' expect th' arrival of his foes.
Few minutes he had lain perdue,
To guard his desp'rate avenue,
Before he heard a dreadful shout,
As loud as putting to the rout,
With which impatiently alarm'd,
He fancy'd th' enemy had storm'd,
And, after ent'ring, SIDROPHEL
Was fall'n upon the guards pell-mell
He therefore sent out all his senses,
To bring him in intelligences,
Which vulgars, out of ignorance,
Mistake for falling in a trance;
But those that trade in geomancy,
Affirm to be the strength of fancy;
In which the Lapland Magi deal,
And things incredible reveal.
Mean while the foe beat up his quarters,
And storm'd the out-works of his fortress:
And as another, of the same
Degree and party, in arms and fame,
That in the same cause had engag'd,
At war with equal conduct wag'd,
By vent'ring only but to thrust
His head a span beyond his post,
B' a gen'ral of the cavaliers
Was dragg'd thro' a window by th' ears;

So he was serv'd in his redoubt,
And by the other end pull'd out.

Soon as they had him at their mercy,
They put him to the cudgel fiercely,
As if they'd scorn'd to trade or barter,
By giving or by taking quarter:
They stoutly on his quarters laid,
Until his scouts came in t' his aid.
For when a man is past his sense,
There's no way to reduce him thence,
But twinging him by th' ears or nose,
Or laying on of heavy blows;
And if that will not do the deed,
To burning with hot irons proceed.
No sooner was he come t' himself,
But on his neck a sturdy elf
Clapp'd, in a trice, his cloven hoof,
And thus attack'd him with reproof;
Mortal, thou art betray'd to us
B' our friend, thy Evil Genius,
Who, for thy horrid perjuries,
Thy breach of faith, and turning lies,
The Brethren's privilege (against
The wicked) on themselves, the Saints,
Has here thy wretched carcase sent
For just revenge and punishment;
Which thou hast now no way to lessen,
But by an open, free confession;
For if we catch thee failing once,
'Twill fall the heavier on thy bones.

What made thee venture to betray,
And filch the lady's heart away?
To Spirit her to matrimony? —
That which contracts all matches — money.
It was th' inchantment oft her riches
That made m' apply t' your croney witches,
That, in return, wou'd pay th' expence,
The wear and tear of conscience;
Which I cou'd have patch'd up, and turn'd,
For the hundredth part of what I earn'd.

Didst thou not love her then? Speak true.
No more (quoth he) than I love you. —
How would'st th' have us'd her, and her money? —
First turn'd her up to alimony;
And laid her dowry out in law,

To null her jointure with a flaw,
Which I before-hand had agreed
T' have put, on purpose in the deed;
And bar her widow's making over
T' a friend in trust, or private lover.

What made thee pick and chuse her out,
T' employ their sorceries about? —
That which makes gamesters play with those
Who have least wit, and most to lose.

But didst thou scourge thy vessel thus,
As thou hast damn'd thyself to us?

I see you take me for an ass:
'Tis true, I thought the trick wou'd pass
Upon a woman well enough,
As 't has been often found by proof,
Whose humours are not to be won,
But when they are impos'd upon.
For love approves of all they do
That stand for candidates, and woo.

Why didst thou forge those shameful lies
Of bears and witches in disguise?

That is no more than authors give
The rabble credit to believe:
A trick of following their leaders,
To entertain their gentle readers;
And we have now no other way
Of passing all we do or say
Which, when 'tis natural and true,
Will be believ'd b' a very few,
Beside the danger of offence,
The fatal enemy of sense.

Why did thou chuse that cursed sin,
Hypocrisy, to set up in?

Because it is in the thriving'st calling,
The only Saints-bell that rings all in;
In which all churches are concern'd,
And is the easiest to be learn'd:
For no degrees, unless th' employ't,
Can ever gain much, or enjoy't:
A gift that is not only able
To domineer among the rabble,

But by the laws impower'd to rout,
And awe the greatest that stand out;
Which few hold forth against, for fear
Their hands should slip, and come too near;
For no sin else among the Saints
Is taught so tenderly against.

What made thee break thy plighted vows? —
That which makes others break a house,
And hang, and scorn ye all, before
Endure the plague of being poor.

Quoth he, I see you have more tricks
Than all your doating politicks,
That are grown old, and out of fashion,
Compar'd with your New Reformation;
That we must come to school to you,
To learn your more refin'd, and new.

Quoth he, If you will give me leave
To tell you what I now perceive,
You'll find yourself an arrant chouse,
If y' were but at a Meeting-House. —
'Tis true, quoth he, we ne'er come there,
Because, w' have let 'em out by th' year.

Truly, quoth he, you can't imagine
What wond'rous things they will engage in
That as your fellow-fiends in Hell
Were angels all before they fell,
So are you like to be agen,
Compar'd with th' angels of us men.

Quoth he, I am resolv'd to be
Thy scholar in this mystery;
And therefore first desire to know
Some principles on which you go.

What makes a knave a child of God,
And one of us? — A livelihood.
What renders beating out of brains,
And murder, godliness? — Great gains.

What's tender conscience? — 'Tis a botch,
That will not bear the gentlest touch;
But breaking out, dispatches more
Than th' epidemical'st plague-sore.

What makes y' encroach upon our trade,
And damn all others? — To be paid.

What's orthodox, and true, believing
Against a conscience? — A good living.

What makes rebelling against Kings
A Good Old Cause? — Administrings.

What makes all doctrines plain and clear? —
About two hundred pounds a year.

And that which was prov'd true before,
Prove false again? — Two hundred more.

What makes the breaking of all oaths
A holy duty? — Food and cloaths.

What laws and freedom, persecution? —
B'ing out of pow'r, and contribution.

What makes a church a den of thieves? —
A dean and chapter, and white sleeves.

Ad what would serve, if those were gone,
To make it orthodox? — Our own.

What makes morality a crime,
The most notorious of the time;
Morality, which both the Saints,
And wicked too, cry out against? —
Cause grace and virtue are within
Prohibited degrees of kin
And therefore no true Saint allows,
They shall be suffer'd to espouse;
For Saints can need no conscience,
That with morality dispense;
As virtue's impious, when 'tis rooted
In nature only, and not imputed
But why the wicked should do so,
We neither know, or care to do.

What's liberty of conscience,
I' th' natural and genuine sense?
'Tis to restore, with more security,
Rebellion to its ancient purity;
And christian liberty reduce
To th' elder practice of the Jews.

For a large conscience is all one,
And signifies the same with none.

It is enough (quoth he) for once,
And has repriev'd thy forfeit bones:
NICK MACHIAVEL had ne'er a trick,
(Though he gave his name to our Old Nick,)
But was below the least of these,
That pass i' th' world for holiness.

This said, the furies and the light
In th' instant vanish'd out of sight,
And left him in the dark alone,
With stinks of brimstone and his own.

The Queen of Night, whose large command
Rules all the sea, and half the land,
And over moist and crazy brains,
In high spring-tides, at midnight reigns,
Was now declining to the west,
To go to bed, and take her rest;
When HUDIBRAS, whose stubborn blows
Deny'd his bones that soft repose,
Lay still expecting worse and more,
Stretch'd out at length upon the floor;
And though he shut his eyes as fast
As if h' had been to sleep his last,
Saw all the shapes that fear or wizards
Do make the Devil wear for vizards,
And pricking up his ears, to hark
If he cou'd hear too in the dark,
Was first invaded with a groan
And after in a feeble tone,
These trembling words: Unhappy wretch!
What hast thou gotten by this fetch;
For all thy tricks, in this new trade,
Thy holy brotherhood o' th' blade?
By sauntring still on some adventure,
And growing to thy horse a Centaure?
To stuff thy skin with swelling knobs
Of cruel and hard-wooded drubs?
For still th' hast had the worst on't yet,
As well in conquest as defeat.
Night is the sabbath of mankind,
To rest the body and the mind,
Which now thou art deny'd to keep,
And cure thy labour'd corpse with sleep.
The Knight, who heard the words, explain'd,

As meant to him, this reprimand,
Because the character did hit
Point-blank upon his case so fit;
Believ'd it was some drolling spright,
That staid upon the guard that night,
And one of those h' had seen, and felt
The drubs he had so freely dealt;
When, after a short pause and groan,
The doleful Spirit thus went on:

This 'tis t' engage with dogs and bears
Pell-mell together by the ears,
And, after painful bangs and knocks,
To lie in limbo in the stocks,
And from the pinnacle of glory
Fall headlong into purgatory.

(Thought he, this devil's full of malice,
That in my late disasters rallies:)
Condemn'd to whipping, but declin'd it,
By being more heroic-minded:
And at a riding handled worse,
With treats more slovenly and coarse:
Engag'd with fiends in stubborn wars,
And hot disputes with conjurers;
And when th' hadst bravely won the day,
Wast fain to steal thyself away.

(I see, thought he, this shameless elf
Wou'd fain steal me too from myself,
That impudently dares to own
What I have suffer'd for and done,)
And now but vent'ring to betray,
Hast met with vengeance the same way.

Thought he, how does the Devil know
What 'twas that I design'd to do?
His office of intelligence,
His oracles, are ceas'd long since;
And he knows nothing of the Saints,
But what some treacherous spy acquaints.
This is some pettifogging fiend,
Some under door-keeper's friend's friend,
That undertakes to understand,
And juggles at the second-hand;
And now would pass for Spirit Po,
And all mens' dark concerns foreknow.
I think I need not fear him for't;

These rallying devils do no hurt.
With that he rouz'd his drooping heart,
And hastily cry'd out, What art?
A wretch (quoth he) whom want of grace
Has brought to this unhappy place.

I do believe thee, quoth the Knight;
Thus far I'm sure th' art in the right;
And know what 'tis that troubles thee,
Better than thou hast guess'd of me.
Thou art some paultry, black-guard spright,
Condemn'd to drudg'ry in the night
Thou hast no work to do in th' house
Nor half-penny to drop in shoes;
Without the raising of which sum,
You dare not be so troublesome,
To pinch the slatterns black and blue,
For leaving you their work to do.
This is your bus'ness good Pug-Robin;
And your diversion dull dry-bobbing,
T' entice fanaticks in the dirt,
And wash them clean in ditches for't;
Of which conceit you are so proud,
At ev'ry jest you laugh aloud,
As now you wou'd have done by me,
But that I barr'd your raillery.

Sir (quoth the voice) y'are no such Sophi
As you would have the world judge of ye.
If you design to weigh our talents
I' the standard of your own false balance,
Or think it possible to know
Us ghosts as well as we do you;
We, who have been the everlasting
Companions of your drubs and basting,
And never left you in contest,
With male or female, man or beast,
But prov'd as true t' ye, and entire,
In all adventures, as your Squire.

Quoth he, That may be said as true
By the idlest pug of all your crew:
For none cou'd have betray'd us worse
Than those allies of ours and yours.
But I have sent him for a token
To your Low-Country HOGEN-MOGEN,
To whose infernal shores I hope
He'll swing like skippers in a rope.

And, if y' have been more just to me
(As I am apt to think) than he,
I am afraid it is as true,
What th' ill-affected say of you:
Y' have spous'd the Covenant and Cause,
By holding up your cloven paws.

Sir, quoth the voice, 'tis true, I grant,
We made and took the Covenant;
But that no more concerns the Cause
Than other perj'ries do the laws,
Which when they're prov'd in open court,
Wear wooden peccadillo's for't:
And that's the reason Cov'nanters
Hold up their hands like rogues at bars.

I see, quoth HUDIBRAS, from whence
These scandals of the Saints commence,
That are but natural effects
Of Satan's malice, and his sects,
Those Spider-Saints, that hang by threads,
Spun out o' th' intrails of their heads.

Sir, quoth the voice, that may as true
And properly be said of you,
Whose talents may compare with either,
Or both the other put together.
For all the Independents do,
Is only what you forc'd 'em to;
You, who are not content alone
With tricks to put the Devil down,
But must have armies rais'd to back
The gospel-work you undertake;
As if artillery, and edge-tools,
Were the only engines to save souls;
While he, poor devil, has no pow'r
By force to run down and devour;
Has ne'er a Classis; cannot sentence
To stools or poundage of repentance;
Is ty'd up only to design,
T' entice, and tempt, and undermine,
In which you all his arts out-do,
And prove yourselves his betters too.
Hence 'tis possessions do less evil
Than mere temptations of the Devil,
Which, all the horrid'st actions done,
Are charg'd in courts of law upon;
Because unless they help the elf,

He can do little of himself;
And therefore where he's best possess'd
Acts most against his interest;
Surprizes none, but those wh' have priests
To turn him out, and exorcists,
Supply'd with spiritual provision,
And magazines of ammunition
With crosses, relicks, crucifixes,
Beads, pictures, rosaries, and pixes;
The tools of working our salvation
By mere mechanick operation;
With holy water, like a sluice,
To overflow all avenues.
But those wh' are utterly unarm'd
T' oppose his entrance, if he storm'd,
He never offers to surprize,
Although his falsest enemies;
But is content to be their drudge,
And on their errands glad to trudge
For where are all your forfeitures
Entrusted in safe hands but ours?
Who are but jailors of the holes,
And dungeons where you clap up souls;
Like under-keepers, turn the keys,
T' your mittimus anathemas;
And never boggle to restore
The members you deliver o're
Upon demand, with fairer justice
Than all your covenanting Trustees;
Unless to punish them the worse,
You put them in the secular pow'rs,
And pass their souls, as some demise
The same estate in mortgage twice;
When to a legal Utlegation
You turn your excommunication,
And for a groat unpaid, that's due,
Distrain on soul and body too.

Thought he, 'tis no mean part of civil
State prudence to cajole the Devil
And not to handle him too rough,
When h' has us in his cloven hoof.

T' is true, quoth he, that intercourse
Has pass'd between your friends and ours;
That as you trust us, in our way,
To raise your members, and to lay,
We send you others of our own,

Denounc'd to hang themselves or drown;
Or, frighted with our oratory,
To leap down headlong many a story
Have us'd all means to propagate
Your mighty interests of state;
Laid out our spiritual gifts to further
Your great designs of rage and murther.
For if the Saints are nam'd from blood,
We only have made that title good;
And if it were but in our power,
We should not scruple to do more,
And not be half a soul behind
Of all dissenters of mankind.

Right, quoth the voice, and as I scorn
To be ungrateful, in return
Of all those kind good offices,
I'll free you out of this distress,
And set you down in safety, where
It is no time to tell you here.
The cock crows, and the morn grows on,
When 'tis decreed I must be gone;
And if I leave you here till day,
You'll find it hard to get away.

With that the Spirit grop'd about,
To find th' inchanted hero out,
And try'd with haste to lift him up;
But found his forlorn hope, his crup,
Unserviceable with kicks and blows,
Receiv'd from harden'd-hearted foes.
He thought to drag him by the heels,
Like Gresham carts, with legs for wheels;
But fear, that soonest cures those sores
In danger of relapse to worse,
Came in t' assist him with it's aid
And up his sinking vessel weigh'd.
No sooner was he fit to trudge,
But both made ready to dislodge.
The Spirit hors'd him like a sack
Upon the vehicle his back;
And bore him headlong into th' hall,
With some few rubs against the wall
Where finding out the postern lock'd,
And th' avenues as strongly block'd,
H' attack'd the window, storm'd the glass,
And in a moment gain'd the pass;
Thro' which he dragg'd the worsted souldier's

Fore-quarters out by the head and shoulders;
And cautiously began to scout,
To find their fellow-cattle out.
Nor was it half a minute's quest,
E're he retriev'd the champion's beast,
Ty'd to a pale, instead of rack;
But ne'er a saddle on his back,
Nor pistols at the saddle-bow,
Convey'd away the Lord knows how,
He thought it was no time to stay,
And let the night too steal away;
But in a trice advanc'd the Knight
Upon the bare ridge, bolt upright:
And groping out for RALPHO's jade,
He found the saddle too was stray'd,
And in the place a lump of soap,
On which he speedily leap'd up;
And turning to the gate the rein,
He kick'd and cudgell'd on amain.
While HUDIBRAS, with equal haste,
On both sides laid about as fast,
And spurr'd as jockies use to break,
Or padders to secure, a neck
Where let us leave 'em for a time,
And to their Churches turn our rhyme;
To hold forth their declining state,
Which now come near an even rate.

PART III

CANTO II

THE ARGUMENT

The Saints engage in fierce Contests
About their Carnal interests;
To share their sacrilegious Preys,
According to their Rates of Grace;
Their various Frenzies to reform,
When Cromwel left them in a Storm
Till, in th' Effigy of Rumps, the Rabble
Burns all their Grandees of the Cabal.

The learned write, an insect breeze
Is but a mungrel prince of bees,

That falls before a storm on cows,
And stings the founders of his house;
From whose corrupted flesh that breed
Of vermin did at first proceed.
So e're the storm of war broke out,
Religion spawn'd a various rout
Of petulant Capricious sects,
The maggots of corrupted texts,
That first run all religion down,
And after ev'ry swarm its own.
For as the Persian Magi once
Upon their mothers got their sons,
That were incapable t' enjoy
That empire any other way;
So PRESBYTER begot the other
Upon the good old Cause, his mother,
Then bore then like the Devil's dam,
Whose son and husband are the same.
And yet no nat'ral tie of blood
Nor int'rest for the common good
Cou'd, when their profits interfer'd,
Get quarter for each other's beard.
For when they thriv'd, they never fadg'd,
But only by the ears engag'd:
Like dogs that snarl about a bone,
And play together when they've none,
As by their truest characters,
Their constant actions, plainly appears.
Rebellion now began, for lack
Of zeal and plunders to grow slack;
The Cause and covenant to lessen,
And Providence to b' out of season:
For now there was no more to purchase
O' th' King's Revenue, and the Churches,
But all divided, shar'd, and gone,
That us'd to urge the Brethren on;
Which forc'd the stubborn'st for the Cause,
To cross the cudgels to the laws,
That what by breaking them th' had gain'd.
By their support might be maintain'd;
Like thieves, that in a hemp-plot lie
Secur'd against the hue-and-cry;
For PRESBYTER and INDEPENDANT
Were now turn'd plaintiff and defendant;
Laid out their apostolic functions
On carnal orders and injunctions;
And all their precious Gifts and Graces
On outlawries and scire facias;

At Michael's term had many a trial,
Worse than the Dragon and St. Michael,
Where thousands fell, in shape of fees,
Into the bottomless abyss.
For when like brethren, and like friends,
They came to share their dividends,
And ev'ry partner to possess
His Church and State Joint-Purchases,
In which the ablest Saint, and best,
Was nam'd in trust by all the rest,
To pay their money; and, instead
Of ev'ry Brother, pass the deed;
He strait converted all his gifts
To pious frauds and holy shifts;
And settled all the other shares
Upon his outward man and's heirs;
Held all they claim'd as forfeit lands,
Deliver'd up into his hands,
And pass'd upon his conscience,
By Pre-intail of Providence;
Impeach'd the rest for reprobates,
That had no titles to estates,
But by their spiritual attaints
Degraded from the right of Saints.
This b'ing reveal'd, they now begun
With law and conscience to fall on,
And laid about as hot and brain-sick
As th' Utter Barrister of SWANSWICK;
Engag'd with moneybags as bold
As men with sand bags did of old;
That brought the lawyers in more fees
Than all unsanctify'd Trustees;
Till he who had no more to show
I' th' case receiv'd the overthrow;
Or both sides having had the worst,
They parted as they met at first.

Poor PRESBYTER was now reduc'd,
Secluded, and cashier'd, and chous'd
Turn'd out, and excommunicate
From all affairs of Church and State;
Reform'd t' a reformado Saint,
And glad to turn itinerant,
To stroll and teach from town to town,
And those he had taught up, teach down.
And make those uses serve agen
Against the new-enlighten'd men,
As fit as when at first they were

Reveal'd against the CAVALIER;
Damn ANABAPTIST and FANATIC,
As pat as Popish and Prelatic;
And with as little variation,
To serve for any Sect i' th' nation.
The Good Old Cause, which some believe
To be the Dev'l that tempted EVE
With Knowledge, and does still invite
The world to mischief with new Light,
Had store of money in her purse
When he took her for bett'r or worse;
But now was grown deform'd and poor,
And fit to be turn'd out of door.

The INDEPENDENTS (whose first station
Was in the rear of reformation,
A mungrel kind of church-dragoons,
That serv'd for horse and foot at once;
And in the saddle of one steed
The Saracen and Christian rid;
Were free of ev'ry spiritual order,
To preach, and fight, and pray, and murder)
No sooner got the start to lurch
Both disciplines, of War and Church
And Providence enough to run
The chief commanders of 'em down,
But carry'd on the war against
The common enemy o' th' Saints,
And in a while prevail'd so far,
To win of them the game of war,
And be at liberty once more
T' attack themselves, as th' had before.

For now there was no foe in arms,
T' unite their factions with alarms,
But all reduc'd and overcome,
Except their worst, themselves at home,
Wh' had compass'd all they pray'd, and swore,
And fought, and preach'd, and plunder'd for;
Subdu'd the Nation, Church, and State,
And all things, but their laws and hate:
But when they came to treat and transact,
And share the spoil of all th' had ransackt,
To botch up what th' had torn and rent,
Religion and the Government,
They met no sooner, but prepar'd
To pull down all the war had spar'd
Agreed in nothing, but t' abolish,

Subvert, extirpate, and demolish.
For knaves and fools b'ing near of kin
As Dutch Boors are t' a Sooterkin,
Both parties join'd to do their best
To damn the publick interest,
And herded only in consults,
To put by one another's bolts;
T' out-cant the Babylonian labourers,
At all their dialects of jabberers,
And tug at both ends of the saw,
To tear down Government and Law.
For as two cheats, that play one game,
Are both defeated of their aim;
So those who play a game of state,
And only cavil in debate,
Although there's nothing lost or won,
The publick bus'ness is undone;
Which still the longer 'tis in doing,
Becomes the surer way to ruin.

This, when the ROYALISTS perceiv'd,
(Who to their faith as firmly cleav'd,
And own'd the right they had paid down
So dearly for, the Church and Crown,)
Th' united constanter, and sided
The more, the more their foes divided.
For though out-number'd, overthrown
And by the fate of war run down)
Their duty never was defeated,
Nor from their oaths and faith retreated;
For loyalty is still the same,
Whether it win or lose the game;
True as the dial to the sun,
Although it be not shin'd upon.
But when these brethren in evil,
Their adversaries, and the Devil,
Began once more to shew them play,
And hopes, at least, to have a day,
They rally'd in parades of woods,
And unfrequented solitudes;
Conven'd at midnight in out-houses,
T' appoint new-rising rendezvouzes,
And with a pertinacy unmatch'd,
For new recruits of danger watch'd.
No sooner was one blow diverted,
But up another party started;
And, as if nature too, in haste
To furnish out supplies as fast,

Before her time, had turn'd destruction
T' a new and numerous production,
No sooner those were overcome,
But up rose others in their room,
That, like the Christian faith, increast
The more, the more they were supprest
Whom neither chains, nor transportation,
Proscription, sale, or confiscation,
Nor all the desperate events
Of former try'd experiments
Nor wounds cou'd terrify, nor mangling,
To leave off loyalty and dangling;
Nor death (with all his bones) affright
From vent'ring to maintain the right,
From staking life and fortune down
'Gainst all together, for the Crown;
But kept the title of their cause
From forfeiture, like claims in laws
And prov'd no prosp'rous usurpation
Can ever settle in the nation;
Until, in spight of force and treason,
They put their loyalty in possession;
And by their constancy and faith,
Destroy 'd the mighty men of Gath.

Toss'd in a furious hurricane,
Did OLIVER give up his reign;
And was believ'd, as well by Saints,
As mortal men and miscreants,
To founder in the Stygian Ferry;
Until he was retriev'd by STERRY,
Who, in a faise erroneous dream,
Mistook the New Jerusalem
Prophanely for the apocryphal
False Heaven at the end o' th' Hall;
Whither it was decreed by Fate
His precious reliques to translate.
So ROMULUS was seen before
B' as orthodox a Senator;
From whose divine illumination
He stole the Pagan revelation.

Next him his Son and Heir Apparent
Succeeded, though a lame vicegerent;
Who first laid by the Parliament,
The only crutch on which he leant;
And then sunk underneath the State,
That rode him above horseman's weight.

And now the Saints began their reign,
For which th' had yearn'd so long in vain,
And felt such bowel-hankerings,
To see an empire all of Kings.
Deliver'd from the Egyptian awe
Of Justice, Government, and Law,
And free t' erect what spiritual Cantons
Should be reveal'd, or Gospel Hans-Towns,
To edify upon the ruins
Of JOHN of LEYDEN'S old Out-goings;
Who for a weather-cock hung up,
Upon the Mother Church's top;
Was made a type, by Providence,
Of all their revelations since;
And now fulfill'd by his successors,
Who equally mistook their measures
For when they came to shape the model,
Not one could fit another's noddle;
But found their Light and Gifts more wide
From fadging than th' unsanctify'd;
While ev'ry individual brother
Strove hand to fist against another;
And still the maddest, and most crackt,
Were found the busiest to transact
For though most hands dispatch apace,
And make light work, (the proverb says,)
Yet many diff'rent intellects
Are found t' have contrary effects;
And many heads t' obstruct intrigues,
As slowest insects have most legs.

Some were for setting up a King;
But all the rest for no such thing,
Unless KING JESUS. Others tamper'd
For FLEETWOOD, DESBOROUGH, and LAMBERT;
Some for the Rump; and some, more crafty,
For Agitators, and the safety;
Some for the Gospel, and massacres
Of Spiritual Affidavit-makers,
That swore to any human regence,
Oaths of supremacy and allegiance;
Yea, though the ablest swearing Saint
That vouch'd the Bulls o' th' Covenant:
Others for pulling down th' high-places
Of Synods and Provincial Classes,
That us'd to make such hostile inroads
Upon the Saints, like bloody NIMRODS

Some for fulfilling prophecies,
And th' expiration of th' excise
And some against th' Egyptian bondage
Of holy-days, and paying poundage:
Some for the cutting down of groves,
And rectifying bakers' loaves:
And some for finding out expedients
Against the slav'ry of obedience.
Some were for Gospel Ministers,
And some for Red-coat Seculars,
As men most fit t' hold forth the word,
And wield the one and th' other sword.
Some were for carrying on the work
Against the Pope, and some the Turk;
Some for engaging to suppress,
The Camisado of surplices,
That gifts and dispensations hinder'd,
And turn'd to th' Outward Man the Inward;
More proper for the cloudy night
Of Popery than Gospel Light.
Others were for abolishing
That tool of matrimony, a ring,
With which th' unsanctify'd bridegroom
Is marry'd only to a thumb;
(As wise as ringing of a pig,
That us'd to break up ground, and dig;)
The bride to nothing but her will,
That nulls the after-marriage still
Some were for th' utter extirpation
Of linsey-woolsey in the nation;
And some against all idolizing
The Cross in shops-books, or Baptizing
Others to make all things recant
The Christian or Surname of Saint;
And force all churches, streets, and towns,
The holy title to renounce.
Some 'gainst a Third Estate of Souls,
And bringing down the price of coals:
Some for abolishing black-pudding,
And eating nothing with the blood in;
To abrogate them roots and branches;
While others were for eating haunches
Of warriors, and now and then,
The flesh of Kings and mighty men
And some for breaking of their bones
With rods of ir'n, by secret ones:
For thrashing mountains, and with spells
For hallowing carriers' packs and bells:

Things that the legend never heard of,
But made the wicked sore afear'd of.

The quacks of Government (who sate
At th' unregarded helm of State,
And understood this wild confusion
Of fatal madness and delusion,
Must, sooner than a prodigy,
Portend destruction to be nigh)
Consider'd timely how t' withdraw,
And save their wind-pipes from the law;
For one rencounter at the bar
Was worse than all th' had 'scap'd in war;
And therefore met in consultation
To cant and quack upon the nation;
Not for the sickly patient's sake,
For what to give, but what to take;
To feel the pulses of their fees,
More wise than fumbling arteries:
Prolong the snuff of life in pain,
And from the grave recover — Gain.

'Mong these there was a politician
With more heads than a beast in vision,
And more intrigues in ev'ry one
Than all the whores of Babylon:
So politic, as if one eye
Upon the other were a spy,
That, to trepan the one to think
The other blind, both strove to blink;
And in his dark pragmatick way,
As busy as a child at play.
H' had seen three Governments run down,
And had a hand in ev'ry one;
Was for 'em and against 'em all,
But barb'rous when they came to fall
For, by trepanning th' old to ruin,
He made his int'rest with the new one
Play'd true and faithful, though against
His conscience, and was still advanc'd.
For by the witchcraft of rebellion
Transform'd t' a feeble state-camelion,
By giving aim from side to side,
He never fail'd to save his tide,
But got the start of ev'ry state,
And at a change ne'er came too late;
Cou'd turn his word, and oath, and faith,
As many ways as in a lath;

By turning, wriggle, like a screw,
Int' highest trust, and out, for new.
For when h' had happily incurr'd,
Instead of hemp, to be preferr'd,
And pass'd upon a government,
He pay'd his trick, and out he went
But, being out, and out of hopes
To mount his ladder (more) of ropes,
Wou'd strive to raise himself upon
The publick ruin, and his own;
So little did he understand
The desp'rate feats he took in hand.
For when h' had got himself a name
For fraud and tricks, he spoil'd his game;
Had forc'd his neck into a noose,
To shew his play at fast and loose;
And when he chanc'd t' escape, mistook
For art and subtlety, his luck.
So right his judgment was cut fit,
And made a tally to his wit,
And both together most profound
At deeds of darkness under-ground;
As th' earth is easiest undermin'd
By vermin impotent and blind.

By all these arts, and many more,
H' had practis'd long and much before,
Our state artificer foresaw
Which way the world began to draw.
For as old sinners have all points
O' th' compass in their bones and joints,
Can by their pangs and aches find
All turns and changes of the wind,
And better than by NAPIER's bones
Feel in their own the age of moons;
So guilty sinners in a state
Can by their crimes prognosticate,
And in their consciences feel pain
Some days before a show'r of rain.
He therefore wisely cast about,
All ways he cou'd, t' ensure his throat;
And hither came, t' observe and smoke
What courses other riskers took
And to the utmost do his best
To save himself, and hang the rest.
To match this Saint, there was another
As busy and perverse a Brother,
An haberdasher of small wares

In politicks and state affairs;
More Jew than Rabbi ACHITOPHEL,
And better gifted to rebel:
For when h' had taught his tribe to 'spouse
The Cause, aloft, upon one house,
He scorn'd to set his own in order,
But try'd another, and went further;
So suddenly addicted still
To's only principle, his will,
That whatsoe'er it chanc'd to prove,
Nor force of argument cou'd move;
Nor law, nor cavalcade of Holborn,
Could render half a grain less stubborn.
For he at any time would hang
For th' opportunity t' harangue;
And rather on a gibbet dangle,
Than miss his dear delight, to wrangle;
In which his parts were so accomplisht,
That, right or wrong, he ne'er was non-plusht;
But still his tongue ran on, the less
Of weight it bore, with greater ease;
And with its everlasting clack
Set all men's ears upon the rack.
No sooner cou'd a hint appear,
But up he started to picqueer,
And made the stoutest yield to mercy,
When he engag'd in controversy.
Not by the force of carnal reason,
But indefatigable teazing;
With vollies of eternal babble,
And clamour, more unanswerable.
For though his topics, frail and weak,
Cou'd ne'er amount above a freak,
He still maintain'd 'em, like his faults,
Against the desp'ratest assaults;
And back'd their feeble lack of sense,
With greater heat and confidence?
As bones of Hectors, when they differ,
The more they're cudgel'd grow the stiffer.
Yet when his profit moderated,
The fury of his heat abated.
For nothing but his interest
Cou'd lay his Devil of Contest.
It was his choice, or chance; or curse,
T' espouse the Cause for bett'r or worse,
And with his worldly goods and wit,
And soul and body, worship'd it:
But when he found the sullen trapes

Possess'd with th' Devil, worms, and claps;
The Trojan mare, in foal with Greeks,
Not half so full of jadish tricks;
Though squeamish in her outward woman,
As loose and rampant as Dol Common;
He still resolv'd to mend the matter,
T' adhere and cleave the obstinater;
And still the skittisher and looser
Her freaks appear'd, to sit the closer.
For fools are stubborn in their way,
As coins are harden'd by th' allay:
And obstinacy's ne'er so stiff
As when 'tis in a wrong belief.
These two, with others, being met,
And close in consultation set,
After a discontented pause,
And not without sufficient cause,
The orator we nam'd of late,
Less troubled with the pangs of State
Than with his own impatience,
To give himself first audience,
After he had a while look'd wise,
At last broke silence, and the ice.

Quoth he, There's nothing makes me doubt
Our last out-goings brought about,
More than to see the characters
Of real jealousies and fears
Not feign'd, as once, but, sadly horrid,
Scor'd upon ev'ry Member's forehead;
Who, 'cause the clouds are drawn together,
And threaten sudden change of weather,
Feel pangs and aches of state-turns,
And revolutions in their corns;
And, since our workings-out are cross'd,
Throw up the Cause before 'tis lost.
Was it to run away we meant,
When, taking of the Covenant,
The lamest cripples of the brothers
Took oaths to run before all others;
But in their own sense only swore
To strive to run away before;
And now would prove, that words and oath
Engage us to renounce them both?
'Tis true, the Cause is in the lurch,
Between a Right and Mungrel-Church;
The Presbyter and Independent,
That stickle which shall make an end on't;

As 'twas made out to us the last
Expedient — (I mean Marg'ret's Fast,)
When Providence had been suborn'd,
What answer was to be return'd.
Else why should tumults fright us now,
We have so many times come through?
And understand as well to tame,
As when they serve our turns t'inflame:
Have prov'd how inconsiderable
Are all engagements of the rabble,
Whose frenzies must be reconcil'd
With drums and rattles, like a child;
But never prov'd so prosperous
As when they were led on by us
For all our scourging of religion
Began with tumult and sedition;
When hurricanes of fierce commotion
Became strong motives to devotion;
(As carnal seamen, in a storm,
Turn pious converts, and reform;)
When rusty weapons, with chalk'd edges,
Maintain'd our feeble privileges;
And brown-bills levy'd in the City,
Made bills to pass the Grand Committee;
When zeal, with aged clubs and gleaves,
Gave chace to rochets and white sleeves,
And made the Church, and State, and Laws,
Submit t' old iron and the Cause.
And as we thriv'd by tumults then,
So might we better now agen,
If we knew how, as then we did,
To use them rightly in our need:
Tumults, by which the mutinous
Betray themselves instead of us.
The hollow-hearted, disaffected,
And close malignant are detected,
Who lay their lives and fortunes down
For pledges to secure our own;
And freely sacrifice their ears
T' appease our jealousies and fears;
And yet, for all these providences
W' are offer'd, if we had our senses;
We idly sit like stupid blockheads,
Our hands committed to our pockets;
And nothing but our tongues at large,
To get the wretches a discharge:
Like men condemn'd to thunder-bolts,
Who, ere the blow, become mere dolts;

Or fools besotted with their crimes,
That know not how to shift betimes,
And neither have the hearts to stay,
Nor wit enough to run away;
Who, if we cou'd resolve on either,
Might stand or fall at least together;
No mean or trivial solace
To partners in extreme distress;
Who us'd to lessen their despairs,
By parting them int' equal shares;
As if the more they were to bear,
They felt the weight the easier;
And ev'ry one the gentler hung,
The more he took his turn among.
But 'tis not come to that, as yet,
If we had courage left, or wit;
Who, when our fate can be no worse,
Are fitted for the bravest course;
Have time to rally, and prepare
Our last and best defence, despair;
Despair, by which the gallant'st feats
Have been atchiev'd in greatest straits,
And horrid'st danger safely wav'd,
By being courageously out-brav'd;
As wounds by wider wounds are heal'd,
And poisons by themselves expell'd:
And so they might be now agen,
If we were, what we shou'd be, men;
And not so dully desperate,
To side against ourselves with Fate;
As criminals, condemn'd to suffer,
Are blinded first, and then turn'd over.
This comes of breaking Covenants,
And setting up Exauns of Saints,
That fine, like aldermen, for grace,
To be excus'd the efficace.
For Spiritual men are too transcendent,
That mount their banks for Independent,
To hang like MAHOMET in th' air,
Or St. IGNATIUS at his prayer,
By pure geometry, and hate
Dependence upon Church or State;
Disdain the pedantry o' th' letter;
And since obedience is better
(The Scripture says) than sacrifice,
Presume the less on't will suffice;
And scorn to have the moderat'st stints
Prescrib'd their peremptory hints,

Or any opinion, true or false,
Declar'd as such, in doctrinals
But left at large to make their best on,
Without b'ing call'd t' account or question,
Interpret all the spleen reveals;
As WHITTINGTON explain'd the bells;
And bid themselves turn back agen
Lord May'rs of New Jerusalem;
But look so big and over-grown,
They scorn their edifiers t' own,
Who taught them all their sprinkling lessons,
Their tones, and sanctified expressions
Bestow'd their Gifts upon a Saint,
Like Charity on those that want;
And learn'd th' apocryphal bigots
T' inspire themselves with short-hand notes;
For which they scorn and hate them worse
Than dogs and cats do sow-gelders.
For who first bred them up to pray,
And teach, the House of Commons Way?
Where had they all their gifted phrases,
But from our CALAMYS and CASES?
Without whose sprinkling and sowing,
Who e'er had heard of NYE or OWEN?
Their dispensations had been stifled,
But for our ADONIRAM BYFIELD;
And had they not begun the war,
Th' had ne'er been sainted, as they are:
For Saints in peace degenerate,
And dwindle down to reprobate;
Their zeal corrupts, like standing water,
In th' intervals of war and slaughter;
Abates the sharpness of its edge,
Without the power of sacrilege.
And though they've tricks to cast their sins
As easy as serpents do their skins,
That in a while grow out agen,
In peace they turn mere carnal men,
And from the most refin'd of saints,
As naturally grow miscreants,
As barnacles turn SOLAND geese
In th' Islands of the ORCADES.
Their dispensation's but a ticket,
For their conforming to the wicked;
With whom the greatest difference
Lies more in words, and shew, than sense.
For as the Pope, that keeps the gate
Of Heaven, wears three crowns of state;

So he that keeps the gate of Hell,
Proud CERBERUS, wears three heads as well;
And if the world has any troth
Some have been canoniz'd in both.
But that which does them greatest harm,
Their spiritual gizzards are too warm,
Which puts the over-heated sots
In fevers still, like other goats.
For though the Whore bends Hereticks
With flames of fire, like crooked sticks,
Our Schismaticks so vastly differ,
Th' hotter th' are, they grow the stiffer;
Still setting off their spiritual goods
With fierce and pertinacious feuds.
For zeal's a dreadful termagant,
That teaches Saints to tear and rant,
And Independents to profess
The doctrine of dependences:
Turns meek, and secret, sneaking ones,
To raw-heads fierce and bloody-bones:
And, not content with endless quarrels
Against the wicked, and their morals,
The GIBELLINES, for want of GUELPHS,
Divert their rage upon themselves.
For now the war is not between
The Brethren and the Men of Sin,
But Saint and Saint, to spill the blood
Of one another's brotherhood;
Where neither side can lay pretence
To liberty of conscience,
Or zealous suff'ring for the cause,
To gain one groat's-worth of applause;
For though endur'd with resolution,
'Twill ne'er amount to persecution.
Shall precious Saints, and secret ones,
Break one another's outward bones,
And eat the flesh of Brethren,
Instead of Kings and mighty men?
When fiends agree among themselves,
Shall they be found the greatest elves?
When BELL's at union with the DRAGON,
And BAAL-PEOR friends with DAGON,
When savage bears agree with bears,
Shall secret ones lug Saints by th' ears,
And not atone their fatal wrath,
When common danger threatens both?
Shall mastiffs, by the coller pull'd,
Engag'd with bulls, let go their hold,

And Saints, whose necks are pawn'd at stake,
No notice of the danger take?
But though no pow'r of Heav'n or Hell
Can pacify phanatick zeal,
Who wou'd not guess there might be hopes,
The fear of gallowses and ropes,
Before their eyes, might reconcile
Their animosities a while;
At least until th' had a clear stage,
And equal freedom to engage,
Without the danger of surprize
By both our common enemies?

This none but we alone cou'd doubt,
Who understand their workings out;
And know them, both in soul and conscience,
Giv'n up t' as reprobate a nonsense
As spiritual out-laws, whom the pow'r
Of miracle can ne'er restore
We, whom at first they set up under,
In revelation only of plunder,
Who since have had so many trials
Of their encroaching self-denials,
That rook'd upon us with design
To out-reform, and undermine;
Took all our interest and commands
Perfidiously out of our hands;
Involv'd us in the guilt of blood
Without the motive gains allow'd,
And made us serve as ministerial,
Like younger Sons of Father BELIAL;
And yet, for all th' inhuman wrong
Th' had done us and the Cause so long,
We never fail to carry on
The work still as we had begun;
But true and faithfully obey'd
And neither preach'd them hurt, nor pray'd;
Nor troubled them to crop our ears,
Nor hang us like the cavaliers;
Nor put them to the charge of gaols,
To find us pill'ries and cart's-tails,
Or hangman's wages, which the State
Was forc'd (before them) to be at,
That cut, like tallies, to the stumps,
Our ears for keeping true accompts,
And burnt our vessels, like a new
Seal'd peck, or bushel, for b'ing true;
But hand in hand, like faithful brothers,

Held for the Cause against all others,
Disdaining equally to yield
One syllable of what we held,
And though we differ'd now and then
'Bout outward things, and outward men,
Our inward men, and constant frame
Of spirit, still were near the same;
And till they first began to cant
And sprinkle down the Covenant,
We ne'er had call in any place,
Nor dream'd of teaching down free grace,
But join'd our gifts perpetually
Against the common enemy.
Although 'twas ours and their opinion,
Each other's Church was but a RIMMON;
And yet, for all this gospel-union,
And outward shew of Church-communion,
They'll ne'er admit us to our shares
Of ruling Church or State affairs;
Nor give us leave t' absolve, or sentence
T' our own conditions of repentance;
But shar'd our dividend o' th' Crown,
We had so painfully preach'd down;
And forc'd us, though against the grain,
T' have calls to teach it up again:
For 'twas but justice to restore
The wrongs we had receiv'd before;
And when 'twas held forth in our way,
W' had been ungrateful not to pay;
Who, for the right w' have done the nation,
Have earn'd our temporal salvation;
And put our vessels in a way
Once more to come again in play.
For if the turning of us out
Has brought this Providence about,
And that our only suffering
Is able to bring in the King,
What would our actions not have done,
Had we been suffer'd to go on?
And therefore may pretend t' a share,
At least; in carrying on th' affair.
But whether that be so, or not,
W' have done enough to have it thought;
And that's as good as if w' had done't,
And easier pass't upon account:
For if it be but half deny'd,
'Tis half as good as justifi'd.
The world is nat'rally averse

To all the truth it sees or hears
But swallows nonsense, and a lie,
With greediness and gluttony
And though it have the pique, and long,
'Tis still for something in the wrong;
As women long, when they're with child,
For things extravagant and wild;
For meats ridiculous and fulsome,
But seldom any thing that's wholesome;
And, like the world, men's jobbernoles
Turn round upon their ears, the poles;
And what they're confidently told,
By no sense else can be control'd.
And this, perhaps, may prove time means
Once more to hedge-in Providence,
For as relapses make diseases
More desp'rate than their first accesses,
If we but get again in pow'r,
Our work is easier than before
And we more ready and expert
I' th' mystery to do our part.
We, who did rather undertake
The first war to create than make,
And when of nothing 'twas begun,
Rais'd funds as strange to carry 't on;
Trepann'd the State, and fac'd it down
With plots and projects of our own;
And if we did such feats at first,
What can we now we're better vers'd?
Who have a freer latitude,
Than sinners give themselves, allow'd,
And therefore likeliest to bring in,
On fairest terms, our discipline;
To which it was reveal'd long since,
We were ordain'd by Providence;
When three Saints Ears, our predecessors,
The Cause's primitive Confessors,
B'ing crucify'd, the nation stood
In just so many years of blood;
That, multiply'd by six, exprest
The perfect number of the beast,
And prov'd that we must be the men
To bring this work about agen;
And those who laid the first foundation,
Compleat the thorough Reformation:
For who have gifts to carry on
So great a work, but we alone?
What churches have such able pastors,

And precious, powerful, preaching masters?
Possess'd with absolute dominions
O'er brethren's purses and opinions?
And trusted with the double keys
Of Heaven and their warehouses;
Who, when the Cause is in distress,
Can furnish out what sums they please,
That brooding lie in bankers' hands,
To be dispos'd at their commands;
And daily increase and multiply,
With doctrine, use, and usury:
Can fetch in parties (as in war
All other heads of cattle are)
From th' enemy of all religions,
As well as high and low conditions,
And share them, from blue ribbands, down
To all blue aprons in the town;
From ladies hurried in calleches,
With cor'nets at their footmens' breeches,
To bawds as fat as Mother Nab;
All guts and belly, like a crab.
Our party's great, and better ty'd
With oaths and trade than any side,
Has one considerable improvement,
To double fortify the Cov'nant:
I mean our Covenant to purchase
Delinquents titles, and the Churches;
That pass in sale, from hand to hand,
Among ourselves, for current land;
And rise or fall, like Indian actions,
According to the rate of factions
Our best reserve for Reformation,
When new out-goings give occasion;
That keeps the loins of Brethren girt
The Covenant (their creed) t' assert;
And when th' have pack'd a Parliament,
Will once more try th' expedient:
Who can already muster friends,
To serve for members, to our ends,
That represent no part o' th' nation,
But Fisher's-Folly Congregation;
Are only tools to our intrigues,
And sit like geese to hatch our eggs;
Who, by their precedents of wit,
T' out-fast, out-loiter, and out-sit,
Can order matters underhand,
To put all bus'ness to a stand;
Lay publick bills aside for private,

And make 'em one another drive out;
Divert the great and necessary,
With trifles to contest and vary;
And make the Ration represent,
And serve for us, in Parliament
Cut out more work than can be done.
In PLATO'S year, but finish none;
Unless it be the Bulls of LENTHAL,
That always pass'd for fundamental;
Can set up grandee against grandee,
To squander time away, and bandy;
Make Lords and Commoners lay sieges
To one another's privileges,
And, rather than compound the quarrel,
Engage to th' inevitable peril
Of both their ruins; th' only scope
And consolation of our hope;
Who though we do not play the game,
Assist as much by giving aim:
Can introduce our ancient arts,
For heads of factions t' act their parts;
Know what a leading voice is worth,
A seconding, a third, or fourth
How much a casting voice comes to,
That turns up trump, of ay, or no;
And, by adjusting all at th' end,
Share ev'ry one his dividend
An art that so much study cost,
And now's in danger to be lost,
Unless our ancient virtuosos,
That found it out, get into th' Houses.
These are the courses that we took
To carry things by hook or crook;
And practis'd down from forty-four,
Until they turn'd us out of door
Besides the herds of Boutefeus
We set on work without the House;
When ev'ry knight and citizen
Kept legislative journeymen,
To bring them in intelligence
From all points of the rabble's sense,
And fill the lobbies of both Houses
With politick important buzzes:
Set committees of cabals,
To pack designs without the walls;
Examine, and draw up all news,
And fit it to our present use.
Agree upon the plot o' th' farce,

And ev'ry one his part rehearse,
Make Q's of answers, to way-lay
What th' other pasties like to say
What repartees, and smart reflections,
Shall be return'd to all objections;
And who shall break the master-jest,
And what, and how, upon the rest
Held pamphlets out, with safe editions,
Of proper slanders and seditions;
And treason for a token send,
By Letter to a Country Friend;
Disperse lampoons, the only wit
That men, like burglary, commit;
Wit falser than a padder's face,
That all its owner does betrays;
Who therefore dares not trust it when
He's in his calling to be seen;
Disperse the dung on barren earth,
To bring new weeds of discord forth;
Be sure to keep up congregations,
In spight of laws and proclamations:
For Charlatans can do no good
Until they're mounted in a crowd;
And when they're punish'd, all the hurt
Is but to fare the better for't;
As long as confessors are sure
Of double pay for all th' endure;
And what they earn in persecution,
Are paid t' a groat in contribution.
Whence some Tub-Holders-forth have made
In powd'ring-tubs their richest trade;
And while they kept their shops in prison,
Have found their prices strangely risen.
Disdain to own the least regret
For all the Christian blood w' have let;
'Twill save our credit, and maintain
Our title to do so again;
That needs not cost one dram of sense,
But pertinacious impudence.
Our constancy t' our principles,
In time will wear out all things else;
Like marble statues rubb'd in pieces
With gallantry of pilgrims' kisses;
While those who turn and wind their oaths,
Have swell'd and sunk, like other froths;
Prevail'd a while, but 'twas not long
Before from world to world they swung:
As they had turn'd from side to side,

And as the changelings liv'd, they dy'd.

This said, th' impatient States-monger
Could now contain himself no longer;
Who had not spar'd to shew his piques
Against th' haranguer's politicks,
With smart remarks of leering faces,
And annotations of grimaces.
After h' had administer'd a dose
Of snuff-mundungus to his nose,
And powder'd th' inside of his skull,
Instead of th' outward jobbernol,
He shook it with a scornful look
On th' adversary, and thus he spoke:

In dressing a calves head, although
The tongue and brains together go,
Both keep so great a distance here,
'Tis strange if ever they come near;
For who did ever play his gambols
With such insufferable rambles
To make the bringing in the KING,
And keeping of him out, one thing?
Which none could do, but those that swore
T' as point-plank nonsense heretofore:
That to defend, was to invade;
And to assassinate, to aid
Unless, because you drove him out,
(And that was never made a doubt,)
No pow'r is able to restore,
And bring him in, but on your score
A spiritual doctrine, that conduces
Most properly to all your uses.
'Tis true, a scorpions oil is said
To cure the wounds the vermine made;
And weapons, drest with salves, restore
And heal the hurts they gave before;
But whether Presbyterians have
So much good nature as the salve,
Or virtue in them as the vermine,
Those who have try'd them can determine.
Indeed, 'th pity you should miss
Th' arrears of all your services,
And for th' eternal obligation
Y' have laid upon th' ungrateful nation,
Be us'd so unconscionably hard,
As not to find a just reward,
For letting rapine loose, and murther,

To rage just so far, but no further;
And setting all the land on fire,
To burn't to a scantling, but no higher;
For vent'ring to assassinate,
And cut the throats, of Church and State,
And not be allow'd the fittest men
To take the charge of both agen:
Especially, that have the grace
Of self-denying, gifted face;
Who when your projects have miscarry'd,
Can lay them, with undaunted forehead,
On those you painfully trepann'd,
And sprinkled in at second hand;
As we have been, to share the guilt
Of Christian Blood, devoutly spilt;
For so our ignorance was flamm'd
To damn ourselves, t' avoid being damn'd;
Till finding your old foe, the hangman,
Was like to lurch you at back-gammon
And win your necks upon the set,
As well as ours, who did but bet,
(For he had drawn your ears before,
And nick'd them on the self-same score,)
We threw the box and dice away,
Before y' had lost us, at foul play;
And brought you down to rook, and lie,
And fancy only, on the by;
Redeem'd your forfeit jobbernoles
From perching upon lofty poles;
And rescu'd all your outward traitors
From hanging up like aligators;
For which ingeniously y' have shew'd
Your Presbyterian gratitude:
Would freely have paid us home in kind,
And not have been one rope behind.
Those were your motives to divide,
And scruple, on the other side.
To turn your zealous frauds, and force,
To fits of conscience and remorse;
To be convinc'd they were in vain,
And face about for new again;
For truth no more unveil'd your eyes,
Than maggots are convinc'd to flies
And therefore all your lights and calls
Are but apocryphal and false,
To charge us with the consequences
Of all your native insolences,
That to your own imperious wills

Laid Law and Gospel neck and heels;
Corrupted the Old Testament,
To serve the New for precedent
T' amend its errors, and defects,
With murther, and rebellion texts;
Of which there is not any one
In all the Book to sow upon
And therefore (from your tribe) the Jews
Held Christian doctrine forth, and use;
As Mahomet (your chief) began
To mix them in the Alchoran:
Denounc'd and pray'd, with fierce devotion,
And bended elbows on the cushion;
Stole from the beggars all your tones,
And gifted mortifying groans;
Had Lights where better eyes were blind,
As pigs are said to see the wind
Fill'd Bedlam with predestination,
And Knights-bridge with illumination:
Made children, with your tones, to run for't,
As bad as bloody-bones, or LUNSFORD:
While women, great with child, miscarry'd,
For being to malignants marry'd
Transform'd all wives to DALILAHS
Whose husbands were not for the Cause;
And turn'd the men to ten horn'd cattle,
Because they came not out to battle
Made taylors' prentices turn heroes,
For fear of being transform'd to MEROZ:
And rather forfeit their indentures,
Than not espouse the Saints' adventures.
Could transubstantiate, metamorphose,
And charm whole herds of beasts, like Orpheus;
Inchant the King's and Churches lands
T' obey and follow your commands;
And settle on a new freehold,
As MARCLY-HILL had done of old:
Could turn the Covenant, and translate
The gospel into spoons and plate:
Expound upon all merchants' cashes,
And open th' intricatest places
Could catechize a money-box,
And prove all powches orthodox;
Until the Cause became a DAMON,
And PYTHIAS the wicked Mammon.

And yet, in spight of all your charms
To conjure legion up in arms,

And raise more devils in the rout
Than e'er y' were able to cast out,
Y' have been reduc'd, and by those fools
Bred up (you say) in your own schools;
Who, though but gifted at your feet,
Have made it plain, they have more wit;
By whom y' have been so oft trepann'd,
And held forth out of all command,
Out-gifted, out-impuls'd, out-done,
And out-reveal'd at carryings-on;
Of all your dispensations worm'd,
Out-Providenc'd, and out-reform'd;
Ejected out of Church and State,
And all things, but the peoples' hate;
And spirited out of th' enjoyments
Of precious, edifying employments,
By those who lodg'd their Gifts and Graces,
Like better bowlers, in your places;
All which you bore with resolution,
Charg'd on th' accompt of persecution;
And though most righteously opprest,
Against your wills, still acquiesc'd;
And never hum'd and hah'd sedition,
Nor snuffled treason, nor misprision.
That is, because you never durst;
For had you preach'd and pray'd your worst,
Alas! you were no longer able
To raise your posse of the rabble:
One single red-coat centinel
Out-charm'd the magick of the spell;
And, with his squirt-fire, could disperse
Whole troops with chapter rais'd and verse.
We knew too well those tricks of yours,
To leave it ever in your powers;
Or trust our safeties, or undoings,
To your disposing of out-goings;
Or to your ordering Providence,
One farthing's-worth of consequence.
For had you pow'r to undermine,
Or wit to carry a design,
Or correspondence to trepan,
Inveigle, or betray one man,
There's nothing else that intervenes,
And bars your zeal to use the means
And therefore wond'rous like, no doubt,
To bring in Kings, or keep them out.
Brave undertakers to restore,
That cou'd not keep yourselves in pow'r;

T' advance the int'rests of the Crown,
That wanted wit to keep your own.

'Tis true, you have (for I'd be loth
To wrong ye) done your parts in both,
To keep him out, and bring him in,
As grace is introduc'd by sin;
For 'twas your zealous want of sense,
And sanctify'd impertinence,
Your carrying business in a huddle,
That forc'd our rulers to new-model;
Oblig'd the State to tack about,
And turn you, root and branch, all out;
To reformado, one and all,
T' your great Croysado General.
Your greedy slav'ring to devour,
Before 'twas in your clutches, pow'r,
That sprung the game you were to set,
Before y' had time to draw the net;
Your spight to see the Churches' lands
Divided into other hands,
And all your sacrilegious ventures
Laid out in tickets and debentures;
Your envy to he sprinkled down,
By Under-Churches in the town;
And no course us'd to stop their mouths,
Nor th' Independents' spreading growths
All which consider'd, 'tis most true
None bring him in so much as you
Who have prevail'd beyond their plots,
Their midnight juntos, and seal'd knots
That thrive more by your zealous piques,
Than all their own rash politicks
And you this way may claim a share
In carrying (as you brag) th' affair;
Else frogs and toads, that croak'd the Jews
From PHARAOH and his brick-kilns loose,
And flies and mange, that set them free
From task-masters and slavery,
Were likelier to do the feat,
In any indiff'rent man's conceit
For who e'er heard of restoration
Until your thorough Reformation?
That is, the King's and Churches' land
Were sequester'd int' other hands:
For only then, and not before,
Your eyes were open'd to restore.
And when the work was carrying on,

Who cross'd it, but yourselves alone?
As by a world of hints appears,
All plain and extant as your ears.

But first, o' th' first: The Isle of WIGHT
Will rise up, if you should deny't;
Where HENDERSON, and th' other masses,
Were sent to cap texts, and put cases;
To pass for deep and learned scholars,
Although but paltry Ob and Sollers:
As if th' unseasonable fools
Had been a coursing in the schools;
Until th' had prov'd the Devil author
O' th' Covenant, and the Cause his daughter,
For when they charg'd him with the guilt
Of all the blood that had been spilt,
They did not mean he wrought th' effusion,
In person, like Sir PRIDE, or HUGHSON,
But only those who first begun
The quarrel were by him set on;
And who could those be but the Saints,
Those Reformation Termagants?
But e'er this pass'd, the wise debate
Spent so much time, it grew too late;
For OLIVER had gotten ground,
T' inclose him with his warriors round
Had brought his Providence about,
And turn'd th' untimely sophists out,
Nor had the UXBRIDGE bus'ness less
Of nonsense in't, or sottishness,
When from a scoundrel Holder-forth,
The scum as well as son o' th' earth,
Your mighty Senators took law;
At his command, were forc'd t' withdraw,
And sacrifice the peace o' th' nation
To doctrine, use and application.
So when the SCOTS, your constant cronies,
Th' espousers of your Cause and monies,
Who had so often, in your aid,
So many ways been soundly paid,
Came in at last for better ends,
To prove themselves your trusty friends,
You basely left them, and the Church
They train'd you up to, in the lurch,
And suffer'd your own tribe of Christians
To fall before, as true Philistines.
This shews what utensils y' have been,
To bring the King's concernments in;

Which is so far from being true,
That none but he can bring in you:
And if he take you into trust,
Will find you most exactly just:
Such as will punctually repay
With double interest, and betray.

Not that I think those pantomimes,
Who vary action with the times,
Are less ingenious in their art,
Than those who dully act one part;
Or those who turn from side to side,
More guilty than the wind and tide.
All countries are a wise man's home,
And so are governments to some,
Who change them for the same intrigues
That statesmen use in breaking leagues;
While others, in old faiths and troths,
Look odd as out-of-fashion'd cloths;
And nastier in an old opinion,
Than those who never shift their linnen.

For true and faithful's sure to lose,
Which way soever the game goes;
And whether parties lose or win,
Is always nick'd, or else hedg'd in:
While pow'r usurp'd, like stol'n delight,
Is more bewitching than the right;
And when the times begin to alter,
None rise so high as from the halter.

And so may we, if w' have but sense
To use the necessary means;
And not your usual stratagems
On one another, Lights and Dreams
To stand on terms as positive,
As if we did not take, but give:
Set up the Covenant on crutches,
'Gainst those who have us in their clutches,
And dream of pulling churches down,
Before w' are sure to prop our own:
Your constant method of proceeding,
Without the carnal mans of heeding;
Who 'twixt your inward sense and outward,
Are worse, than if y' had none, accoutred.
I grant, all courses are in vain,
Unless we can get in again;
The only way that's left us now;

But all the difficulty's, How?
'Tis true, w' have money, th' only pow 'r
That all mankind falls down before;
Money, that, like the swords of kings,
Is the last reason of all things;
And therefore need not doubt our play
Has all advantages that way;
As long as men have faith to sell,
And meet with those that can pay well;
Whose half-starv'd pride, and avarice,
One Church and State will not suffice
T' expose to sale, beside the wages
Of storing plagues to after-ages.
Nor is our money less our own,
Than 'twas before we laid it down;
For 'twill return, and turn t' account,
If we are brought, in play upon't:
Or but, by casting knaves, get in,
What pow 'r can hinder us to win?
We know the arts we us'd before,
In peace and war, and something more;
And by th' unfortunate events,
Can mend our next experiments:
For when w' are taken into trust,
How easy are the wisest choust?
Who see but th' outsides of our feats,
And not their secret springs and weights;
And while they're busy at their ease,
Can carry what designs we please.
How easy is it to serve for agents,
To prosecute our old engagements?
To keep the Good Old Cause on foot,
And present power from taking root?
Inflame them both with false alarms
Of plots and parties taking arms;
To keep the Nation's wounds too wide
From healing up of side to side;
Profess the passionat'st concerns
For both their interests by turns;
The only way to improve our own,
By dealing faithfully with none;
(As bowls run true, by being made
On purpose false, and to be sway'd:)
For if we should be true to either,
'Twould turn us out of both together;
And therefore have no other means
To stand upon our own defence,
But keeping up our ancient party

In vigour, confident and hearty:
To reconcile our late dissenters,
Our brethren, though by other venters;
Unite them, and their different maggots,
As long and short sticks are in faggots,
And make them join again as close
As when they first began t' espouse;
Erect them into separate
New Jewish tribes, in Church and State;
To join in marriage and commerce,
And only among themselves converse;
And all that are not of their mind,
Make enemies to all mankind:
Take all religions in and stickle
From Conclave down to Conventicle;
Agreeing still, or disagreeing,
According to the Light in being.
Sometimes for liberty of conscience,
And spiritual mis-rule, in one sense;
But in another quite contrary,
As dispensations chance to vary;
And stand for, as the times will bear it,
All contradictions of the Spirit:
Protect their emissaries, empower'd
To preach sedition and the word;
And when they're hamper'd by the laws,
Release the lab'rers for the Cause,
And turn the persecution back
On those that made the first attack;
To keep them equally in awe,
From breaking or maintaining law:
And when they have their fits too soon,
Before the full-tides of the moon,
Put off their zeal t' a fitter season
For sowing faction in and treason;
And keep them hooded, and their Churches,
Like hawks from baiting on their perches,
That, when the blessed time shall come
Of quitting BABYLON and ROME,
They may be ready to restore
Their own Fifth Monarchy once more.

Meanwhile be better arm'd to fence
Against revolts of Providence.
By watching narrowly, and snapping
All blind sides of it, they happen
For if success could make us Saints,
Or ruin turn'd us miscreants:

A scandal that wou'd fall too hard
Upon a few, and. unprepar'd.

These are the courses we must run,
Spight of our hearts, or be undone;
And not to stand on terms and freaks,
Before we have secur'd our necks;
But do our work, as out of sight,
As stars by day, and suns by night;
All licence of the people own,
In opposition to the Crown;
And for the Crown as fiercely side,
The head and body to divide;
The end of all we first design'd,
And all that yet remains behind
Be sure to spare no publick rapine,
On all emergencies, that happen;
For 'tis as easy to supplant
Authority as men in want;
As some of us, in trusts, have made
The one hand with the other trade;
Gain'd vastly by their joint endeavour;
The right a thief; the left receiver;
And what the one, by tricks, forestall'd,
The other, by as sly, retail'd.
For gain has wonderful effects
T' improve the Factory of Sects;
The rule of faith in all professions.
And great DIANA of the EPHESIANS;
Whence turning of Religion's made
The means to turn and wind a trade:
And though some change it for the worse,
They put themselves into a course;
And draw in store of customers,
To thrive the better in commerce:
For all Religions flock together,
Like tame and wild fowl of a feather;
To nab the itches of their sects,
As jades do one another's necks.
Hence 'tis, Hypocrisy as well
Will serve t' improve a Church as ZEAL:
As Persecution or Promotion,
Do equally advance Devotion.

Let business, like ill watches, go
Sometime too fast, sometime too slow;
For things in order are put out
So easy, Ease itself will do't;

But when the feat's design'd and meant,
What miracle can bar th' event?
For 'tis more easy to betray,
Than ruin any other way.
All possible occasions start
The weighty'st matters to divert;
Obstruct, perplex, distract, intangle,
And lay perpetual trains to wrangle.
But in affairs of less import,
That neither do us good nor hurt,
And they receive as little by,
Out-fawn as much, and out-comply;
And seem as scrupulously just,
To bait our hooks for greater trust;
But still be careful to cry down
All publick actions, though our own:
The least miscarriage aggravate,
And charge it all upon the Sate;
Express the horrid'st detestation,
And pity the distracted nation
Tell stories scandalous and false,
I' th' proper language of cabals,
Where all a subtle statesman says,
Is half in words, and half in face;
(As Spaniards talk in dialogues
Of heads and shoulders, nods and shrugs:)
Entrust it under solemn vows
Of mum, and silence, and the rose,
To be retail'd again in whispers,
For th' easy credulous to disperse.

Thus far the Statesman — When a shout,
Heard at a distance, put him out;
And straight another, all aghast,
Rush'd in with equal fear and haste;
Who star'd about, as pale as death,
And, for a while, as out of breath;
Till having gather'd up his wits,
He thus began his tale by fits.

That beastly rabble — that came down
From all the garrets — in the town,
And stalls, and shop-boards — in vast swarms,
With new-chalk'd bills — and rusty arms,
To cry the Cause — up, heretofore,
And bawl the BISHOPS — out of door,
Are now drawn up — in greater shoals,
To roast — and broil us on the coals,

And all the Grandees — of our Members
Are carbonading — on the embers;
Knights, Citizens, and Burgesses —
Held forth by Rumps — of Pigs and Geese,
That serve for Characters — and Badges.
To represent their Personages:
Each bonfire is a funeral pile,
In which they roast, and scorch, and broil,
And ev'ry representative
Have vow'd to roast — and broil alive:

And 'tis a miracle, we are not
Already sacrific' d incarnate.
For while we wrangle here, and jar,
W' are grilly'd all at TEMPLE-BAR:
Some on the sign-post of an ale-house,
Hang in effigy, on the gallows;
Made up of rags, to personate
Respective Officers of State;
That henceforth they may stand reputed,
Proscrib'd in law, and executed;
And while the Work is carrying on
Be ready listed under DON,
That worthy patriot, once the bellows,
And tinder-box, of all his fellows;
The activ'st Member of the Five,
As well as the most primitive;
Who, for his faithful service then
Is chosen for a Fifth agen:
(For since the State has made a Quint
Of Generals, he's listed in't.)
This worthy, as the world will say,
Is paid in specie, his own way;
For, moulded to the life in clouts,
Th' have pick'd from dung-hills hereabouts,
He's mounted on a hazel bavin,
A cropp'd malignant baker gave 'm;
And to the largest bone-fire riding,
They've roasted COOK already and PRIDE in;
On whom in equipage and state,
His scarecrow fellow-members wait,
And march in order, two and two,
As at thanksgivings th' us'd to do;
Each in a tatter'd talisman,
Like vermin in effigie slain.

But (what's more dreadful than the rest)
Those Rumps are but the tail o' th' Beast,

Set up by Popish engineers,
As by the crackers plainly appears;
For none but Jesuits have a mission
To preach the faith with ammunition,
And propagate the Church with powder:
Their founder was a blown-up Soldier.
These spiritual pioneers o' th' Whore's,
That have the charge of all her stores,
Since first they fail'd in their designs,
To take in Heav'n by springing mines,
And with unanswerable barrels
Of gunpowder dispute their quarrels,
Now take a course more practicable,
By laying trains to fire the rabble,
And blow us up in th' open streets,
Disguis'd in Rumps, like Sambenites;
More like to ruin, and confound,
Than all the doctrines under ground.

Nor have they chosen Rumps amiss
For symbols of State-mysteries;
Though some suppose 'twas but to shew
How much they scorn'd the Saints, the few;
Who, 'cause they're wasted to the stumps,
Are represented best by Rumps.
But Jesuits have deeper reaches
In all their politick far-fetches,
And from the Coptick Priest, Kircherus,
Found out this mystick way to jeer us.
For, as th' Egyptians us'd by bees
T' express their antick PTOLOMIES;
And by their stings, the swords they wore,
Held forth authority and power;
Because these subtil animals
Bear all their int'rests in their tails;
And when they're once impar'd in that,
Are banish'd their well-order'd state;
They thought all governments were best
By Hieroglyphick Rumps exprest.

For, as in bodies natural,
The rump's the fundament of all;
So, in a commonwealth, or realm,
The government is call'd the helm;
With which, like vessels under sail,
They're turn'd and winded by the tail;
The tail, which birds and fishes steer
Their courses with through sea and air;

To whom the rudder of the rump is
The same thing with the stern and compass.
This shews how perfectly the Rump
And Commonwealth in nature jump.
For as a fly, that goes to bed,
Rests with his tail above his head,
So in this mungrel state of ours;
The rabble are the supreme powers;
That hors'd us on their backs, to show us
A jadish trick at last, and throw us.

The learned Rabbins of the Jews
Write there's a bone, which they call leuz,
I' th' rump of man, of such a virtue,
No force in nature can do hurt to;
And therefore at the last great day,
All th' other members shall, they say,
Spring out of this, as from a seed
All sorts of vegetals proceed;
From whence the learned sons of art
Os Sacrum justly stile that part.
Then what can better represent
Than this Rump Bone the Parliament;
That, alter several rude ejections,
And as prodigious resurrections,
With new reversions of nine lives,
Starts up, and like a cat revives?

But now, alas! they're all expir'd,
And th' House, as well as Members, fir'd;
Consum'd in kennels by the rout,
With which they other fires put out:
Condemn'd t' ungoverning distress,
And paultry, private wretchedness;
Worse than the Devil, to privation,
Beyond all hopes of restoration;
And parted, like the body and soul,
From all dominion and controul.
We, who cou'd lately with a look
Enact, establish, or revoke;
Whose arbitrary nods gave law,
And frowns kept multitudes in awe;
Before the bluster of whose huff,
All hats, as in a storm, flew off;
Ador'd and bowed to by the great,
Down to the footman and valet;
Had more bent knees than chapel-mats,
And prayers than the crowns of hats;

Shall now be scorn'd as wretchedly;
For ruin's just as low as high;
Which might be suffer'd, were it all
The horror that attends our fall:
For some of us have scores more large
Than heads and quarters can discharge;
And others, who, by restless scraping,
With publick frauds, and private rapine,
Have mighty heaps of wealth amass'd,
Would gladly lay down all at last;
And to be but undone, entail
Their vessels on perpetual jail;
And bless the Dev'l to let them farms
Of forfeit souls on no worse terms.

This said, a near and louder shout
Put all th' assembly to the rout,
Who now begun t' out-run their fear,
As horses do from whom they bear;
But crowded on with so mach haste,
Until th' had block'd the passage fast,
And barricado'd it with haunches
Of outward men, and bulks, and paunches,
That with their shoulders strove to squeeze,
And rather save a crippled piece
Of all their crush'd and broken members,
Than have them grilled on the embers;
Still pressing on with heavy packs
Of one another on their backs:
The van-guard could no longer hear
The charges of the forlorn rear,
But, born down headlong by the rout,
Were trampled sorely under foot:
Yet nothing prov'd so formidable
As the horrid cookery of the rabble;
And fear, that keeps all feeling out,
As lesser pains are by the gout,
Reliev'd 'em with a fresh supply
Of rallied force enough to fly,
And beat a Tuscan running-horse,
Whose jockey-rider is all spurs.

PART III

CANTO III

THE ARGUMENT

The Knight and squire's prodigious Flight
To quit th' inchanted Bow'r by Night.
He plods to turn his amorous Suit
T' a Plea in Law, and prosecute
Repairs to Counsel, to advise
'Bout managing the Enterprise;
But first resolves to try by Letter,
And one more fair Address, to get her.

Who wou'd believe what strange bugbears
Mankind creates itself of fears
That spring like fern, that insect weed,
Equivocally, without seed;
And have no possible foundation,
But merely in th' imagination;
And yet can do more dreadful feats
Than hags, with all their imps and teats
Make more bewitch and haunt themselves
Than all their nurseries of elves?
For fear does things so like a witch,
'Tis hard t' unriddle which is which:
Sets up Communities of senses,
To chop and change intelligences;
As Rosicrucian virtuosos
Can see with ears, and hear with noses;
And when they neither see nor hear,
Have more than both supply'd by fear
That makes 'em in the dark see visions,
And hag themselves with apparitions;
And when their eyes discover least,
Discern the subtlest objects best
Do things not contrary, alone,
To th' course of nature, but its own;
The courage of the bravest daunt,
And turn poltroons as valiant:
For men as resolute appear
With too much as too little fear
And when they're out of hopes of flying,
Will run away from death by dying;
Or turn again to stand it out,
And those they fled, like lions, rout.

This HUDIBRAS had prov'd too true,
Who, by the furies left perdue,
And haunted with detachments, sent

From Marshal Legion's regiment,
Was by a fiend, as counterfeit,
Reliev'd and rescu'd with a cheat;
When nothing but himself, and fear,
Was both the imp and conjurer;
As, by the rules o' th' virtuosi,
It follows in due form of poesie.

Disguis'd in all the masks of night,
We left our champion on his flight,
At blind man's buff, to grope his way,
In equal fear of night and day,
Who took his dark and desp'rate course,
He knew no better than his horse;
And, by an unknown Devil led,
(He knew as little whither,) fled.
He never was in greater need,
Nor less capacity, of speed;
Disabled, both in man and beast,
To fly and run away his best;
To keep the enemy, and fear,
From equal falling on his rear.
And though with kicks and bangs he ply'd
The further and the nearer side,
(As seamen ride with all their force,
And tug as if they row'd the horse,
And when the hackney sails most swift,
Believe they lag, or run a-drift,)
So, though he posted e'er so fast,
His fear was greater than his haste:
For fear, though fleeter than the wind,
Believes 'tis always left behind.
But when the morn began t' appear,
And shift t' another scene his fear,
He found his new officious shade,
That came so timely to his aid,
And forc'd him from the foe t' escape,
Had turn'd itself to RALPHO's shape;
So like in person, garb, and pitch,
'Twas hard t' interpret which was which.

For RALPHO had no sooner told
The Lady all he had t' unfold,
But she convey'd him out of sight,
To entertain the approaching Knight;
And, while he gave himself diversion,
T' accommodate his beast and person,
And put his beard into a posture

At best advantage to accost her,
She order'd th' anti-masquerade
(For his reception) aforesaid:
But when the ceremony was done,
The lights put out, and furies gone,
And HUDIBRAS, among the rest,
Convey'd away, as RALPHO guess'd,
The wretched caitiff, all alone,
(As he believ'd) began to moan,
And tell his story to himself,
The Knight mistook him for an elf;
And did so still till he began
To scruple at RALPH's Outward Man;
And thought, because they oft agreed
T' appear in one another's stead,
And act the Saint's and Devil's part
With undistinguishable art,
They might have done so now, perhaps,
And put on one another's shapes
And therefore, to resolve the doubt,
He star'd upon him, and cry'd out,
What art? My 'Squire, or that bold Sprite
That took his place and shape to-night?
Some busy indepenent pug,
Retainer to his Synagogue?
Alas! quoth he, I'm none of those,
Your bosom friends, as you suppose;
But RALPH himself, your trusty 'Squire,
Wh' has dragg'd your Dunship out o' th' mire,
And from th' inchantments of a widow,
Wh' had turn'd you int' a beast, have freed you;
And, though a prisoner of war,
Have brought you safe where you now are;
Which you would gratefully repay
Your constant Presbyterian way.

That's stranger (quoth the Knight) and stranger.
Who gave thee notice of my danger?

Quoth he, Th' infernal Conjurer
Pursu'd and took me prisoner;
And knowing you were hereabout,
Brought me along to find you out;
Where I, in hugger-mugger hid,
Have noted all they said or did:
And though they lay to him the pageant,
I did not see him, nor his agent;
Who play'd their sorceries out of sight,

T' avoid a fiercer second fight.
But didst thou see no Devils then?
Not one (quoth he) but carnal men,
A little worse than fiends in hell,
And that She-Devil Jezebel,
That laugh'd and tee-he'd with derision,
To see them take your deposition.

What then (quoth HUDIBRAS) was he
That play'd the Dev'l to examine me?
A rallying weaver in the town,
That did it in a parson's gown;
Whom all the parish take for gifted;
But, for my part, I ne'er believ'd it:
In which you told them all your feats,
Your conscientious frauds and cheats;
Deny'd your whipping, and confest
The naked truth of all the rest,
More plainly than the Rev'rend Writer,
That to our Churches veil'd his Mitre;
All which they took in black and white,
And cudgell'd me to under-write.

What made thee, when they all were gone,
And none but thou and I alone,
To act the Devil, and forbear
To rid me of my hellish fear?

Quoth he, I knew your constant rate
And frame of sp'rit too obstinate
To be by me prevail'd upon
With any motives of my own;
And therefore strove to counterfeit
The Dev'l a-while, to nick your wit;
The Devil, that is your constant crony,
That only can prevail upon ye;
Else we might still have been disputing,
And they with weighty drubs confuting.

The Knight who now began to find
Th' had left the enemy behind,
And saw no farther harm remain,
But feeble weariness and pain;
Perceiv'd, by losing of their way,
Th' had gain'd th' advantage of the day;
And, by declining of the road,
They had, by chance, their rear made good;
He ventur'd to dismiss his fear,

That parting's wont to rent and tear,
And give the desperat'st attack
To danger still behind its back.
For having paus'd to recollect,
And on his past success reflect,
T' examine and consider why,
And whence, and how, they came to fly,
And when no Devil had appear'd,
What else, it cou'd be said, he fear'd;
It put him in so fierce a rage,
He once resolv'd to re-engage;
Toss'd like a foot-ball back again,
With shame and vengeance, and disdain.
Quoth he, it was thy cowardice
That made me from this leaguer rise
And when I'd half reduc'd the place,
To quit it infamously base
Was better cover'd by the new
Arriv'd detachment then I knew;
To slight my new acquests, and run
Victoriously from battles won;
And reck'ning all I gain'd or lost,
To sell them cheaper than they cost;
To make me put myself to flight,
And conqu'ring run away by night
To drag me out, which th' haughty foe
Durst never have presum'd to do
To mount me in the dark, by force,
Upon the bare ridge of my horse;
Expos'd in querpo to their rage,
Without my arms and equipage;
Lest, if they ventur'd to pursue,
I might th' unequal fight renew;
And, to preserve thy Outward Man,
Assum'd my place, and led the van.

All this quoth RALPH, I did, 'tis true,
Not to preserve my self, but you;
You, who were damn'd to baser drubs
Than wretches feel in powd'ring tubs.
To mount two-wheel'd carroches, worse
Than managing a wooden-horse
Dragg'd out through straiter holes by th' ears,
Eras'd or coup'd for perjurers;
Who, though th' attempt had prov'd in vain,
Had had no reason to complain:
But since it prosper'd, 'tis unhandsome
To blame the hand that paid our ransome,

And rescu'd your obnoxious bones
From unavoidable battoons.
The enemy was reinforc'd,
And we disabled, and unhors'd,
Disarm'd, unqualify'd for fight,
And no way left but hasty flight,
Which though as desp'rate in th' attempt,
Has giv'n you freedom to condemn't.
But were our bones in fit condition
To reinforce the expedition,
'Tis now unseasonable, and vain,
To think of falling on again.
No martial project to surprize
Can ever be attempted twice;
Nor cast design serve afterwards,
As gamesters tear their losing-cards,
Beside, our bangs of man and beast
Are fit for nothing now but rest;
And for a-while will not be able
To rally, and prove serviceable;
And therefore I, with reason, chose
This stratagem t' amuse our foes;
To make an honourable retreat,
And wave a total sure defeat;
For those that fly may fight again,
Which he can never do that's slain.
Hence timely running's no mean part
Of conduct in the martial art;
By which some glorious feats atchieve,
As citizens by breaking thrive;
And cannons conquer armies, while
They seem to draw off and recoil;
Is held the gallantest course, and bravest
To great exploits, as well as safest;
That spares th' expence of time and pains,
And dangerous beating out of brains;
And in the end prevails as certain
As those that never trust to fortune;
But make their fear do execution
Beyond the stoutest resolution;
As earthquakes kill without a blow,
And, only trembling, overthrow,
If th' ancients crown'd their bravest men
That only sav'd a citizen,
What victory could e'er be won,
If ev'ry one would save but one
Or fight endanger'd to be lost,
Where all resolve to save the most?

By this means, when a battle's won,
The war's as far from being done;
For those that save themselves, and fly,
Go halves, at least, i' th' victory;
And sometimes, when the loss is small,
And danger great, they challenge all;
Print new additions to their feats,
And emendations in Gazettes;
And when, for furious haste to run,
They durst not stay to fire a gun,
Have done't with bonfires, and at home
Made squibs and crackers overcome;
To set the rabble on a flame,
And keep their governors from blame;
Disperse the news the pulpit tells,
Confirm'd with fire-works and with bells;
And though reduc'd to that extream,
They have been forc'd to sing Te Deum;
Yet, with religious blasphemy,
By flattering Heaven with a lie
And for their beating giving thanks,
Th' have rais'd recruits, and fill'd their banks;
For those who run from th' enemy,
Engage them equally to fly;
And when the fight becomes a chace,
Those win the day that win the race
And that which would not pass in fights,
Has done the feat with easy flights;
Recover'd many a desp'rate campaign
With Bordeaux, Burgundy, and Champaign;
Restor'd the fainting high and mighty
With brandy-wine and aqua-vitae;
And made 'em stoutly overcome
With bachrach, hoccamore, and mum;
Whom the uncontroul'd decrees of fate
To victory necessitate;
With which, although they run or burn
They unavoidably return:
Or else their sultan populaces
Still strangle all their routed Bassas.

Quoth HUDIBRAS, I understand
What fights thou mean'st at sea and land,
And who those were that run away,
And yet gave out th' had won the day;
Although the rabble sous'd them for't,
O'er head and ears in mud and dirt.
'Tis true, our modern way of war

Is grown more politick by far,
But not so resolute, and bold,
Nor ty'd to honour, as the old.
For now they laugh at giving battle,
Unless it be to herds of cattle;
Or fighting convoys of provision,
The whole design o' the expedition:
And not with downright blows to rout
The enemy, but eat them out:
As fighting, in all beasts of prey,
And eating, are perform'd one way,
To give defiance to their teeth
And fight their stubborn guts to death;
And those atchieve the high'st renown,
That bring the others' stomachs down,
There's now no fear of wounds, nor maiming;
All dangers are reduc'd to famine;
And feats of arms, to plot, design,
Surprize, and stratagem, and mine;
But have no need nor use of courage,
Unless it be for glory or forage:
For if they fight, 'tis but by chance,
When one side vent'ring to advance,
And come uncivilly too near,
Are charg'd unmercifully i' th' rear;
And forc'd with terrible resistance,
To keep hereafter at a distance;
To pick out ground to incamp upon,
Where store of largest rivers run,
That serve, instead of peaceful barriers,
To part th' engagements of their warriors;
Where both from side to side may skip,
And only encounter at bo-peep:
For men are found the stouter-hearted,
The certainer th' are to be parted,
And therefore post themselves in bogs,
As th' ancient mice attack'd the frogs,
And made their mortal enemy,
The water-rat, their strict ally.
For 'tis not now, who's stout and bold,
But who bears hunger best, and cold;
And he's approv'd the most deserving,
Who longest can hold out at starving;
And he that routs most pigs and cows,
The formidablest man of prowess.
So th' emperor CALIGULA,
That triumph'd o'er the British Sea,
Took crabs and oysters prisoners,

Lobsters, 'stead of cuirasiers,
Engag'd his legions in fierce bustles
With periwinkles, prawns, and muscles;
And led his troops with furious gallops,
To charge whole regiments of scallops
Not like their ancient way of war,
To wait on his triumphal carr
But when he went to dine or sup
More bravely eat his captives up;
And left all war, by his example,
Reduc'd to vict'ling of a camp well.

Quoth RALPH, By all that you have said,
And twice as much that I cou'd add,
'Tis plain you cannot now do worse,
Than take this out-of-fashion'd course;
To hope, by stratagem, to woo her,
Or waging battle to subdue her
Though some have done it in romances,
And bang'd them into amorous fancies;
As those who won the AMAZONS,
By wanton drubbing of their bones;
And stout Rinaldo gain'd his bride,
By courting of her back and side.
But since those times and feats are over,
They are not for a modern lover,
When mistresses are too cross-grain'd
By such addresses to be gain'd;
And if they were, wou'd have it out
With many another kind of bout.
Therefore I hold no course s' infeasible,
As this of force to win the JEZEBEL;
To storm her heart, by th' antick charms
Of ladies errant, force of arms;
But rather strive by law to win her,
And try the title you have in her.
Your case is clear; you have her word,
And me to witness the accord
Besides two more of her retinue
To testify what pass'd between you;
More probable, and like to hold,
Than hand, or seal, or breaking gold;
For which so many, that renounc'd
Their plighted contracts, have been trounc'd
And bills upon record been found,
That forc'd the ladies to compound;
And that, unless I miss the matter,
Is all the bus'ness you look after.

Besides, encounters at the bar
Are braver now than those in war,
In which the law does execution
With less disorder and confusion
Has more of honour in't, some hold
Not like the new way, but the old
When those the pen had drawn together,
Decided quarrels with the feather,
And winged arrows kill'd as dead,
And more than bullets now of lead.
So all their combats now, as then,
Are manag'd chiefly by the pen;
That does the feat with braver vigours,
In words at length, as well as figures;
Is judge of all the world performs
In voluntary feats of arms
And whatsoe'er's atchiev'd in fight,
Determines which is wrong or right:
For whether you prevail, or lose
All must be try'd there in the close;
And therefore 'tis not wise to shun
What you must trust to ere y' have done.

The law, that settles all you do,
And marries where you did but woo;
That makes the most perfidious lover
A lady, that's as false, recover;
And if it judge upon your side,
Will soon extend her for your bride;
And put her person, goods, or lands,
Or which you like best int' your hands.

For law's the wisdom of all ages,
And manag'd by the ablest sages;
Who, though their bus'ness at the bar
Be but a kind of civil war,
In which th' engage with fiercer dudgeons
Than e'er the GRECIANS did and TROJANS,
They never manage the contest
T' impair their public interest;
Or by their controversies lessen
The dignity of their profession:
Not like us Brethren, who divide
Our Commonwealth, the Cause, and Side;
And though w' are all as near of kindred
As th' outward man is to the inward,
We agree in nothing, but to wrangle
About the slightest fingle-fangle;

While lawyers have more sober sense
Than t' argue at their own expence,
But make their best advantages
Of others' quarrels, like the Swiss;
And, out of foreign controversies,
By aiding both sides, fill their purses;
But have no int'rest in the cause
For which th' engage, and wage the laws;
Nor further prospect than their pay,
Whether they lose or win the day:
And though th' abounded in all ages,
With sundry learned clerks and sages,
Though all their business be dispute,
Which way they canvass ev'ry suit,
Th' have no disputes about their art,
Nor in Polemicks controvert:
While all professions else are found
With nothing but disputes t' abound
Divines of all sorts, and physicians,
Philosophers, mathematicians:
The Galenist and Paracelsian
Condemn the way each other deals in:
Anatomists dissect and mangle,
To cut themselves out work to wrangle
Astrologers dispute their dreams,
That in their sleeps they talk of schemes:
And heralds stickle, who got who
So many hundred years ago.

But lawyers are too wise a nation
T' expose their trade to disputation;
Or make the busy rabble judges
Of all their secret piques and grudges;
In which whoever wins the day,
The whole profession's sure to pay.
Beside, no mountebanks, nor cheats,
Dare undertake to do their feats,
When in all other sciences
They swarm, like insects, and increase.

For what bigot durst ever draw,
By inward light, a deed in law?
Or could hold forth, by revelation,
An answer to a declaration?
For those that meddle with their tools
Will cut their fingers, if they're fools;
And if you follow their advice,
In bills, and answers, and replies,

They'll write a love-letter in chancery,
Shall bring her upon oath to answer ye,
And soon reduce her to b' your wife,
Or make her weary of her life.

The Knight, who us'd with tricks and shifts
To edify by RALPHO's Gifts,
But in appearance cry'd him down,
To make them better seem his own,
(All Plagiaries' constant course
Of sinking when they take a purse),
Resolv'd to follow his advice,
But kept it from him by disguise;
And, after stubborn contradiction,
To counterfeit his own conviction,
And by transition fall upon
The resolution as his own.

Quoth he, This gambol thou advisest
Is of all others the unwisest;
For if I think by law to gain her,
There's nothing sillier or vainer
'Tis but to hazard my pretence,
Where nothing's certain, but th' expence;
To act against myself, and traverse
My suit and title, to her favours
And if she shou'd (which Heav'n forbid)
O'erthrow me, as the fidler did,
What aftercourse have I to take,
'Gainst losing all I have at stake?
He that with injury is griev'd,
And goes to law to be reliev'd,
Is sillier than a sottish chowse,
Who, when thief has robb'd his house,
Applies himself to cunning men,
To help him to his goods agen;
When all he can expect to gain,
Is but to squander more in vain;
And yet I have no other way
But is as difficult to play.
For to reduce her by main force,
Is now in vain; by fair means, worse;
But worst of all, to give her over,
'Till she's as desp'rate to recover
For bad games are thrown up too soon,
Until th' are never to be won.
But since I have no other course,
But is as bad t' attempt, or worse,

He that complies against his will,
Is of his own opinion still;
Which he may adhere to, yet disown,
For reasons to himself best known:
But 'tis not to b' avoided now,
For SIDROPHEL resolves to sue;
Whom I must answer, or begin
Inevitably first with him.
For I've receiv'd advertisement,
By times enough, of his intent;
And knowing he that first complains
Th' advantage of the business gains;
For Courts of Justice understand
The plaintiff to be eldest hand;
Who what he pleases may aver;
The other, nothing, till he swear;
Is freely admitted to all grace,
And lawful favour, by his place;
And, for his bringing custom in,
Has all advantages to win.
I, who resolve to oversee
No lucky opportunity,
Will go to council, to advise
Which way t' encounter, or surprize,
And, after long consideration,
Have found out one to fit th' occasion;
Most apt for what I have to do,
As counsellor and justice too.
And truly so, no doubt, he was,
A lawyer fit for such a case.

An old dull sot, who told the clock
For many years at Bridewell-dock,
At Westminster, and Hicks's-Hall,
And Hiccius Doctius play'd in all;
Where, in all governments and times,
H' had been both friend and foe to crimes,
And us'd two equal ways of gaining
By hind'ring justice or maintaining;
To many a whore gave priviledge,
And whipp'd for want of quarteridge:
Cart-loads of bawds to prison sent
For b'ing behind a fortnight's rent
And many a trusty pimp and croney
To Puddle-dock for want of money;
Engag'd the constable to seize
All those that would not break the peace,
Nor give him back his own foul words,

Though sometimes Commoners or Lords,
And kept 'em prisoners of course,
For being sober at ill hours;
That in the morning he might free
Or bind 'em over for his fee;
Made monsters fine, and puppet-plays,
For leave to practise in their ways;
Farm'd out all cheats, and went a share
With th' headborough and scavenger;
And made the dirt i' th' streets compound
For taking up the publick ground;
The kennel, and the King's highway,
For being unmolested, pay;
Let out the stocks, and whipping-post,
And cage, to those that gave him most;
Impos'd a tax on bakers' ears,
And for false weights on chandelers;
Made victuallers and vintners fine
For arbitrary ale and wine;
But was a kind and constant friend
To all that regularly offend;
As residentiary bawds,
And brokers that receive stol'n goods;
That cheat in lawful mysteries,
And pay church duties and his fees;
But was implacable, and awkward,
To all that interlop'd and hawker'd.

To this brave man the Knight repairs
For council in his law-affairs
And found him mounted in his pew,
With books and money plac'd for shew,
Like nest-eggs to make clients lay,
And for his false opinion pay
To whom the knight, with comely grace,
Put off his hat to put his case
Which he as proudly entertain'd
As th' other courteously strain'd;
And, to assure him 't was not that
He look'd for, bid him put on's hat.

Quoth he, There is one SIDROPHEL,
Whom I have cudgell'd — Very well.
And now he brags t' have beaten me. —
Better and better still, quoth he. —
And vows to stick me to a wall
Where-e'er he meets me — Best of all.
'Tis true, the knave has taken's oath

That I robb'd him — Well done, in troth
When h' has confess'd he stole my cloak,
And pick'd my fob, and what he took;
Which was the cause that made me bang him,
And take my goods again — Marry hang him.
Now whether I should before-hand,
Swear he robb'd me? — I understand.
Or bring my action of conversion
And trover for my goods? — Ah, Whoreson!
Or if 'tis better to indite,
And bring him to his trial? — Right.
Prevent what he designs to do,
And swear for th' State against him? — True.
Or whether he that is defendant
In this case has the better end on't;
Who, putting in a new cross-bill,
May traverse th' action? — Better still.
Then there's a Lady too — Aye, marry
That's easily prov'd accessary;
A widow, who, by solemn vows
Contracted to me for my spouse,
Combin'd with him to break her word,
And has abetted all. — Good Lord
Suborn'd th' aforesaid SIDROPHEL
To tamper with the Dev'l of Hell;
Who put m' into a horrid fear,
Fear of my life. — Make that appear.
Made an assault with fiends and men
Upon my body. — Good agen,
And kept me in a deadly fright,
And false imprisonment, all night
Mean while they robb'd me, and my horse,
And stole my saddle. — Worse and worse.
And made me mount upon the bare ridge,
T' avoid a wretcheder miscarriage.

Sir, quoth the Lawyer, not to flatter ye,
You have as good and fair a battery
As heart can wish, and need not shame
The proudest man alive to claim.
For if th' have us'd you as you say;
Marry, quoth I, God give you joy.
I wou'd it were my case, I'd give
More than I'll say, or you'll believe.
I would so trounce her, and her purse;
I'd make her kneel for better or worse;
For matrimony and hanging here
Both go by destiny so clear,

That you as sure may pick and choose,
As Cross, I win; and, Pile, you lose;
And, if I durst, I would advance
As much in ready maintenance,
As upon any case I've known,
But we that practise dare not own.
The law severely contrabands
Our taking bus'ness off men's hands;
'Tis common barratry, that bears
Point-blank an action 'gainst our ears
And crops them till there is not leather
To stick a pin in left of either;
For which some do the Summer-sault,
And o'er the bar, like tumblers, vault,
But you may swear, at any rate,
Things not in nature, for the State;
For in all courts of justice here
A witness is not said to swear,
But make oath; that is, in plain terms,
To forge whatever he affirms.

(I thank you, quoth the Knight, for that,
Because 'tis to my purpose pat —)
For Justice, though she's painted blind,
Is to the weaker Side inclin'd,
Like Charity; else right and wrong
Could never hold it out so long,
And, like blind Fortune, with a slight
Convey mens' interest and right
From Stiles's pocket into Nokes's,
As easily as Hocus Pocus;
Play fast and loose; make men obnoxious,
And clear again, like Hiccius Doctius.
Then whether you wou'd take her life,
Or but recover her for your wife,
Or be content with what she has,
And let all other matters pass,
The bus'ness to the law's alone,
The proof is all it looks upon:
And you can want no witnesses
To swear to any thing you please,
That hardly get their mere expences
By th' labour of their consciences;
Or letting out to hire their ears
To affidavit customers,
At inconsiderable values,
To serve for jury-men or tallies,
Although retain'd in th' hardest matters,

Of trustees and administrators.

For that, quoth he, let me alone;
W' have store of such, and all our own;
Bred up and tutor'd by our teachers,

The ablest of conscience-stretchers.
That's well, quoth he; but I should guess,
By weighing all advantages,
Your surest way is first to pitch
On BONGEY for a water-witch;
And when y' have hang'd the conjurer,
Y' have time enough to deal with her.
In th' int'rim, spare for no trepans
To draw her neck into the bans
Ply her with love-letters and billets,
And bait 'em well, for quirks and quillets
With trains t' inveigle, and surprize,
Her heedless answers and replies;
And if she miss the mouse-trap lines,
They'll serve for other by-designs;
And make an artist understand
To copy out her seal or hand;
Or find void places in the paper
To steal in something to intrap her
Till, with her worldly goods and body,
Spight of her heart, she has endow'd ye,
Retain all sorts of witnesses,
That ply i' th' Temple under trees;
Or walk the round, with knights o' th' posts,
About the cross-legg'd knights, their hosts;
Or wait for customers between
The pillars-rows in Lincoln's-Inn
Where vouchers, forgers, common-bail,
And affidavit-men, ne'er fail
T' expose to sale all sorts of oaths,
According to their ears and cloaths,
Their only necessary tools,
Besides the Gospel and their souls;
And when y' are furnish'd with all purveys,
I shall be ready at your service.

I would not give, quoth HUDIBRAS,
A straw to understand a case,
Without the admirable skill
To wind and manage it at will;
To vere, and tack, and steer a cause
Against the weather-gage of laws;

And ring the changes upon cases
As plain as noses upon faces,
As you have well instructed me,
For which you've earn'd (here 'tis) your fee.
I long to practise your advice,
And try the subtle artifice;
To bait a letter, as you bid;
As not long after, thus he did
For having pump'd up all his wit,
And humm'd upon it, thus he writ.

AN HEROICAL EPISTLE OF HUDIBRAS TO HIS LADY

I who was once as great as CAESAR,
Am now reduc'd to NEBUCHADNEZZAR;
And from as fam'd a conqueror
As ever took degree in war,
Or did his exercise in battle,
By you turn'd out to grass with cattle:
For since I am deny'd access
To all my earthly happiness
Am fallen from the paradise
Of your good graces, and fair eyes;
Lost to the world, and you, I'm sent
To everlasting banishment;
Where all the hopes I had t' have won
Your heart, b'ing dash'd, will break my own.

Yet if you were not so severe
To pass your doom before you hear,
You'd find, upon my just defence,
How much y' have wrong'd my innocence.
That once I made a vow to you,
Which yet is unperformed, 'tis true:
But not because it is unpaid,
'Tis violated, though delay'd;
Or, if it were, it is no fau't,
So heinous as you'd have it thought;
To undergo the loss of ears,
Like vulgar hackney perjurers
For there's a diff'rence in the case,
Between the noble and the base,
Who always are observ'd t' have done't
Upon as different an account:
The one for great and weighty cause,
To salve in honour ugly flaws;

For none are like to do it sooner
Than those who are nicest of their honour:
The other, for base gain and pay,
Forswear, and perjure by the day;
And make th' exposing and retailing
Their souls and consciences a calling.

It is no scandal, nor aspersion,
Upon a great and noble person,
To say he nat'rally abhorr'd
Th' old-fashion'd trick, To keep his word;
Though 'tis perfidiousness and shame
In meaner men to do the same:
For to be able to forget,
Is found more useful to the great,
Than gout, or deafness, or bad eyes,
To make 'em pass for wond'rous wise.
But though the law on perjurers
Inflicts the forfeiture of ears,
It is not just that does exempt
The guilty, and punish th' innocent;
To make the ears repair the wrong
Committed by th' ungovern'd tongue;
And when one member is forsworn,
Another to be cropt or torn.
And if you shou'd, as you design,
By course of law, recover mine,
You're like, if you consider right,
To gain but little honour by't.
For he that for his lady's sake
Lays down his life or limbs at stake,
Does not so much deserve her favour,
As he that pawns his soul to have her,
This y' have acknowledg'd I have done,
Although you now disdain to own;
But sentence what you rather ought
T' esteem good service than a fau't.
Besides, oaths are not bound to bear
That literal sense the words infer,
But, by the practice of the age,
Are to be judg'd how far th' engage;
And, where the sense by custom's checkt,
Are found void, and of none effect.
For no man takes or keeps a vow
But just as he sees others do;
Nor are th' oblig'd to be so brittle,
As not to yield and bow a little:
For as best-temper'd blades are found,

Before they break, to bend quite round,
So truest oaths are still most tough,
And though they bow, are breaking proof.
Then wherefore should they not b' allow'd
In love a greater latitude?
For as the law of arms approves
All ways to conquest, so should love's;
And not be ty'd to true or false,
But make that justest that prevails
For how can that which is above
All empire, high and mighty love,
Submit its great prerogative
To any other power alive?
Shall love, that to no crown gives place,
Become the subject of a case?
The fundamental law of nature,
Be over-rul'd by those made after?
Commit the censure of its cause
To any but its own great laws?
Love, that's the world's preservative,
That keeps all souls of things alive;
Controuls the mighty pow'r of fate,
And gives mankind a longer date;
The life of nature, that restores
As fast as time and death devours;
To whose free-gift the world does owe,
Not only earth, but heaven too;
For love's the only trade that's driven,
The interest of state in heav'n,
Which nothing but the soul of man
Is capable to entertain.
For what can earth produce, but love
To represent the joys above?
Or who but lovers can converse,
Like angels, by the eye-discourse?
Address and compliment by vision;
Make love and court by intuition?
And burn in amorous flames as fierce
As those celestial ministers?
Then how can any thing offend,
In order to so great an end?
Or heav'n itself a sin resent,
That for its own supply was meant?
That merits, in a kind mistake,
A pardon for th' offence's sake.
Or if it did not, but the cause
Were left to th' injury at laws,
What tyranny can disapprove

There should be equity in love;
For laws that are inanimate,
And feel no sense of love or hate,
That have no passion of their own,
Nor pity to be wrought upon,
Are only proper to inflict
Revenge on criminals as strict
But to have power to forgive,
Is empire and prerogative;
And 'tis in crowns a nobler gem
To grant a pardon than condemn.
Then since so few do what they ought,
'Tis great t' indulge a well-meant fau't.
For why should he who made address,
All humble ways, without success,
And met with nothing, in return,
But insolence, affronts, and scorn,
Not strive by wit to countermine,
And bravely carry his design?
He who was us'd so unlike a soldier,
Blown up with philters of love-powder?
And after letting blood, and purging,
Condemn'd to voluntary scourging;
Alarm'd with many a horrid fright,
And claw'd by goblins in the night;
Insulted on, revil'd, and jeer'd,
With rude invasion of his beard;
And when your sex was foully scandal'd,
As foully by the rabble handled;
Attack'd by despicable foes,
And drub'd with mean and vulgar blows;
And, after all, to be debarr'd
So much as standing on his guard;
When horses, being spurr'd and prick'd,
Have leave to kick for being kick'd?

Or why should you, whose mother-wits
Are furnish'd with all perquisites,
That with your breeding-teeth begin,
And nursing babies, that lie in,
B' allow'd to put all tricks upon
Our cully sex, and we use none?
We, who have nothing but frail vows
Against your stratagems t' oppose;
Or oaths more feeble than your own,
By which we are no less put down?
You wound, like Parthians, while you fly,
And kill with a retreating eye:

Retire the more, the more we press
To draw us into ambushes.
As pirates all false colours wear
T' intrap th' unwary mariner,
So women, to surprise us, spread
The borrow'd flags of white and red;
Display 'em thicker on their cheeks
Than their old grandmothers, the Picts;
And raise more devils with their looks,
Than conjurer's less subtle books;
Lay trains of amorous intrigues,
In tow'rs, and curls, and perriwigs,
With greater art and cunning rear'd,
Than PHILIP NYE's thanksgiving beard,
Prepost'rously t' entice, and gain
Those to adore 'em they disdain;
And only draw 'em in, to clog
With idle names a catalogue.

A lover is, the more he's brave,
T' his mistress but the more a slave;
And whatsoever she commands,
Becomes a favour from her hands;
Which he's obliged t' obey, and must,
Whether it be unjust or just.
Then when he is compell'd by her
T' adventures he would else forbear,
Who with his honour can withstand,
Since force is greater than command?
And when necessity's obey'd,
Nothing can be unjust or bad
And therefore when the mighty pow'rs
Of love, our great ally and yours,
Join'd forces not to be withstood
By frail enamour'd flesh and blood,
All I have done, unjust or ill,
Was in obedience to your will;
And all the blame that can be due,
Falls to your cruelty and you.
Nor are those scandals I confest,
Against my will and interest,
More than is daily done of course
By all men, when they're under force;
When some upon the rack confess
What th' hangman and their prompters please;
But are no sooner out of pain,
Than they deny it all again.
But when the Devil turns confessor,

Truth is a crime he takes no pleasure
To hear, or pardon, like the founder
Of liars, whom they all claim under
And therefore, when I told him none,
I think it was the wiser done.
Nor am I without precedent,
The first that on th' adventure went
All mankind ever did of course,
And daily dues the same, or worse.
For what romance can show a lover,
That had a lady to recover,
And did not steer a nearer course,
To fall a-board on his amours?
And what at first was held a crime,
Has turn'd to honourable in time.

To what a height did infant ROME,
By ravishing of women, come
When men upon their spouses seiz'd,
And freely marry'd where they pleas'd,
They ne'er forswore themselves, nor ly'd.
Nor, in the mind they were in, dy'd;
Nor took the pains t' address and sue,
Nor play'd the masquerade to woo;
Disdain'd to stay for friends' consents;
Nor juggled about settlements:
Did need no license, nor no priest,
Nor friends, nor kindred, to assist;
Nor lawyers, to join land and money
In th' holy state of matrimony,
Before they settled hands and hearts,
Till alimony or death them parts:
Nor wou'd endure to stay until
Th' had got the very bride's good will;
But took a wise and shorter course
To win the ladies, downright force.
And justly made 'em prisoners then,
As they have often since, us men,
With acting plays, and dancing jigs,
The luckiest of all love's intrigues;
And when they had them at their pleasure,
Then talk'd of love and flames at leisure;
For after matrimony's over,
He that holds out but half a lover,
Deserves for ev'ry minute more
Than half a year of love before;
For which the dames in contemplation
Of that best way of application,

Prov'd nobler wives than e'er was known,
By suit or treaty to be won;
And such as all posterity
Cou'd never equal nor come nigh.

For women first were made for men,
Not men for them. — It follows, then,
That men have right to ev'ry one,
And they no freedom of their own
And therefore men have pow'r to chuse,
But they no charter to refuse.
Hence 'tis apparent, that what course
Soe'er we take to your amours,
Though by the indirectest way,
'Tis no injustice, nor foul play;
And that you ought to take that course,
As we take you, for better or worse;
And gratefully submit to those
Who you, before another, chose.
For why should ev'ry savage beast
Exceed his great lord's interest?
Have freer pow'r than he in grace,
And nature, o'er the creature has?
Because the laws he since has made
Have cut off all the pow'r he had;
Retrench'd the absolute dominion
That nature gave him over women;
When all his pow'r will not extend
One law of nature to suspend;
And but to offer to repeal
The smallest clause, is to rebel.
This, if men rightly understood
Their privilege, they wou'd make good;
And not, like sots, permit their wives
T' encroach on their prerogatives;
For which sin they deserve to be
Kept, as they are, in slavery:
And this some precious Gifted Teachers,
Unrev'rently reputed leachers,
And disobey'd in making love,
Have vow'd to all the world to prove,
And make ye suffer, as you ought,
For that uncharitable fau't.
But I forget myself, and rove
Beyond th' instructions of my love.

Forgive me (Fair) and only blame
Th' extravagancy of my flame,

Since 'tis too much at once to show
Excess of love and temper too.
All I have said that's bad and true,
Was never meant to aim at you,
Who have so sov'reign a controul
O'er that poor slave of yours, my soul,
That, rather than to forfeit you,
Has ventur'd loss of heaven too:
Both with an equal pow'r possest,
To render all that serve you blest:
But none like him, who's destin'd either
To have, or lose you, both together.
And if you'll but this fault release
(For so it must be, since you please)
I'll pay down all that vow, and more,
Which you commanded, and I swore,
And expiate upon my skin
Th' arrears in full of all my sin.
For 'tis but just that I should pay
Th' accruing penance for delay,
Which shall be done, until it move
Your equal pity and your love.

The Knight, perusing this Epistle,
Believ'd h' had brought her to his whistle;
And read it like a jocund lover,
With great applause t' himself, twice over;
Subscrib'd his name, but at a fit
And humble distance to his wit;
And dated it with wond'rous art,
Giv'n from the bottom of his heart;
Then seal'd it with his Coat of Love,
A smoaking faggot — and above,
Upon a scroll — I burn, and weep;
And near it — For her Ladyship;
Of all her sex most excellent,
These to her gentle hands present.
Then gave it to his faithful Squire,
With lessons how t' observe and eye her.

She first consider'd which was better,
To send it back, or burn the letter.
But guessing that it might import,
Though nothing else, at least her sport,
She open'd it, and read it out,
With many a smile and leering flout:
Resolv'd to answer it in kind,
And thus perform'd what she design'd.

THE LADY'S ANSWER TO THE KNIGHT

That you're a beast, and turn'd to grass,
Is no strange news, nor ever was;
At least to me, who once you know,
Did from the pound replevin you,
When both your sword and spurs were won
In combat by an Amazon.
That sword, that did (like Fate) determine
Th' inevitable death of vermine,
And never dealt its furious blows,
But cut the throats of pigs and cows,
By TRULLA was, in single fight,
Disarm'd and wrested from its knight;
Your heels degraded of your spurs,
And in the stocks close prisoners;
Where still they'd lain, in base restraint,
If I, in pity of your complaint,
Had not on honourable conditions,
Releast 'em from the worst of prisons
And what return that favour met
You cannot (though you wou'd) forget;
When, being free, you strove t' evade
The oaths you had in prison made;
Forswore yourself; and first deny'd it,
But after own'd and justify'd it
And when y' had falsely broke one vow,
Absolv'd yourself by breaking two.
For while you sneakingly submit,
And beg for pardon at our feet,
Discourag'd by your guilty fears,
To hope for quarter for your ears,
And doubting 'twas in vain to sue,
You claim us boldly as your due;
Declare that treachery and force,
To deal with us, is th' only course;
We have no title nor pretence
To body, soul, or conscience;
But ought to fall to that man's share
That claims us for his proper ware.
These are the motives which, t' induce
Or fright us into love, you use.
A pretty new way of gallanting,
Between soliciting and ranting;

Like sturdy beggars, that intreat
For charity at once, and threat.
But since you undertake to prove
Your own propriety in love,
As if we were but lawful prize
In war between two enemies,
Or forfeitures, which ev'ry lover,
That wou'd but sue for, might recover,
It is not hard to understand
The myst'ry of this bold demand,
That cannot at our persons aim,
But something capable of claim.

'Tis not those paultry counterfeit
French stones, which in our eyes you set,
But our right diamonds, that inspire
And set your am'rous hearts on fire.
Nor can those false St. Martin's beads,
Which on our lips you lay for reds,
And make us wear, like Indian dames,
Add fuel to your scorching flames;
But those true rubies of the rock,
Which in our cabinets we lock.
'Tis not those orient pearls our teeth,
That you are so transported with;
But those we wear about our necks,
Produce those amorous effects.
Nor is't those threads of gold, our hair,
The periwigs you make us wear,
But those bright guineas in our chests,
That light the wild fire in your breasts.
These love-tricks I've been vers'd in so,
That all their sly intrigues I know,
And can unriddle, by their tones,
Their mystick cabals and jargones;
Can tell what passions, by their sounds,
Pine for the beauties of my grounds;
What raptures fond and amorous
O' th' charms and graces of my house;
What extasy and scorching flame,
Burns for my money in my name;
What from th' unnatural desire
To beasts and cattle takes its fire;
What tender sigh, and trickling tear,
Longs for a thousand pounds a year;
And languishing transports are fond
Of statute, mortgage, bill, and bond.

These are th' attracts which most men fall
Inamour'd, at first sight, withal
To these th' address with serenades,
And court with balls and masquerades;
And yet, for all the yearning pain
Y' have suffer'd for their loves in vain,
I fear they'll prove so nice and coy
To have, and t' hold and to enjoy
That all your oaths and labour lost,
They'll ne'er turn ladies of the post.
This is not meant to disapprove
Your judgment in your choice of love;
Which is so wise, the greatest part
Of mankind study 't as an art;
For love shou'd, like a deodand,
Still fall to th' owner of the land;
And where there's substance for its ground,
Cannot but be more firm and sound
Than that which has the slightest basis
Of airy virtue, wit, and graces;
Which is of such thin subtlety,
It steals and creeps in at the eye,
And, as it can't endure to stay,
Steals out again as nice a way.

But love, that its extraction owns
From solid gold and precious stones
Must, like its shining parents, prove
As solid and as glorious love.
Hence 'tis you have no way t'express
Our charms and graces but by these:
For what are lips, and eyes, and teeth,
Which beauty invades and conquers with,
But rubies, pearls, and diamonds,
With which a philter-love commands?

This is the way all parents prove,
In managing their childrens' love;
That force 'em t' intermarry and wed,
As if th' were bur'ing of the dead;
Cast earth to earth, as in the grave,
To join in wedlock all they have:
And when the settlement's in force,
Take all the rest for better or worse;
For money has a power above
The stars and fate to manage love;
Whose arrows, learned poets hold,
That never miss, are tipp'd with gold.

And though some say, the parents' claims
To make love in their childrens' names,
Who many times at once provide
The nurse, the husband, and the bride
Feel darts and charms, attracts and flames,
And woo and contract in their names;
And as they christen, use to marry 'em,
And, like their gossips, answer for 'em;
Is not to give in matrimony,
But sell and prostitute for money;
'Tis better than their own betrothing,
Who often do't for worse than nothing;
And when th' are at their own dispose,
With greater disadvantage choose.
All this is right; but for the course
You take to do't, by fraud or force,
'Tis so ridiculous, as soon
As told, 'tis never to be done;
No more than setters can betray,
That tell what tricks they are to play.
Marriage, at best, is but a vow,
Which all men either break or bow:
Then what will those forbear to do,
Who perjure when they do but woo?
Such as before-hand swear and lie
For earnest to their treachery;
And, rather than a crime confess,
With greater strive to make it less;
Like thieves, who, after sentence past,
Maintain their innocence to the last;
And when their crimes were made appear
As plain as witnesses can swear,
Yet, when the wretches come to die,
Will take upon their death a lie,
Nor are the virtues you confest
T' your ghostly father, as you guest,
So slight as to be justify'd
By being as shamefully deny'd,
As if you thought your word would pass
Point-blank on both sides of a case;
Or credit were not to be lost
B' a brave Knight-Errant of the Post,
That eats perfidiously his word,
And swears his ears through a two inch board:
Can own the same thing, and disown,
And perjure booty, Pro and Con:
Can make the Gospel serve his turn,
And help him out, to be forsworn;

When 'tis laid hands upon, and kist,
To be betray'd and sold like Christ.
These are the virtues in whose name
A right to all the world you claim,
And boldly challenge a dominion,
In grace and nature, o'er all women;
Of whom no less will satisfy
Than all the sex your tyranny,
Although you'll find it a hard province,
With all your crafty frauds and covins,
To govern such a num'rous crew,
Who, one by one, now govern you:
For if you all were SOLOMONS,
And wise and great as he was once,
You'll find they're able to subdue
(As they did him) and baffle you.

And if you are impos'd upon
'Tis by your own temptation done,
That with your ignorance invite;
And teach us how to use the slight.
For when we find y' are still more taken
With false attracts of our own making;
Swear that's a rose, and that a stone,
Like sots, to us that laid it on,
And what we did but slightly prime,
Most ignorantly daub in rhime;
You force us, in our own defences,
To copy beams and influences;
To lay perfections on the graces,
And draw attracts upon our faces;
And, in compliance to your wit,
Your own false jewels counterfeit.
For, by the practice of those arts
We gain a greater share of hearts;
And those deserve in reason most
That greatest pains and study cost;
For great perfections are, like heaven,
Too rich a present to be given.
Nor are these master-strokes of beauty
To be perform'd without hard duty,
Which, when they're nobly done and well,
The simple natural excell.
How fair and sweet the planted rose
Beyond the wild in hedges grows!
For without art the noblest seeds
Of flow'rs degen'rate into weeds.
How dull and rugged, e're 'tis ground

And polish'd, looks a diamond!
Though Paradise were e'er so fair,
It was not kept so without care.
The whole world, without art and dress,
Would be but one great wilderness;
And mankind but a savage herd,
For all that nature has conferr'd.
This does but rough-hew, and design;
Leaves art to polish and refine.
Though women first were made for men,
Yet men were made for them agen;
For when (outwitted by his wife)
Man first turn'd tenant but for life,
If women had not interven'd,
How soon had mankind had an end!
And that it is in being yet,
To us alone you are in debt.
And where's your liberty of choice,
And our unnatural No Voice?
Since all the privilege you boast,
And falsly usurp'd, or vainly lost,
Is now our right; to whose creation
You owe your happy restoration:
And if we had not weighty cause
To not appear, in making laws,
We could, in spite of all your tricks,
And shallow, formal politicks,
Force you our managements t' obey,
As we to yours (in shew) give way.
Hence 'tis that, while you vainly strive
T' advance your high prerogative,
You basely, after all your braves,
Submit, and own yourselves our slaves;
And 'cause we do not make it known,
Nor publickly our int'rest own,
Like sots, suppose we have no shares
In ord'ring you and your affairs;
When all your empire and command
You have from us at second hand
As if a pilot, that appears
To sit still only while he steers,
And does not make a noise and stir
Like ev'ry common mariner,
Knew nothing of the card, nor star,
And did not guide the man of war;
Nor we, because we don't appear
In councils, do not govern there;
While, like the mighty PRESTER JOHN,

Whose person none dares look upon,
But is preserv'd in close disguise,
From being made cheap to vulgar eyes,
W' enjoy as large a pow'r unseen,
To govern him, as he does men;
And in the right of our Pope JOAN,
Make Emp'rors at our feet fall down;
Or JOAN DE PUCEL'S braver name,
Our right to arms and conduct claim;
Who, though a Spinster, yet was able
To serve FRANCE for a Grand Constable.

We make and execute all laws;
Can judge the judges and the cause;
Prescribe all rules of right or wrong
To th' long robe, and the longer tongue;
'Gainst which the world has no defence;
But our more pow'rful eloquence.
We manage things of greatest weight
In all the world's affairs of state
Are ministers of war and peace,
That sway all nations how we please.
We rule all churches and their flocks,
Heretical and orthodox;
And are the heavenly vehicles
O' th' spirits in all conventicles.
By us is all commerce and trade
Improv'd, and manag'd, and decay'd;
For nothing can go off so well,
Nor bears that price, as what we sell.
We rule in ev'ry publique meeting,
And make men do what we judge fitting;
Are magistrates in all great towns,
Where men do nothing but wear gowns.
We make the man of war strike sail,
And to our braver conduct veil,
And, when h' has chac'd his enemies,
Submit to us upon his knees.
Is there an officer of state
Untimely rais'd, or magistrate,
That's haughty and imperious?
He's but a journeyman to us.
That as he gives us cause to do't,
Can keep him in, or turn him out.

We are your guardians, that increase
Or waste your fortunes how we please;
And, as you humour us, can deal

In all your matters, ill or well.

'Tis we that can dispose alone,
Whether your heirs shall be your own,
To whose integrity you must,
In spight of all your caution, trust;
And, 'less you fly beyond the seas,
Can fit you with what heirs we please;
And force you t' own 'em, though begotten
By French Valets or Irish Footmen.
Nor can the vigorousest course
Prevail, unless to make us worse;
Who still, the harsher we are us'd,
Are further off from b'ing reduc'd;
And scorn t' abate, for any ills,
The least punctilios of our wills.
Force does but whet our wits t' apply
Arts, born with us, for remedy;
Which all your politicks, as yet,
Have ne'er been able to defeat:
For when y' have try'd all sorts of ways,
What fools d' we make of you in plays!
While all the favours we afford,
Are but to girt you with the sword,
To fight our battles in our steads,
And have your brains beat out o' your heads;
Encounter, in despite of nature,
And fight at once, with fire and water,
With pirates, rocks, and storms, and seas,
Our pride and vanity t' appease;
Kill one another, and cut throats,
For our good graces, and best thoughts;
To do your exercise for honour,
And have your brains beat out the sooner;
Or crack'd, as learnedly, upon
Things that are never to be known;
And still appear the more industrious,
The more your projects are prepost'rous;
To square the circle of the arts,
And run stark mad to shew your parts;
Expound the oracle of laws,
And turn them which way we see cause
Be our solicitors and agents,
And stand for us in all engagements.

And these are all the mighty pow'rs
You vainly boast to cry down ours;
And what in real value's wanting,

Supply with vapouring and ranting;
Because yourselves are terrify'd,
And stoop to one another's pride,
Believe we have as little wit
To be out-hector'd, and submit;
By your example, lose that right
In treaties which we gain'd in fight;
And, terrify'd into an awe,
Pass on ourselves a Salique law:

Or, as some nations use, give place,
And truckle to your mighty race;
Let men usurp th' unjust dominion,
As if they were the better women.

GLOSSARY

Advowtry: Adultery
Animalia: Animals (L.)
Arsie-versie: Upside-down
Aruspicy: Prophesying, fortune-telling
Bachrach: Wine from Bacharach, in Germany
Bavin: A bundle of firewood
Boutefeu: Arsonist or (literal or metaphorical) firebrand
Cacodaemon: An evil Spirit
Caldes'd: Cheated
Calendae: The st or nd of the month
Calleche: A carriage with two wheels and a folding hood
Camelion: A giraffe
Camisado: An attack by night, during which the attackers wore shirts over their armour so they could recognise one another
Cane & Angue pejus: Worse than a dog or a snake (L.)
Caperdewsie: The stocks
Capoch'd: Pulled off the hoods
Caprich: A caprice
Carbonading: Thrashing, beating
Carroch: A stately or luxurious carriage
Catasta: The stocks
Cawdie: A military cadet
Cawdle: Soup or gruel
Ceruse: White lead used as a cosmetic
Champaign: Champagne wine
Champain: Countryside
Chous'd, choust, chows'd: Cheated
Chowse: A cheat's victim
Classis: The elders and pastors of all the Presbyterian

congregations in a district

Coincidere: To come together (L.)

Congees: Bows, curtseys

Conster: Construe, explain

Conventicle: Secret or illegal religious meetings

Covins: Conspiracies

Cucking-stool: A stool to which a malefactor (often an unfaithful wife) was tied, to be exposed to public ridicule, or ducked in a pond or river.

Curship: The title of being a cur — pun on "worship"

Curule: An ivory chair used as a mayor's throne

Deletory: That which wipes out or destroys

Deodand: In English law an article which had caused a man's death was ordered by the court to be a forfeited as a deodand (Ad Deo dandum - to be given to God). Before the reformation it or its value was given to the Church; afterwards to the local landowner.

Dewtry: A stupefying drink made from the Indian thorn-apple fruit.

Dialectico: A philosophical point of argument

Dictum factum: No sooner said than done (L.)

Disparo: To separate (L.)

Donzel: A young page or squire

Drazel: A slut

Ducatoon: An Italian silver coin, worth about shillings.

Ejusdem generis: Of the same kind (L.)

Enucleate: To explain the meaning of

Ex parte: On behalf of (L.)

Exaun: A religious establishment not under the authority of the local bishop

Fadging: Fitting

Feme-covert: A woman under the protection of a husband (a legal term)

Ferk: Beat, whip

Festina lente: Make haste slowly (L.)

Fingle-fangle: A whimsical or fantastic idea

Fother: A cart-load

Fulhams: Loaded dice

Ganzas: The birds which the hero of a popular romance harnessed to take him to the moon

Genethliack: A caster of horoscopes

Geomancy: Divination by interpreting the patterns of lines drawn at random on the ground or on paper.

Gleave: A spear or halberd

Granado: A grenade

Grilly'd: Grilled

Grincam: Syphilis

Guep: Go on! — said to a horse or as an expression of derision.

Habergeon: A chain-mail shirt

Haut-gousts: Tasty things

Headborough: A constable

Hiccius Doctius: A nonsense word used by jugglers, conjurers etc., hence, any kind of trick or dishonest dealing

Hight: Called, named

Hoccamore: Wine from Hochheim, in Germany

Horary: Hourly

Huckle: The hip
Hugonots: French Calvinists
Hypocondries: The upper abdomen, between the breastbone and the navel
Id est: That is (L.)
Idem: The same (L.)
Illation: Inference, deduction
In eodem subjecto: Thrown together in the same place (L.)
In querpo: Naked
Jobbernol(e): A thick head or blockhead
Jure divino: By God's law (L.)
Langued: Heraldic term meaning, with a tongue of a particular colour e.g. langued gules - with a red tongue
Lathy: Thin, like a lath
Linsey-woolsey : A cloth of mixed wool and linen threads
Linstock: A stick for holding a gunner's match
L'Ombre: A card game
Longees: Lunges
Lustrations: Ceremonials of ritual purification by washing
Mainprize: To stand surety for someone
Manicon: A plant (deadly nightshade) or its extract, believed to cause insanity when taken
Manto: Mantua, a kind of woman's loose gown
Martlet: A swallow or martin
Mazzard: The head
Meazle: A spot or pustule
Mira de lente: Wonderfully slow (L.)
Mordicus: With the teeth (L.)
Morpion: A crab-louse
Mundungus: Bad tobacco
Nare olfact: Nostril (L.)
Neat (noun): A calf or cow
Negatur: It is denied (L.)
Nimmer: A petty thief
Omnibus nervis: With every sinew (L.)
Oppugn: Attack or fight against
Orcades: The Orkneys
pacquet-male: Large wallet
Padder: A thief
Pari Libra: Equally (L.)
Pathic: Passively homosexual
Pernicion: Total ruin
Petronel: A short carbine or large pistol
Picqueer: Skirmish or quarrel
Pigsney: A term of endearment for a woman, "darling"
Plus satis: More than enough (L.)
Poesie: Poetry
Pullen: Poultry
Punese: A bed-bug
Pursy: Rich

Quarteridge: A tax or payment due quarterly
Quatenus: So far as (it is) (L.)
Quillets: Verbal points or quibbles
Rampiers: Ramparts
Rationalia: Thinking creatures (L.)
Rochet: A bishop's white gown or surplice
Satis: Enough
Sault: Jump
Scire facias: To know the appearance of (L.)
Sedes Stercoraria: Filthier seat (L.)
Seisin: A token of ownership, formally handed over when property is sold.
Shanker: A venereal sore, chancre
Slubberdegullion: A dirty, slovenly person
Soland geese: Barnacle geese (Branta leucopsis)
Staffier: A footman
Stentrophonick: Loud, as from a megaphone
Stum: A mixture of wine and grape juice
Suggill'd: Beaten severely
Sui juris: Independently (L.)
Swound: A swoon
Synodical: Arising from or of the nature of a synod - a meeting of bishops etc. of the Anglican Church
Tantundem dat tantidem: So much of that gives so much of this = they are exactly the same (L.)
Tarsel: A male falcon
Theorbo: A kind of lute with two necks
Totidem verbis: In just as many words (L.)
Trapes: Tripes
Trepan: To trap
Trigon: A set of signs of the Zodiac at -degree angles to each other
Tussis pro crepitu: A cough for a fart (L.)
Velis & remis: By sail and oar (L.)
Veni, Vidi, Vici : I came, I saw, I conquered (L.)
Versal: Universal
Videlicet: That is, viz. (L.)
Vitiligation: Argument, quarrelling
Vizard: A mask or disguise
Welkin: The sky
Whiffler: A ceremonial guard who cleared the way for a mayor or other official
Whinyard: A short sword
Ycleped: Named
Yerst: Erst, formerly

Samuel Butler – A Short Biography

Samuel Butler was born on 4th December 1835 at the village rectory in Langar, Nottinghamshire, to the Rev. Thomas Butler, himself the son of Dr. Samuel Butler, then headmaster of Shrewsbury School and later Bishop of Lichfield.

The young Butler's immediate family created an oppressive home environment that was largely antagonistic (he later chronicled this in 'The Way of All Flesh'). It was said that Thomas Butler, to make up for having been a servile son, became a bullying and overbearing father. The relationship with his mother was better, but not by much.

His education began at home and included frequent beatings, as was all too common at the time. Samuel wrote later that his parents were "brutal and stupid by nature." He later wrote that his father "never liked me, nor I him; from my earliest recollections I can call to mind no time when I did not fear him and dislike him …. I have never passed a day without thinking of him many times over as the man who was sure to be against me."

Under his parents' parochial influence, he was set to follow his father into the priesthood. He was sent to Shrewsbury at the age of twelve, where he did not enjoy the hard life and its routines.

From there, in 1854, he went to St John's College, Cambridge, where he obtained a first in Classics in 1858. The graduate society of St John's was later named the Samuel Butler Room in his honour.

After Cambridge he went to live in an impoverished parish in London 1858–59 as preparation for his ordination into the Anglican clergy; there he uneasily discovered that baptism made no apparent difference to the morals and behaviour of his new peers. He began to question his faith. This experience would later serve as inspiration for his work 'The Fair Haven'. His correspondence with his father about the issue failed to set his mind at rest, inciting instead his father's wrath.

As a result, the young Butler emigrated in September 1859, on the ship Roman Emperor to New Zealand. In common with many British settlers of privileged origins, he wanted to put as much distance as possible between himself and his family. He was determined to change his life and removing himself from the toxic relationship of family seemed the one thing in his control.

He wrote of his arrival and life as a sheep farmer on Mesopotamia Station in 'A First Year in Canterbury Settlement' (1863). After a few years of farming he sold his farm and made a handsome profit. The chief achievement of these years however was not farming or money but his ability to write. In these years were gathered the source materials and the first drafts for much of his masterpiece 'Erewhon'.

'Erewhon' revealed Butler's long interest in Darwin's theories of biological evolution. In 1863, four years after Darwin published 'On the Origin of Species', the editor of The Press, a New Zealand newspaper, published a letter titled 'Darwin among the Machines.' Written by Butler but signed Cellarius (q.v.,) it compares human evolution to machine evolution. Rather startlingly it projected that machines would eventually replace man: "In the course of ages we shall find ourselves the inferior race."

But Butler was not a devoted admirer of Darwin. Indeed he spent much time criticising him. In part this was due to Butler's complicated relationship with his own father and grandfather percolating through. He was of the belief that Darwin had used some of the work pioneered by his own father and grandfather and not sufficiently credited it. Butler was an evolutionist, just not of the Darwin kind.

Butler returned to England in 1864, settling in rooms in Clifford's Inn, near Fleet Street, where he would live for the rest of his life.

In 1872, he published his Utopian novel 'Erewhon' anonymously, causing some speculation as to the identity of the author. When Butler revealed himself, 'Erewhon' made him a well-known figure, more because of this speculation than for its literary merits, which remain undisputed.

In 1839 his grandfather Dr Butler had left Samuel property he owned at Whitehall in Shrewsbury on the condition that he survived his own father and his aunt, Dr Butler's daughter Harriet Lloyd. While at Cambridge in 1857 he sold the Whitehall mansion and six acres to his cousin Thomas Bucknall Lloyd, but kept the remaining land surrounding the mansion. His aunt died in 1880 and his father's death in 1886 resolved his financial problems for the last sixteen years of his own life.

There has been some speculation as to why Butler never married. For many years he made regular visits to a woman, Lucie Dumas, where he paid for sex but this seems overshadowed by his intense male friendships, which is reflected in several of his works.

His first significant male friendship was with the young Charles Pauli, whom he met in New Zealand; they both returned to England in 1864 and took neighbouring apartments in Clifford's Inn. Butler now paid Pauli a regular pension to finance his study of the law. This payment continued long after the friendship had cooled. With Pauli's death in 1892, Butler was shocked to learn that Pauli had benefited from mirror arrangements with other men and had died wealthy. He left nothing to Butler.

After 1878, Butler became close friends with Henry Festing Jones. Butler took him on as his literary assistant and travelling companion, at a salary of £200 a year. Jones kept his own lodgings but the two men saw each other daily, working together on music and writing projects during the day, and attending concerts and the theatre in the evenings. They were also frequent visitors to Europe. After Butler's death, Jones edited Butler's notebooks for publication and later published his own biography of Butler in 1919.

Butler was partial to indulging himself, holidaying in Italy every summer and producing his works on the Italian landscape and art. His close interest in the art of the Sacri Monti is reflected in 'Alps and Sanctuaries of Piedmont' and the 'Canton Ticino' (1881) and 'Ex Voto' (1888).

Another significant friendship was with Hans Rudolf Faesch, a Swiss student who stayed with them in London for two years, improving his English, before departing East for Singapore. Butler and Jones both wept when he left on his travels in early 1895. Butler subsequently wrote a very emotional poem, "In Memoriam H. R. F.", which was offered for publication to several leading English magazines. With the Oscar Wilde trial, and its revelations of homosexual behaviour among the literati now being aired, Butler feared association and hastily withdrew the poem.

He wrote a number of other books, including a moderately successful sequel, 'Erewhon Revisited'. His masterpiece and semi-autobiographical novel 'The Way of All Flesh' did not appear in print until after his death. Butler thought its tone of satirical attack on Victorian morality too contentious and shied away from further potential problems.

Samuel Butler died aged 66 on 18th June 1902 at a nursing home in St John's Wood Road, London. He was cremated at Woking Crematorium, and accounts say his ashes were either dispersed or buried in an unmarked grave.

George Bernard Shaw and E.M. Forster were great admirers of the later works of Samuel Butler, who brought a new form into Victorian literature of utopian/dystopian literature.

Butler belonged to no literary school, and although respected was not the subject of any literary devotion during his lifetime. Although an amateur student of religion and evolution his writings and controversial assertions shut him out from these opposing factions of church and science which played such a large role in late Victorian cultural life: "In those days one was either a religionist or a Darwinian, but he was neither." His later influence on literature came mainly through 'The Way of All Flesh', which Butler began in 1870 and finished after some revisions in 1885 but was unpublished on his explicit wishes until 1903. Despite the decades of its incubation it was still fresh and modern especially in its use of psychoanalytical thought.

Whether it be in his satire and fiction, his studies on the evidences of Christianity, his works on evolutionary thought or in his various other writings, a consistent theme runs through Butler's work, stemming largely from his personal struggle with the stifling of his own nature by his parents, which led him on to seek more general principles of growth, development and purpose. That struggle resulted in a literary career that is still respected to this day.

Samuel Butler – A Concise Bibliography

Darwin among the Machines (1863, largely incorporated into Erewhon)
Lucubratio Ebria (1865)
Erewhon, or Over the Range (1872)
Life and Habit (1878).
Evolution, Old and New; Or, the theories of Buffon, Dr. Erasmus Darwin, and Lamarck, as compared with that of Charles Darwin (1879)
Unconscious Memory (1880)
Alps and Sanctuaries of Piedmont and the Canton Ticino (1881)
Luck or Cunning as the Main Means of Organic Modification? (1887)
Ex Voto; An Account of the Sacro Monte or New Jerusalem at Verallo-Sesia (1888)
The Authoress of the Odyssey (1897)
The Iliad of Homer, Rendered into English Prose (1898)
Shakespeare's Sonnets Reconsidered (1899)
The Odyssey of Homer (1900)
Erewhon Revisited Twenty Years Later: By the Original Discoverer of the Country & His Son (1901)
The Way of All Flesh (1903, also entitled Ernest Pontifex; or, The Way of All Flesh)
God the Known and God the Unknown (1909)
The Note-Books of Samuel Butler (1912)
The Fair Haven (1913, considers inconsistencies between the Gospels)
A First Year in Canterbury Settlement With Other Early Essays (1914)

www.ingramcontent.com/pod-product-compliance
Lightning Source LLC
Chambersburg PA
CBHW060232050426
42448CB00009B/1413